THE SECRET HISTORY
OF AL-QA'IDA

Abdel Bari Atwan

ABACUS

First published in Great Britain in 2006 by Saqi Books
This paperback edition published in 2007 by Abacus
Reprinted 2007 (four times)

A CIP catalogue record for this book
is available from the British Library.

ISBN 978-0-349-12035-5

Papers used by Abacus are natural, recyclable products
made from wood grown in sustainable forests and certified
in accordance with the rules of the Forest Stewardship Council

Typeset in Garamond by M Rules
Printed and bound in Great Britain by
Clays Ltd, St Ives plc
Paper supplied by Hellefoss AS, Norway

Abacus
An imprint of
Little, Brown Book Group
100 Victoria Embankment
London EC4Y 0DY

An Hachette Livre UK Company

www.littlebrown.co.uk

To my family: Basima, Khalid,
Nada and Kareem
In memory of my mother, Zarifa Atwan,
who died in the Rafah refugee camp in the
Gaza Strip in August 2003.

Contents

Acknowledgements

My thanks first and foremost go to Susan de Muth for her meticulous research. Dr Azzam Tamimi and Said Aburish provided invaluable input and useful feedback on the text. Thanks also to Haitham al-Zobaidi, Yasser al-Sirri, Dr Muhammad al-Masari, Dr Saad al-Faqih, Peter Bergen, Fu'ad Husayn, Hala Jaber and, last but by no means least, to Pat Sundram, my personal assistant, and to the rest of the staff at *al-Quds al-Arabi*.

I also wish to thank my brother, Kamal Atwan, who funded my education. Without his support and encouragement throughout my life, I would not have achieved all that he made possible.

Many other people were involved in this project; they know who they are, and to them, also, thanks.

Preface

The suicide bombings that brought death and chaos to central London on 7 July 2005 were a savage reminder that al-Qaʿida still represents the most potent threat to Western security and stability in recent years. It is my opinion that Western governments – in particular the US of President George W. Bush and the UK of Prime Minister Tony Blair – do not fully understand the level of this threat, why it has arisen or how to deal with it effectively.

As an Arab Muslim who has lived in London for thirty years, working as a journalist specializing in Middle Eastern politics, I believe I bring a unique perspective to the story of al-Qaʿida and its impact on Western civilization. I understand both Muslim and Western ways of life and am certain that cooperation, not confrontation, is the only way forward. If the West genuinely wants to remove the terrorist threat posed by al-Qaʿida it must first understand the nature and political roots of what has now become an ideological network with franchises all over the world. It must also consider how to deal with legitimate grievances and establish channels for meaningful dialogue.

This book seeks to make a contribution to this process by looking at the genesis, membership, ambitions, influence and strategy of al-Qaʿida in an objective and analytical manner.

I do not endorse or in any way support al-Qaʿida's agenda. By going into many aspects of the network that have not been discussed in depth before, I am seeking only to explore and, where possible, explain and analyse. This book is a presentation of my first-hand knowledge of al-Qaʿida and its leaders and is the result of many years' observation, study and experiences, visiting al-Qaʻida camps and interviewing key players.

The terrifying events in London proved that al-Qaʻida has changed and expanded, that it has a long-term strategy which it is patiently and doggedly pursuing.

Al-Qaʻida's new structure, whereby small independent groups that subscribe to its ideology can form locally and operate with little or no reference to the core leadership, is not a sign that the organization is weakened – as some optimistic commentators have suggested. Quite the opposite: by expanding horizontally, al-Qaʻida is rapidly becoming bigger and stronger. Its ideology and strategy are widely available on the Internet, making it very easy for any one of its branches or affiliated groups to operate strictly within its framework in any place and at any time, without the need for a licence or approval.

George W. Bush has often said that he sent American troops to Iraq to fight al-Qaʻida there in order to prevent the network from attacking the US itself. Three and a half years after the invasion of Iraq al-Qaʻida has managed not only to hurt US-friendly Arab countries with attacks in Taba and Sharm El-Sheikh in Egypt, Aqaba in Jordan and Casablanca in Morocco, but is casting its shadow of menace ever closer to the US itself via Istanbul, Madrid and London.

The US has already spent $337 billion on its military adventure in Iraq, but al-Qaʻida seems impervious to this costly 'war on terror'. In fact, it has used this war for its own ends: Iraq has become its training ground. American foreign policy is the best recruitment officer al-Qaʻida has ever had.

It is sadly ironic that in the name of spreading moderation in the Muslim world and isolating radicalism in order to starve al-Qaʻida of oxygen, the American and British governments have achieved exactly the opposite. In many ways al-Qaʻida has effected more change on Western societies than vice versa, provoking draconian legislation in Britain and the US and a change of government in the 2004 Spanish general election, to cite the most obvious examples.

The notion that Muslims hate the American people or Western civilization is dangerous and erroneous. What many do hate is American foreign policy, and they are not alone in that. To take one example, in May 2005 thirty-three leaders from Arab League and South American nations met for the first time in Brazil with the intention of forming new alliances to counter what they see as US global hegemony. In Europe, to take another, support for the US-led war in Iraq is less than 10 per cent in countries like Spain and Greece. Equally erroneous is the idea that the world is in the grip of a 'clash of civilizations'. At this moment in history there is no Islamic civilization to speak of, only a preponderance of pro-Western corrupt dictatorships with little to speak of in the way of democracy or economic productivity.

The organization might have changed, but al-Qa'ida's complaints and demands have not. Western leaders need to seriously consider these, not deny them, as Tony Blair has done with his stubborn refusal to accept that the London bombings are in any way connected with his support for the US's project in the Middle East. Why did the Spanish people make that connection following the carnage on their transport system on 11 March 2004 and vote to change the government that had backed the US invasion of Iraq? Why, as Osama bin Laden himself asks, hasn't al-Qa'ida attacked countries like Sweden?

One does not have to be a genius or even a clever analyst to answer these questions. Osama bin Laden and Ayman al-Zawahiri have outlined these matters in the clearest possible terms and the grievances of the Muslim world that they use to justify their bloody attacks are long-standing.

Consider bin Laden's address to the American people five days before the 4 November elections in 2004. In it he describes the genesis of 11 September and states quite clearly that his campaign against the US 'started in 1982 when America permitted the Israelis to invade Lebanon and the American Sixth Fleet helped them in that . . . I couldn't forget those moving scenes, blood and severed limbs, women and children sprawled everywhere. Houses destroyed along with their occupants and high-rises demolished . . . as I looked at those demolished towers in Lebanon, it entered my mind that we should punish the oppressor in kind and that we should destroy towers in America'.

In the same message, broadcast on al-Jazeera, bin Laden condemns 'the sanctions that led to the deaths of millions in Iraq and the greatest mass slaughter of children mankind has ever known, by Bush Sr, and millions of pounds of bombs and explosives hurled at millions of children – also in Iraq – by Bush Jr, in order to remove an old agent and replace him with a new puppet to assist in the pilfering of Iraq's oil and other outrages'.

I utterly condemn the attacks on innocent citizens in the West. I have lived in London for most of my adult life and love this city and its people. I support and appreciate Western democracy and civilization with its pillars of fairness, an independent judicial system, civil liberties, freedom of expression and equality of opportunities. But I do question whether or not Western leaders are right to expose their people to grave danger for what appear to be dubious, ill-defined political and economic ends.

It is my contention that leaders like President Bush and Prime Minister Blair are increasingly at odds with the wishes and interests of the people they are meant to be serving. This is all within the al-Qa'ida master plan, as I discuss in this book, and Osama bin Laden will not fail to exploit this fatal breach when he judges the time is right.

My purpose in writing this book is to establish what al-Qa'ida is or has become, what it wants, what its capabilities are and how the West can answer its complaints and challenges. I consider the ferocious campaign in Iraq and how that country has become a breeding ground for the most ruthless and militant al-Qa'ida fighters we have ever seen. Furthermore, Iraq, Pakistan and Afghanistan are now the platforms from which international operations are launched – I am thinking of the recent attacks on Madrid, London, Sharm El-Sheikh and Aqaba, all of which have traceable links back to al-Qaʿidaʾs central leadership. Al-Qaʿida is not only attempting to destabilize the Western world, but the whole of the stagnated Middle East.

In other chapters I look at the role of the Internet and the emergence of 'cyber-*jihad*' as a form of warfare; I examine the history and phenomenon of the suicide bomber, and consider al-Qaʿidaʾs economic strategy. Saudi Arabia and the US in particular have much to fear from al-Qaʿida as it pursues a highly intelligent project to implode oppressive regimes and bleed Western economies into bankruptcy by forcing up the price of oil and engaging them in wars of attrition costing billions of dollars.

This book begins with a personal record of time spent with Osama bin Laden while he was still one of the world's most wanted men, on his way to becoming *the* most wanted. He is now also one of the world's most written-about people, yet has remained, paradoxically, an enigma in many respects. No history of al-Qaʿida can properly begin without an in-depth look at its founder and guide. The first two chapters of this book provide both a portrait of the man and describe his development as the prime exponent of *jihad* today; readers already familiar with bin Laden's biography will find much here that is new.

In my travels throughout the Middle East I have observed the growing significance bin Laden and al-Qaʿida have for many of the world's 1.3 billion Muslims. The war with al-Qaʿida is asymmetric, but complacency on the part of the West will not win it. Osama bin Laden and al-Qaʿida have patience on their side, a long-term strategy and a steadfast ideology. If the West is to engage with al-Qaʿida, it needs first to understand it.

We ignore al-Qaʿida at our peril. It is not going to go away.

Inside the Lair:
With bin Laden at Tora Bora

At the time in which the events recorded in this chapter took place, Afghanistan was in complete turmoil. The Taliban (backed by Pakistan) had seized Kabul in September 1996 after two years of civil war with the ousted government, the Islamic State of Afghanistan. But the country remained completely unstable, with opposing warlords grappling for power outside the main cities.

The Strange Invitation

In 1996 I spent three days with Osama bin Laden at his hideout in Tora Bora, the only Western-based journalist to have spent such a significant amount of time with him before or since. This trip was undoubtedly the strangest assignment I have ever undertaken in a career spanning more than thirty years, and explains my enduring interest in bin Laden and al-Qaʻida.

From 1994 to 1998, bin Laden had an office in London's Oxford Street. This was the UK branch of his organization, the Advice and Reform Committee, which was set up to lobby for change in Saudi Arabia, and not connected to al-Qaʻida. It was managed by Khaled al-Fawwaz, who was arrested by Scotland Yard in 1998 for his alleged part in planning the al-Qaʻida bombings of US embassies in Nairobi, Kenya, and Dar-es-Salaam,

Tanzania, charges which he has continued to deny.

Arab journalists in the know referred to al-Fawwaz as 'bin Laden's ambassador to Britain'. In November 1996 he came to the offices of the newspaper *al-Quds al-Arabi*, where I am Editor-in-Chief, and after some courteous preliminaries and beating around the bush asked if I would be interested in travelling to Afghanistan to interview bin Laden, who had recently gone into hiding. This unanticipated suggestion intrigued me: bin Laden was already well on his way to being US Public Enemy Number One, and was much discussed in Arab circles as a paradoxical militant figure, charismatic, wealthy and extremely dangerous.

Usually it is the journalist who requests an interview but in this – as in all matters – bin Laden had his own way of doing things. He seems to have developed a very good sense of how to use the media over the years, and when he decided to declare war on the US, he wanted it to be known the world over. He instructed al-Fawwaz to invite other selected media professionals for interviews, too. From the newspaper sector, only the British journalist Robert Fisk of the *Independent* and I were chosen. Bin Laden had great respect for Fisk on account of his daring articles criticizing US policy on Israel and its support for corrupt regimes around the world. Al-Fawwaz told me I was picked because bin Laden admired my uncompromising criticism of certain Arab regimes, and because of my opposition to the 1991 Gulf war. Moreover, *al-Quds al-Arabi* is the only truly independent Arab daily. The Arab newspaper industry is completely dominated by Saudi interests, and mine was one of very few that would be able to publish an interview with Osama bin Laden.

(Among broadcast networks, the BBC was contacted, but its directors declined because they did not consider bin Laden's profile high enough to warrant despatching a television crew to Afghanistan. The American network CBS also missed its opportunity for similar reasons. But British Channel Four welcomed the idea and sent a crew; I met the producer at a hotel in Jalalabad when I, too, was on my way to meet bin Laden. We were both very secretive about our reasons for being there.

CNN reporter Peter Bergen was the only broadcast journalist at that stage to appreciate the immense significance of bin Laden. He was very enthusiastic when approached by al-Fawwaz, and persuaded his bosses that this was an important assignment. I learned afterwards that bin Laden's men did not trust the CNN crew, suspecting CIA infiltration. The crew was blindfolded and taken to a makeshift camp in a remote area; the interview lasted for less than an hour – apparently bin Laden had been very tense.)

I politely replied to al-Fawwaz that I appreciated the offer, but would have to give the matter some thought. There were several reasons for my hesitation, most of them involving fears for my own safety. Afghanistan at the time had been in the grip of a crushing civil war, and total lawlessness reigned. There was no security, no police and no government. Crime was at unprecedented levels and kidnapping commonplace: if no ransom was forthcoming the warlords' men would kill you for $5 in your pocket. Since I do not speak Pashtu, and few in Afghanistan speak Arabic or English (my only two languages), I did not feel confident of being able to talk my way out of such a situation.

I was also concerned that I might be followed by secret service agents of any one of a number of countries who were hunting bin Laden at the time. He was not as famous, or infamous, as he is today, but he stood accused of two attacks inside his native Saudi Arabia – the Riyadh bombing of 1995 and the truck-bomb attack on the American base at Khobar, which killed nineteen US soldiers in 1996. He was certainly considered extremely dangerous by various regimes from the US to Pakistan and had been the object of several Saudi assassination attempts. If I unwittingly led intelligence operatives to bin Laden, I myself would most probably be killed in the attack. On the other hand, if bin Laden's men won the battle they would inevitably consider me a spy, with grisly consequences: a real no-win scenario. However, I already had a very strong intuition that bin

Laden would prove to be a phenomenon of immense historical significance in the Muslim world. I knew that several high-profile Western journalists had been trying to gain access to him, with limited success. I was being offered unlimited access and a trip to his base; I could not pass up the opportunity for such a scoop.

Two weeks later a bearded man whispered in my ear that arrangements had been made. I was to fly to the frontier city of Peshawar, in Pakistan just across the border from Afghanistan, and on arrival check in at the Pearl Continental Hotel and call a man named 'Faisal' whose number had been scrawled on a piece of paper for me. This was the only information I was given in advance about my trip.

Utmost Security

I knew from the outset that I couldn't tell anybody where I was going or what I was doing. Such knowledge would be dangerous for them, dangerous for me and dangerous for the whole assignment. Fortunately al-Jazeera, with excellent timing, invited me to take part in a televised debate in Qatar, which provided me with a legitimate reason to be travelling to the region.

Only one person – my second-in-command at *al-Quds al-Arabi* – knew where I was really going. Even my wife and children had no idea. As soon as the debate was over, I told my colleagues in Qatar that I was going on a short vacation to Dubai, 'to relax'. Nothing could have been further from the truth.

Peshawar

I arrived in Peshawar late the next evening. As I stood at the reception desk checking in at the Pearl Continental Hotel and feeling very clandestine, I was horrified to hear a familiar Saudi voice calling my name. I turned round to find myself being enthusiastically kissed and greeted by an old acquaintance. Swiftly the whole group of Saudis he was with engulfed me, and everyone wanted to know what on Earth I was doing in such a strange place. I am not popular in Saudi Arabia, having been a critic of the regime there for many years; I was very afraid that if I aroused suspicions, they would alert the Saudi security forces and I would be followed, and my real purpose discovered.

Playing for time, I asked what they themselves were doing in Peshawar. 'We are part of a delegation,' my unwanted companion replied. 'We've been on a fact-finding mission in Afghanistan.'

'Me too,' I said, grateful for this prompt. 'I start my fact-finding mission tomorrow.'

'They should have sent someone else, Abdel Bari,' the man commented. 'It's an extremely dangerous country and security is nonexistent.' He continued to unnerve me (and, I'm sorry to add, bore me) with his tales for several hours.

It was past midnight when I was finally able to lock the door to my room and unroll the tiny scrap of paper that contained Faisal's number. A rather terse voice answered immediately: 'Be ready at 10 AM tomorrow morning. Nothing else. The phone is not safe.'

Crossing the Border

At 10 AM Faisal knocked on the door of my hotel room. He was a bearded, dark-skinned young man of medium build, dressed in Pakistani-style clothes. He said very little, but I thought I detected a Saudi accent, from Jeddah or possibly Mecca; I might be wrong.

Faisal had brought me an Afghan costume to wear for our journey. This consisted of baggy trousers, a long shirt and a turban. The turban in particular made me feel very self-conscious, as I had never worn such a thing in my life. At that time Pakistani security forces were preventing Arabs from entering Afghanistan, but Faisal assured me that in these clothes I would easily pass for a Pashtun tribal leader. I was not convinced, but put them on as quickly as I could – which was not an easy matter in the case of the turban, which had to be secured round the head in a very complicated fashion. (I still have these garments in my wardrobe at home in London, and prefer them to any Armani suit, as they always trigger memories of this adventure and of the Afghan mountains.)

As I dressed Faisal hurriedly told me the arrangements: two Taliban would smuggle me across the checkpoints and borders between Peshawar and Jalalabad, where others would take over the mission of delivering me to bin Laden. No indication whatsoever was given as to where bin Laden might be found.

I was already well aware that the trip would be extremely hazardous. We were going into the mountainous borderlands which are completely controlled by lawless, warring tribes whose daily business is kidnapping, robbery and murder. I also knew that if my true Arab identity was discovered by Pakistani security forces, I would be in the gravest danger. Into this cocktail of fear, Faisal casually tossed an extra ingredient: several roads we would be taking to avoid certain checkpoints were likely to be mined. I was duly scared to death.

Faisal told me to leave all my things in the hotel room – I was to take nothing with me. In my new clothes, and accompanied by Faisal, I went to the bus station, where we met the two Taliban as promised. Humble in their manner, not yet twenty years old and completely unarmed in a land where even children carry guns, these were not the most reassuring escorts through the dangers ahead. Faisal left us, and we squeezed into a small Toyota pickup with fifteen other passengers. The driver, who was a young man, screeched off at great speed in a cloud of dust.

My two Taliban companions spoke neither Arabic nor any language but their own. As I spoke no Pashtu, we communicated silently during the journey, using gestures and pointing, sometimes punctuating our mute conversation with smiles of relief each time we safely crossed a Pakistani checkpoint.

I had noticed, however, that they were unable to conceal their merriment whenever they glanced at my costume and turban. I wondered if they knew the nature of my trip or if they thought I was a heroin smuggler, an arms dealer or some poor fellow wishing to join the *jihad* in a country where *jihad* seems never-ending. Though my attire was very much in keeping with those around me I felt self-conscious and awkward. My fellow passengers looked at me curiously and several times I caught the assistant driver eyeing me with suspicion in the wing mirror. I realized that this was because my garments were so clean, uncrumpled and obviously brand-new.

The youthful driver raced with the wind, his rusty old vehicle screeching round the terrifying mountain hairpin bends at acrobatic angles. Pakistan was in a state of emergency, and security was intense. We were stopped at numerous roadblocks, but we managed to get through them all. Nor did we fall prey to marauding tribes. With quite unbelievable luck we arrived without incident at the Khyber Pass, where the border crossing was a pathway not wider than ten metres between two mountains.

We had to disembark and walk past the Pakistani soldiers and intelligence officers who lined the way, scrutinizing everyone who passed through but stopping only those who were carrying luggage or suspicious items. Since I was carrying nothing more than a small knapsack containing a camera and a tape recorder, we passed through unchallenged. It may well also have been that as the Taliban was on such good terms with Pakistan, and with its army in particular, my two companions had more impressive credentials than any diplomatic passport.

About half a kilometre down the path we came to the Afghan side of the border crossing. This consisted of little more than a scarcely noticeable soiled white rag hanging from a stick. Next to this welcome banner sat a ghost of a man, bearded and turbaned, who spoke to no one and behaved as though none of this had anything to do with him. We re-boarded the vehicle and soon passed a cemetery where twenty or thirty red and green Islamic and Arab flags fluttered round the entrance. Someone explained that this was where the Arab *mujahedin* who had fallen in the *jihad* against the Soviet Union were buried. (The successful Afghan *jihad* against the Soviet invasion lasted ten years, from 1979–89.) I asked the driver to stop, and we wandered awhile among the graves, deciphering names and Qur'anic verses. There were fighters from Egypt, Yemen, Saudi Arabia and other Arab countries; the name of the battle in which each had fallen was inscribed on the graves. It was a testament to how the *jihad* had united people from all over the Muslim world.

We came to a small market town. Seeing a restaurant by the side of the road, my two companions began pointing to their mouths as if telling me that they wanted to have lunch. By then it was already 2.30 PM, and realizing I was extremely hungry, I agreed with much vigorous nodding.

The chairs were made from the branches of trees brought straight from the mountains and the table tops were rusty tin. The food was an unidentifiable broth with great pools of grease floating on the surface, containing a piece of meat – God only knows where it came from – and half a potato served in a metal saucer. A few bread buns and some water in three metal cups completed this feast. My two companions belched and praised God several times for the gift of this food. We headed for a nearby mosque to pray. I recognized some of the *imam*'s words, but most were incomprehensible to me.

I had no idea where we were, other than in Afghanistan, but this border town had a bus station where my two companions now led me. They succeeded, being in their own country and by virtue of their affiliation with the Taliban, in seating me in the front seat next to the driver, that is to say, in 'first class'. Out of courtesy and humility they sat behind in 'second class', or at least this how it seemed to me.

The journey from the Pakistani borders to Jalalabad should take about four hours, but this can vary significantly depending on the zeal of the driver, his vehicle and the cooperation of the passengers. Our vehicle was an ancient machine that had survived the Afghan *jihad* and might have even taken part in it one way or another. We had to disembark three times. Burst tyres halted us twice, but on the third occasion the vehicle became immobilized in deep mud. When it became obvious that however furiously the driver revved up the engine it was not going to budge, the shoulders and muscle-power of the passengers had to be deployed to give it that extra boost.

In Pakistan people drive on the left-hand side – they are among the few countries that continue to adhere to this British colonial legacy despite their independence. In Afghanistan, the rules governing traffic circulation are a mystery. It all depends on the mood of the driver and the holes in the road. Like an ageing snake, a vehicle would turn once to the left and once to the right to avoid the craters caused by bombs, tank tracks, floods and other erosion factors, or all of these together.

Afghanistan Under the Taliban

We arrived in Jalalabad suffering from severe neck and back pains, but safe. My two companions took me to the next location on the itinerary, which had clearly involved very thorough forward planning. They deposited their consignment – me – at a safe house in the Jalalabad region, and departed. I never saw them again.

I was offered tea and, as I sat talking to the occupants of this house, I was told that two of the young boys who were clustered round a computer playing Nintendo games were bin Laden's sons, Saad and Muhammad.

I was directed to one of the city's hotels. The illustriously named Ever White Mountain was a shy reminder that Afghanistan had once been settled and stable, a relic of its bygone glory. Spacious and surrounded by gardens full of orange trees and roses, the hotel was empty of guests except for two British television journalists. They joined me for dinner, which this time consisted of broth with either meat or chicken and a choice of rice or bread.

The hotelier was an inquisitive man from Kabul. He had fled to Jalalabad to escape the shelling and had bought the hotel. Because of my costume, he thought I was an Afghan Pashtun, but when I answered him in English he became suspicious and even more curious.

He asked me endless questions about what I was doing in Afghanistan. I tricked him into believing that my father was Pashtun and my mother was English; when he asked me why I did not speak Pashtu, I had the inspiration to claim that my father had died while I was young and that my mother, who spoke nothing but English, had brought me up. My evasiveness was essential if I was to conceal my real objective, and besides, the hotelier's endless interrogation was extremely annoying. I was delighted when he finally stopped asking questions and started analysing the situation in Afghanistan.

It seemed to me he was a supporter of Najibullah (the former pro-Soviet Afghan president, who was ousted in 1992), as he spoke enthusiastically of the man and his leadership qualities. But he praised the Taliban too, appropriately or otherwise, perhaps to secure his safety and avoid trouble. He admitted that their rule had brought security to the city, which had until recently been the domain of highway robbers and thieves – not to mention rival war-lords, whose militias imposed levies on all and sundry; some of these had even committed rape, the worst possible crime in Afghan culture.

Soon after dinner, there was a power cut. We traced our way back to our modestly furnished rooms by candlelight. When I asked the hotelier when the power was likely to be restored, he replied: 'It could be seven minutes, it could be seven days. Allah alone, and then the Taliban, would know best.' When I left the hotel the following afternoon the electricity was still off, and for all I know it might not be back on even now. My night in the Ever White Mountain was torture. It was impossible to sleep because of the insects that shared my bed with me; some of these bedbugs and fleas were of the lethal variety.

On Friday morning, bin Laden's 'envoy' in Jalalabad came to the hotel. He apologized and informed me that 'the Sheikh' could not meet me that day after all, and that I would have to wait. I told him I was in a hurry and had commitments in London that required my presence there on Monday. He appeared understanding and promised he would do his best. That 'envoy' was the Egyptian Abu Hafs al-Misri, also known as Muhammad Atef. He was chief of al-Qa'ida's military operations at that time, though I had no idea of this and he did not enlighten me. He was a very striking-looking person, tall and slender with bright green eyes, dark-skinned, bearded, full of youth and vigour. He was modest, extremely radical and exceptionally polite. I respected his sincerity, humility and profound faith in the issues he believed in. I think he sensed my respect for him.

Later, Abu Hafs was to tell me about the attack on the Egyptian embassy in Islamabad which had taken place in 1995. It was in revenge, he said, for the torture and sexual assault of 'brothers' by Egyptian secret agents inside the embassy. They decided to destroy it, and developed the strategy of sending a small car to blow up the gate, which would then be followed by a tanker packed with 1,500 kg of explosives to blow up the embassy itself. When the same strategy was later employed in the attacks on US embassies in Nairobi and Dar-es-Salaam in 1998, I realized immediately that this was the work of Abu Hafs. (The last time I spoke to him was in the wake of the American bombardment of Tora Bora in November 2001. He telephoned me to issue a communiqué which we published exclusively, confirming that Osama bin Laden was safe, that five Arab *mujahedin* had been 'martyred', and that 'Sheikh bin Laden' swore vengeance on the American regime. Abu Hafs was killed in Kabul shortly afterwards by an American missile.)

At 3 PM a red car pulled in front of the hotel bearing a person I hadn't seen before, a driver and two armed men. I was told we were going to meet 'the Sheikh' and that the journey would be arduous, exhausting and dangerous.

The journey to 'bin Laden's emirate' was indeed arduous. The road was unpaved and passed through mountain and valley villages connected by terrifying rock-strewn spiralling roads. It was my bad luck that we had to tackle this road after nightfall and in pitch darkness. I felt as if we were hurtling into the unknown, driven by a man with a death wish who was also suffering from the delusion that he was on an *Autobahn* and not a series of hairpin bends. From time to time he could not resist the opportunity to show off his acrobatic skills, swinging the screeching vehicle this way and that.

Half way through the journey we had to stop because an enormous rock was blocking the road. 'It has recently fallen from the mountain,' the driver announced cheerfully. My heart sank and I asked him if this was a common occurrence. 'Very much so,' he answered even more cheerfully. 'And there will be more on the way because it is winter now and the soil is very loose.' He then went on to tell us about his friend, Abu Ubaydah, who had been killed on this road a few days earlier when a rock fell on his car and crushed him. I took a deep breath, glanced up at the looming shadowy mountains above and recited *al-Fatihah* (the first *sura* of the Qur'an).

After seven more hours' agony, rock-wrestling and perilous mountain passes we came to a roadblock of a rather different nature. This one was manned by fierce-looking armed Taliban and it was by no means certain whether they would consider us friend or foe. As we slowly drove up to them I could feel my stomach tightening, but I needn't have worried because they hardly cast us a second glance. They didn't ask us what we were doing, where we were going or for any form of identity; they simply waved us through. In actual fact I was never once searched or questioned in the course of my entire journey. I had expected quite the reverse as bin Laden was being hunted by the entire world.

Unlike the very few other journalists who had been taken to meet Osama bin Laden I was not blindfolded as we approached Tora Bora. I took this as a sign that bin Laden considered me worthy of his trust and confidence.

Soon the communications equipment in the car started buzzing. My companion had sent a message ahead that we were approaching. Suddenly a vehicle intercepted us, bristling with armed men and decorated on top with a rocket-propelled grenade (RPG) launcher and a machine gun. I did not find this reassuring, although that, apparently, was the point of this exercise.

Inside the Eagle's Nest: Tora Bora

We finally arrived at the Eagle's Nest, as the Afghan Arabs' base at
Tora Bora was called. ('Afghan Arabs' was the name given to the
mujahedin who flocked from Arab countries to base themselves in
Afghanistan and fight first against the Soviets and later the US invasion. Many of these men later formed the base of al-Qa'ida.) We
were at an altitude of around 3,000 metres, and in the car headlights
I could see several caves had been dug out of the snow-covered
mountainside. I could dimly make out bands of armed *mujahedin*
moving about here and there. I had spent much of my trip in a state
of near-terror, but experienced a sense of relief, even safety, now we
had reached bin Laden's secret lair. (I never once felt that there was
anything to fear from bin Laden or his men.)

The car drew up outside the entrance to one of the caves. A dim
light came from within. A very cold wind struck my face as I got out
and almost blew my turban off towards the mountains. Seeing nothing else in the dark, I hurried towards the lit cave and entered it
alone. A man was there to meet me; I was absolutely astonished to
recognize him as a Syrian writer I knew quite well from London,
Omar Abdel Hakim, also known as Mustafa Setmaryam Nasar and
whose *nom de guerre* is 'Abu Mus'ab al-Suri', a specialist on *jihad* and
Islam. We spoke for a few moments and I learned that he had left
Spain, where he had both citizenship and a wife, to join al-Qa'ida.
Later he was to join the Taliban, and became Mullah Omar's media
advisor. 'Come,' he said, leading the way into another cave. 'The
Sheikh is waiting for you.'

I met Osama bin Laden just before midnight on 23 November.
He was sitting cross-legged on the carpet, a Kalashnikov in his lap.
There were several others present, but I was transfixed by him. It is
always strange to meet someone in the flesh whose image you have
become familiar with in the press, even more so when you know
they are wanted by the world's intelligence agencies. Bin Laden
placed his rifle on the ground and got up. He came towards me with

a warm smile that turned into barely repressed laughter as he took in the way I was dressed. He embraced me warmly and asked about my trip.

I felt like an honoured guest and was treated with the greatest respect. Bin Laden said he hoped I wasn't too tired and promised me that we would have dinner together later. He indicated that I should sit on a bench made out of small branches from the oak trees that covered the mountainsides, nailed together into a makeshift base with a thin mattress on top.

Bin Laden made every effort to put me at ease, and he somehow seemed very familiar to me – perhaps that is the essence of charisma. He chatted informally and explained that Tora Bora had a special significance for him. During the *jihad* against the Soviet Union it had been his main military base, but now he used it as a retreat – a place to think, plan and relax.

I was surprised to find Osama bin Laden, the son of one of the wealthiest Arab families and used to the utmost luxury, in this freezing, humble cave. Even when it had become clear that his base was going to be high in the mountains I still expected to find him, if not in a palace, then perhaps a house – in reasonable accommodation at least. But bin Laden told me he despised money, and had never sought a life of comfort and ease; unlike his brothers, he had always lived modestly.

I complained about how cold it was, and he told me I was lucky it was winter; when Robert Fisk had come there to interview him it had been summer, and the place was full of scorpions. The cave was approximately six metres by four metres. The main feature of the room was an extensive library full of books on Islamic heritage and *tafsir* (Qur'anic commentary). Kalashnikov assault rifles decorated the remaining walls of the cave, hanging from nails here and there.

Osama bin Laden is tall and slender, and was without any apparent physical weakness. He had allowed his beard to grow, and wore Afghan clothing. To protect himself from the cold he wore a padded combat jacket of the type worn by special commando units and often covered this with an Afghan woollen blanket, which hung from his shoulders. He wore either a white turban or sometimes a red scarf on his head.

Bin Laden's manner is one of extreme humility, and I discovered in the two days I spent in his company that he can be very pleasant to be with. His voice is soft, but clear. He is constantly smiling in a reassuring manner that shortens the distance between him and his guest, especially one meeting him for the first time.

During our initial conversation I started complaining about the discomforts of my journey, all the pains I had endured in my back, neck and stomach. He started laughing and told me that he had been at another base, much further up, but had decided to make things easier for me by coming down to meet me half way. I expressed my gratitude.

Suddenly a lot of loud shouting erupted outside, followed by a prolonged burst of furious gunfire. I froze in terror and before I could ask my host what was going on he had rushed outside. More gunshots followed, then I heard the screech of artillery shelling and the sound of rockets being fired. I was convinced that the base was under attack and that my life was about to come to an end. A short while later bin Laden came back in looking completely unperturbed. He apologized for having alarmed me and explained that this was a drill that his men underwent on a regular basis so that they were always on the alert and prepared to respond to emergencies at all times. I was slightly comforted by this, but certainly not reassured.

A Modest Dinner

As our initial conversation came to an end, someone came in to announce that dinner was ready. Since I had been eating so badly since coming to Afghanistan I was looking forward to this meal. I'd imagined that when I met bin Laden we would feast on roast deer or goat. When I considered the facilities available at the Eagle's Nest I tailored these expectations to its spartan reality, and believed chicken perhaps a more likely dish. It was a great surprise to discover that dinner consisted of Arab-style potato chips soaking in a puddle of cottonseed oil; a plate of fried eggs that was scarcely enough for one man, let alone five; salty cheese of a variety long extinct even in the villages of upper Egypt; and some bread buns that must have been made with sand, as my teeth screeched and ground whenever I chewed. After a few bites I pretended that I did not usually eat dinner for health reasons. The men accepted my excuse and carried on eating.

Another meal featured bin Laden's favourite food, bread with yogurt and rice, served with potatoes cooked in tomato sauce. Animal fat floated on the surface, and I could hardly force it down my throat. Afterwards I was sick under a pine tree outside the cave.

(Recently somebody close to bin Laden told me that when I first published an account of this visit in *al-Quds al-Arabi*, bin Laden read it four times. Each time he got to the bit about how awful the food was, he laughed heartily and said that if ever I visited him again he would serve me the very finest stuffed lamb.)

As my companions finished their meal I considered my surroundings and allowed my thoughts to wander. I was puzzled by bin Laden's chosen path in life. What motivates this man, from a well-known and honourable family in possession of billions, to lead such a comfortless life in these inhospitable and dangerous mountains, awaiting attack, capture or death at any moment, hunted by so many regimes? Just then bin Laden began to speak of having no fear of death, of his desire for martyrdom and how it grieved him that he was still alive. When he spoke of his fellow *mujahedin* who had already left and, as they believe, gone to Paradise, his eyes became moist and he was obviously very moved.

We spoke about his wealth, and while he avoided saying exactly how much he was worth he acknowledged that he still, even in hiding, managed an extensive investment portfolio through a complex network of secret contacts. But this wealth, he said, was for the *umma* (the global Islamic community). 'It is the duty of the *umma* as a whole to commit its wealth to the struggle,' he said. I noticed that he rarely spoke of 'Arabs', but always about Islam and the *umma*. 'The *umma* is connected like an electric current,' he said, surprising me with his use of such modern imagery (for here was a man who would wish to take us back 1,500 years in time).

A splendid conversation followed. Bin Laden's media advisor was in the room, and was not happy when 'the Sheikh' began to speak about certain things; he asked me not to write about them, and I have not done so until now. One of the censored conversations concerned the Sudanese government and leadership, which had recently expelled bin Laden from that country at the behest of the US. He complained with a great deal of anger and bitterness in his voice that they were un-Islamic and had betrayed him. He had helped that bankrupt nation financially to the tune of $300 million of his own money. When they asked him to leave he requested that these loans be repaid. 'They told me they had no money,' Bin Laden recalled. 'And that was true. But then they offered to give me corn, wheat and livestock instead, suggesting I could sell these to raise the cash.' Bin Laden's eyes contained both bitterness and merriment as he laughed, asking: 'Who will buy corn and animals from the fugitive Osama bin Laden?'

Bin Laden has a lively sense of humour and often makes jokes at the least expected moments. During a long, angry diatribe against the presence of US forces on the Arabian Peninsula (in Saudi Arabia and the Gulf states) he said their main interest was obviously oil, but that this did not require military pressure: 'Of course we are going to sell them the oil anyway,' he said. 'After all, we cannot drink it.'

He refused to have his voice taped during our interviews. My hand was getting very cramped from constantly writing notes, and I asked him why he didn't offer me the easy alternative of recording the conversation, but I received no answer. His media advisor later explained (off the record, of course) that bin Laden was afraid he might make some grammatical or theological mistakes which, if these were recorded, could be used against him. At that time he was not perfectly versed in Islam but was working towards this goal. I realized how conscious he must be of his image in the Islamic world, and that he desired to be a *mufti* (an authority trained in *shari'ah* [Islamic law], who can pronounce *fatwas* [religious edicts]).

It was after midnight when the other dinner guests left the cave to go to sleep. There were just two beds in the cave; bin Laden offered me one while he himself took the other. This was certainly the most unusual bed I have ever slept in. The mattress was hard and grimy, and must have been twenty years old. The blankets were of a similar age, and the pillow had lost any softness it might once have had. Most alarming was that the mattress lay across several crates of hand grenades and was surrounded by dangling Kalashnikovs and other rifles.

The primitive heating, which was now fired up, consisted of a water tank warmed by a wood stove. A pipe extended from it all the way to the ceiling. This rudimentary system, which is common across Afghanistan, is as effective – if not more so – as any modern central heating equipment in Europe. But despite the comparative warmth of the cave, I was in for another sleepless night. The arsenal that surrounded me made me very tense. Since I know nothing about firearms I was very anxious that something might set them off unintentionally.

Osama bin Laden had no such problems with insomnia. Placing his beloved Kalashnikov on the floor beside his bed he immediately fell into a deep and very peaceful sleep. If I'd been an assassin or bounty hunter, I'd have been in luck. I had no idea at the time that my bedfellow was to become the most notorious man of modern times, and that the price on his head would increase from the relatively modest $1 million at the time I slept so near him to the $25 million offered by the US today.

The wind howled outside like sirens going off all night, and a squint-eyed cock started crowing loudly at 1 AM, producing an unnerving sound the likes of which I had never heard before. Still worse, the *mujahedin* at the base took turns revving the engines of their vehicles, one after the other. When I asked about this in the morning I was told that this was the only way to prevent the diesel freezing in the engines.

At 4 AM things started moving at the base. The resident *imam* called us to *al-Fajr* (dawn prayers). It was intensely beautiful, echoing round the lofty mountains. Some of bin Laden's followers had taken on the names of military commanders from early Islamic conquests, and I felt as though I had stepped back into the past: here was Abu Ubaydah, there Abu Mu'adh, Abu Suhayb, Abu Dharand, Abu al-Walid.

As I hadn't slept a wink, technically I hadn't woken up, but the men brought me a bowl of tepid water all the same, and I was expected to perform the obligatory ablutions Islam requires upon waking and before morning prayers. I was in the company of very religious men, and both ablutions and prayers would have to be performed right then, and not when it suited me. I rose sluggishly and asked: 'Where is the toilet?' They burst out laughing.

'Where do you think you are, the Sheraton?'

But they pointed to some icy ground outside, saying: 'You can fulfil your needs and make your ablutions over there.' It was about -20 degrees Celsius, if not lower; all I remember is that my limbs were completely frozen. God only knows if my ablutions were good or not – but I did my best.

Cannons, Tanks and Nature

As the light slowly crept into my surroundings, all the detail of this Emirate-base became clear. I had boycotted the splendours of nature for the better part of thirty years, but became very enthusiastic when those awe-inspiring mountains were uncloaked. Pine trees embraced the snow-covered mountainsides; fresh air filled the lungs; the shy sun rose steadily out of a scarlet dawn on the distant horizon like the wedding canopy for a tribe's most beautiful girl.

I could see that the base was very well protected: there was an anti-aircraft gun, and tanks and armoured vehicles controlled the approach road. Many hides had been prepared where the *muja-hedin* could conceal themselves for an ambush. They also had rocket launchers and, I had heard, Stinger missiles to combat air raids. I did not actually see those and did not ask about them either, wary of jeopardizing my own safety or arousing the suspicion that I might be a spy.

Breakfast was little different to dinner: the same cheese, or what remained of it, some cane syrup and tea with milk. It was accompanied by recitation from the Qur'an. I observed that bin Laden ate very little, and I never saw him drink tea or coffee, only water.

A Modern Base and an Educated Elite

As I was shown around the lower base I discovered that, in contrast with the primitive accommodation, it was well-equipped with the latest technology and powered by its own small generator. Here were computers and up-to-the-minute communications equipment. Bin Laden had access to the Internet, which was not then ubiquitous as it is now, and said: 'These days the world is becoming like a small village.'

The modernity of bin Laden's communications network was quite at odds with the austerity recommended by the more extreme forms of Islamic fundamentalism and in particular that of his hosts, the Taliban. One of his aides laughed at this observation and said the base was 'a republic within a republic'.

Bin Laden had a huge archive containing data saved in both hard-copy form and computer disks. The archive also included cuttings from the Arab and foreign press. Bin Laden always receives the latest news either by daily wire services from London and the Gulf or newspapers, depending on his whereabouts and circumstances. As

I stood by bin Laden's desk my eyes fell upon a company seal. I couldn't see underneath to decipher which organization this endorsed, but toyed with the idea that it might spell out 'al-Qaʻida'.

The base at Tora Bora had not been used as a training camp for several years. The *mujahedin* around bin Laden at that time were there to protect him from capture or attack. There were men of all ages and from most of the Arab countries, with the majority from the Arabian Peninsula and Egypt; a high percentage came from al-Qasim, Mecca, Medina and the Gulf emirates. They had all taken Islamic names, the most popular being those of the Prophet's companions, in particular those who were given the glad tidings that their places were guaranteed in Paradise. They displayed an immense faith in their Lord and their religion. They had turned their backs on life a long time ago and were in a hurry to get to eternal life in the hereafter. All spoke longingly of the martyrdom they hoped for. I found it remarkable that so many of the *mujahedin* possessed the very highest academic qualifications. There were doctors, engineers and teachers among them, people who had left their families and jobs to join the *jihad.*

Bin Laden did not behave in an authoritarian or even commanding manner – far from it. Yet the respect and esteem in which the *mujahedin* held their leader was immediately apparent. They hung on his every word and always addressed him with the honorific 'Sheikh.' All of them told me they would gladly give their lives to defend him and would exact revenge on any person or group that might harm him. I remember Faisal, the envoy who came to me in Peshawar, telling me that he would be prepared to take bullets in his own chest to shield and protect 'the Sheikh'.

Bin Laden – or 'Abu Abdullah', as his followers and disciples call him – took me on a walk through the mountains adjacent to the base, sporting the Kalashnikov rifle so dear to him. (He told me it had belonged to a Soviet general who was killed in one of the Afghan *jihad* battles.)

We talked about the past, present and future, about corrupt Arab regimes and US injustice against Muslim states. He told me about his days in Sudan and Somalia, about the attempts made on his life by Saudi secret services and the enormous financial rewards he had been offered if he would relinquish his mission and his *jihad*. He said the Saudis had offered to return his passport to him if he would publicly declare that King Fahd was a true Muslim, but he had refused. (All these matters will be discussed more fully elsewhere in this book.)

The End of the Visit

The next day dawned, sunny but freezing cold. Bin Laden took me on a guided tour up the mountain to the rest of the camp. We walked through the trees, and he explained that he loved mountains and could only ever live in such an environment: 'I would rather die than live in a European state,' he declared.

There were several mudbrick houses in clearings with smoke rising from their chimneys. There was a smell of baking bread and the sound of children playing. I could see some of these kids and several women completely veiled from top to toe.

Bin Laden pointed out the very top of the mountain and explained that during the *jihad* it had housed a Soviet base that had complete control of the area and had given the *mujahedin* a lot of trouble. 'We bombed it,' he recalled with great pride, 'and kicked the Soviets out.'

He spoke well of the Soviet fighters, whom he described as 'brave and patient'. This sparked some revelations, which were exclusive at that time. Bin Laden told me that his Afghan Arabs had been involved in the 1993 ambush on American troops in Mogadishu, Somalia. He described how the Somali warlord Mohammed Farah Aidid had been blamed. 'But he denied responsibility, and he was telling the truth about that,' bin Laden said. 'There were successful battles in which we inflicted big losses on the Americans, and we preyed on them in Mogadishu.' He said he thought the US had

displayed a singular lack of courage by pulling out of Somalia immediately afterwards.

Bin Laden also confirmed that al-Qa'ida was behind the June
1996 bombing of the American base at Khobar Towers in Dharan,
Saudi Arabia. A massive 1,500 kg of dynamite exploded in the
military complex housing American forces; nineteen soldiers were
killed and 500 people injured. Bin Laden said he was upset that the
US had subsequently relocated its Saudi military base to al-Kharj,
in the desert south of Riyadh. 'It's a much more remote place,' he
complained. 'In Khobar it was easy to catch them . . . and they
moved so quickly. They did it in under a month.' He said that al-
Qa'ida had had other operations planned for the Khobar Towers
compound.

Bin Laden said that more attacks were in the planning stages
and emphasized that these 'operations', as he called them, took a
long time to prepare. He hinted at a strike at the US on their home
territory, but I confess I did not really register the enormity of what
he implied when he came out with an unforgettable statement: 'We
hope to reach ignition point in the not-too-distant future.' After the
terrible events of 11 September I often thought about the young
mujahedin I had met at Tora Bora and wondered if I had been sitting
next to any of the men who perpetrated those devastating attacks. I
would not be surprised.

The end of my allotted two days with Osama bin Laden had
come, and the same red car arrived to take me back to Jalalabad. I
very much regretted that I could not have spent longer in this
Afghan Arab emirate – I was fascinated by the psychological, political and social dimensions of this group of people and their leader,
but could not have even scratched the surface in such a short space
of time.

After meeting bin Laden, I realized that this was no ordinary
man, and fully expected that he would play a significant role in the
history of his homeland, Saudi Arabia, and the Muslim world in
general. It didn't occur to me for one moment that this polite,

soft-spoken, smiling and apparently gentle person would become the world's most dangerous man, terrorizing Western capitals, inflicting hundreds of billions of dollars' worth of damage on the US, threatening its economic stability and embroiling it in full-scale wars in Afghanistan and Iraq. The experience of meeting the man marked the beginning of my abiding interest in al-Qa'ida, and the close attention I have given all matters concerned with this subject, which informs this book.

Osama bin Laden

The Historical Inevitability of bin Laden

Today the Muslim world is fascinated by bin Laden. When the Qatar-based al-Jazeera satellite television channel broadcasts a video or audio message by him, or a programme about his life, the streets are almost emptied in countries like Saudi Arabia, Egypt, Palestine, Syria and Morocco, as everyone heads indoors to watch or listen to this man who has managed to gain an almost iconic status in the region.

A recent survey showed that as much as 60 per cent of the population in some Arab countries support him. In November 2003, even though the kingdom was experiencing al-Qaʿida attacks first-hand, more than half of all Saudis said they approved of bin Laden's message. In Egypt, where US aid is key to the economy, bin Laden is more popular than George W. Bush.

There was a historical inevitability about the rise of bin Laden, who has become for many the figurehead of a resurgent Muslim identity. For many people in the West this is unthinkable, as there he is presented and perceived as an evil terrorist. Yet it is important to understand how he is viewed by his admirers in the Islamic world. How can the very real threat that al-Qaʿida's ideology represents to global security be countered if its identity and nature remains shrouded in obscurity?

Osama bin Laden is perceived by many Muslims as a brave

champion of revolution and rebellion, a person of mythical proportions with the appeal of a David challenging Goliath. Probably
many of those who currently support him would not endorse either
his extreme violence or the kind of *shari'ah* governance Salafis[1]
would like them to live under, but for the moment these are minor
details for them. After centuries of decline, they view bin Laden as
having brought hope and dignity back to a people under the shadow
of humiliation and exploitation, and having squared up to the bul-
lies of the West, in particular the US: this is how people have
described their feelings about him to me.

Some have compared bin Laden to Jawaharlal Nehru, the great
Indian populist leader; others have likened him to Buddha in that
he, too, renounced wealth, prosperity and comfort in order to live
austerely in the caves of barren mountains. Of course the enormous
difference is that both Nehru and Buddha were pacifists, using only
peaceful means in the pursuit of justice and freedom, whereas bin
Laden has chosen the path of extreme violence and mass murder.

Perhaps Ayatollah Khomeini, the figurehead of the Iranian
Islamic Revolution, is the closest in historical terms to bin Laden.
Khomeini was to some extent bin Laden's role model when he was
in Sudan. He pursued a similar methodology to that of Khomeini
in spreading his message; he issued communiqués, released audio-
cassettes and published written admonitions demanding reform
and calling for the full implementation of *shari'ah* and the com-
batting of corruption. However, in the crucial aspect of theology
they are at odds, as Khomeini was a Shi'i Muslim whereas bin
Laden is Sunni.

The Early Years

Osama bin Laden was born in Riyadh, Saudi Arabia, in 1957. His
mother was of Syrian origin and his father was a self-made construction contractor named Muhammad Awad bin Laden, who
came to the Kingdom of Saudi Arabia from the Hadramaut region

in southern Yemen, where the inhabitants are known for their intelligence, shrewdness, patience and distinctive business talents. Most of the big business families in Saudi Arabia originally hailed from this region. Muhammad bin Laden started as a simple labourer, but within a few years he was rapidly climbing the ladder of success and prosperity, eventually presiding over the biggest construction empire in the Arab world.

More importantly, he became a major behind-the-scenes political player in the kingdom. He established close ties with the ruling family, and when a feud erupted in the mid-1960s between King Saud and his brother Crown Prince Faisal, Muhammad bin Laden played a major role in persuading the king to abdicate in favour of Faisal and leave the country. The state treasury was empty at the time, and the country was on the verge of bankruptcy. Muhammad bin Laden lent the Saudi state tens of millions of dollars to pay the salaries of government employees for more than six months. The grateful ruling family subsequently rewarded him with enormous construction contracts, the most significant of which was the expansion of the Sanctuary in Mecca and the Prophet Muhammad's mosque in Medina.

Osama bin Laden is the forty-third of fifty-three siblings, and twenty-first of twenty-nine brothers. He was ten years old when his father was killed in a plane crash.

When he was six months old his family moved from Riyadh to Hijaz, where he spent his childhood and adolescence. He frequently visited Islam's two holiest cities, Mecca and Medina. This must have had a great impact on him and certainly contributed to the religious faith he exhibits now.

One of bin Laden's brothers informed me that Osama was quiet and aloof as a child. He kept his distance from other children and did not participate with them in their play and clamour. He was intelligent and preferred to stay close to his father, enjoying sitting quietly in his company. He attended many religious meetings, study circles and Qur'anic readings even as a young boy.

Bin Laden has always been very attached to his mother. Born Aliyah Ghanem, she came from a rural family in the northeastern Syrian coastal region of Latakia. Although the region is dominated by Allawi Muslims, the Ghanem family is Sunni. Muhammad bin Laden was introduced to the beautiful Aliyah while on a business trip to Latakia in 1956, and soon afterwards she became his fourth wife. Osama bin Laden is her only son; he spoke to me about her with the greatest warmth and respect.

In 1998 the Saudi government tried to turn bin Laden's admiration for his mother to their advantage, flying her by private jet to Afghanistan in the hope that she might dissuade her son from pursuing *jihad* and talk him into returning to Saudi Arabia. Her mission met with failure, however. It is believed that the last time mother and son met was in January 2001, at the wedding of bin Laden's son to Abu Hafs al-Misri's daughter.

Aliyah is known to follow her son's activities with almost obsessive interest, keeping newspaper cuttings, watching the satellite channels and keeping up to date with his Internet communiqués and statements.

Osama bin Laden used to spend his summer holidays with his uncle Naji in Latakia, and it was there, at age seventeen, that he met his cousin Najua Ghanem, who was to become his first wife. She was fourteen when they married, and moved to Saudi Arabia with him. They have eleven children together.

Bin Laden received his education at Jeddah's primary, intermediate and secondary schools. He then studied economics and business administration at King Abdulaziz University in Jeddah where he received his BA. During his university years, he studied prevalent Islamic ideological trends and learned from such renowned scholars as Muhammad Qutb and Dr Abdullah Azzam.

Osama bin Laden's marriage at the early age of seventeen speaks clearly against the often repeated allegation that he spent his youth travelling to London, Paris, Geneva and Manila in search of thrills. However, one of his brothers did tell me that he went to London at the age of thirteen for an English-language summer course at an Oxford Street language school. Sheikh Muhammad Zaki Badawi, the former director of the Regents Park Islamic Centre in London, confirmed that bin Laden visited the mosque in the early 1980s and delivered several sermons there.

Muhammad bin Laden was in the habit of offering his hospitality to large numbers of pilgrims on their way to Mecca each year. Following his death, two of the older bin Laden brothers decided to do likewise. The pilgrims often included renowned Islamic scholars and thinkers with whom the young Osama was eager to meet and speak. He was greatly influenced by two men in particular. The first was Muhammad Qutb, brother of Sayyid Qutb (who some analysts regard as the spiritual father of Islamic radical groups, and who will later be discussed in detail). The other was Abdullah Azzam, the ideologue of the *jihad* in Afghanistan and a very influential figure among Muslim youths in the 1980s. Both men lectured at the University of Jeddah, teaching Islamic culture, which was a mandatory module for all students.

Afghanistan

Abdullah Azzam became bin Laden's first mentor, providing him with an overview of current events in the Muslim world. He discussed the Soviet occupation of Afghanistan, emphasizing the necessity of liberating that Muslim country from foreign occupation. Azzam organized a secret trip to Pakistan for bin Laden through his own contacts and the young man travelled to Peshawar and Karachi, where he met leaders of the Afghan Islamic groups including Abdul Rasul Sayyaf of the Itihad-i-Islami Baraye Azadi Afghanistan and Burhanuddin Rabbani of the Jama'at-e Islami (both men would later oppose the Taliban, with whom bin Laden formed a *de facto* alliance). This trip lasted for a month and was followed by several others until Osama bin Laden eventually moved to Afghanistan more or less full-time in 1982. Bin Laden brought drilling equipment, diggers and bulldozers from the family firm in Saudi Arabia. This was an immense contribution to the *mujahedin*'s campaign against the Soviet invaders, creating access routes up mountains, levelling ground and digging labyrinthine camps like the one I visited at Tora Bora.

Bin Laden also played a key role fundraising for the *mujahedin* and encouraged thousands of Saudis to volunteer for the *jihad* on his many trips back to Saudi Arabia, where he gave talks and sermons; by then he was already seen as something of a role model. Although he had been born into great wealth, bin Laden did not care for material comforts and had abandoned the lavish lifestyle the majority of his family enjoyed to pursue an Islamic agenda. He was becoming a well-known face in the pages of Arab magazines and newspapers in the Gulf region, celebrated as a heroic *mujahed* who was willing to sacrifice comfort and even his life for the cause and for the principles he believed in.

The Saudi government wholeheartedly supported and backed the Afghan and Arab *mujahedin* fighting the Soviet occupation in Afghanistan. Fundraising committees were formed under the chairmanship of Prince Salman bin Abdul Aziz, the governor of the Riyadh district. *Imams* at mosques were encouraged to deliver fiery sermons exhorting young men to join the fight. Large boxes were placed in mosque courtyards to collect donations from worshippers. I recall being at the mosque on Fridays when thousands were present, and seeing how eagerly they pressed around these boxes to deposit their offerings. The Saudi government itself split the cost of the Afghan war with the US.

In 1984, bin Laden founded Bayt al-Ansar (House of the Supporters) in Peshawar. His mission was to provide a station where newly arrived volunteers for *jihad* could be received before being sent for training. Bin Laden did not have his own training camps at this time, and sent new recruits to one of the Afghan *mujahedin* groups led by men such as Sayyaf, Rabbani or Gulbuddin Hekmatyar, leader of the Afghan Hezb-e Islami party. By 1986 bin

Laden had set up his own training camps in various parts of Afghanistan. In 1988 he established an office to record the names of the *mujahedin* and inform the families of those who were killed. The name of this register was 'al-Qa'ida' ('the base' or 'foundation'), and that is how the organization got its name. Most Islamist sources say that the embryonic al-Qa'ida network was established at this point.

In 1989, in the wake of the withdrawal of Soviet troops, bin Laden returned to Saudi Arabia having received a warning from Pakistani intelligence that he and Abdullah Azzam were being targeted for assassination by the CIA. Two weeks later Azzam, godfather of the Afghan *jihad*, was assassinated along with his two sons.

Saudi Arabia

The Saudi government put bin Laden under house arrest in mid-1990 and banned him from travelling; one of his stud farms was also raided and kept under close observation. The Saudi government had security concerns about bin Laden even at this early stage. His very outspoken public speeches had been recorded on cassette tapes and were widely distributed; in them he warned the Saudi people about the threat posed by the Iraqi Ba'thist regime, which he believed had plans to invade the entire Gulf region. A subsequent letter from bin Laden to Prince Ahmad bin Abdul Aziz, Deputy Minister of the Interior, urging the royal family to recognize the necessity for comprehensive reform, did nothing to endear him to the regime. In the same letter bin Laden predicted that Saddam Hussein would invade Kuwait.

Prince Nawwaf bin Abdul Aziz, Minister of the Interior, was sufficiently interested in this analysis to invite bin Laden to a meeting. However, he did not act upon the warnings. When Saddam eventually did invade Kuwait on 2 August 1990, bin Laden wrote another letter to the minister in which he suggested mobilizing *mujahedin* from various parts of the Muslim world, including his own Afghan Arab veterans, in order to liberate Kuwait. He claimed he could muster an army of 100,000 men. This letter was ignored.

Bin Laden told me that the Saudi government's decision to invite US troops to defend the kingdom and liberate Kuwait was the biggest shock of his entire life. He could not believe that the House of Al Saud could welcome the deployment of 'infidel' forces on Arabian Peninsula soil, within the proximity of the Holy Places, for the first time since the inception of Islam.

Bin Laden also feared that by welcoming US troops onto Arab land the Saudi government would be subjecting the country to foreign occupation – in an exact replay of the course of events in Afghanistan, when the Communist government in Kabul invited Russian troops into the country. Just as bin Laden had taken up arms to fight the Soviet troops in Afghanistan, he now decided to take up arms to confront the US troops on the Arabian Peninsula. At this point bin Laden decided to stop advising the Saudi officials on what actions they should or should not take. He felt communication with them had become utterly futile.

Bin Laden now had two main aims: renowned Saudi cleric Sheikh bin Uthaymin had issued a *fatwa* stating that it was obligatory for every Muslim, particularly those from the Arabian Peninsula, to prepare for battle against the 'invaders'. Bin Laden decided to use this *fatwa* as a means of mobilizing youths to travel to Afghanistan and train for combat, and a considerable number of Saudis heeded the call.

He also decided to assemble the largest possible number of scholars in an independent religious establishment that could become an authoritative frame of reference for the people, in lieu of the official Senior Scholars' Association (the *ulama*, or religious authorities). Bin Laden no longer had faith in the Saudi *ulama* whose religious rulings, he felt, were in response to requests from the government rather than based on truthful interpretations of the *shari'ah*. He now sought an independent *fatwa* on whether or not it was permissible for the Saudi rulers to seek the assistance of foreign troops.

Meanwhile, bin Laden had decided to leave his homeland indefinitely. There was one problem – his passport had been confiscated. He made use of his family's close connections with the royal family to get permission to travel to Pakistan, where he said he had to wind down some of his businesses. After a considerable amount of stalling, he was eventually granted permission to make a single trip and was issued a passport.

Sudan

Arriving in Pakistan, bin Laden travelled over the border into Afghanistan, where he discovered that the *mujahedin*, who had fought together as comrades, were now engaged in bitter and violent feuding between rival Afghan warlords. Initially, bin Laden tried to calm down the situation, advising the Arab *mujahedin* not to get involved and trying to mediate between the Afghan faction leaders in the hope of resolving the disputes among them. However, all he got for his efforts were death threats, and he decided to move to Sudan. The Islamic National Salvation Revolution Party had taken power there in a 1989 military coup, and bin Laden thought he would be able to operate freely there.

Bin Laden headed for Sudan in total secrecy in December 1991, travelling in a private jet with a number of his comrades. His companies undertook several construction and agricultural projects, and he paved the way for his own 'political *jihad*'. He started to give interviews and issued press releases inciting Islamic revolution. He invested massive amounts of his own money in large-scale construction projects such as building the Port Sudan airport and the 400-km 'Defiance Highway' between Port Sudan and Khartoum. He also invested heavily in agricultural projects in the al-Jazeera district, cultivating thousands of acres of land producing wheat and sunflowers. He told me that his personal investments in Sudan amounted to some $200 million. The projects were also subsidized by the Saudi government.

Bin Laden employed many of the Afghan Arabs who had fought with him against the Soviet Union on these projects and encouraged them to move their families over to Sudan. Many were Egyptians, and members of the extremely radical Islamic Jihad and Jama'at Islamiyah groups. This alarmed the Egyptian government, which launched a vicious press campaign against the Saudi government, accusing it of supporting and funding terrorism. The Saudi government bowed to pressure and stripped bin Laden of his citizenship, disowning him and suspending all funding to projects carried out in Sudan by bin Laden's companies under the pretext of punishing the Sudanese regime for supporting Saddam Hussein's invasion of Kuwait.

Bin Laden described to me the time he spent in Sudan as one of the most important and fruitful in his life. In Khartoum he met Islamic scholars from all over the Muslim world, including Sudan's own Hassan al-Turabi, who was in the process of establishing a new political organization opposed to the US, uniting religious and secular members alike. The Arab Islamic People's Congress held its first conference in Khartoum in 1991. Participants represented a wide range of opinions and beliefs, and included such prominent figures as Gulbuddin Hekmatyar; Abdul Rasul Sayyaf; Yasser Arafat, Chair of the Palestine Liberation Organization; Nayif Hawatimah, founder and Secretary General of the Democratic Front for the Liberation of Palestine; Fatih al-Shiqaqi, leader of the Palestinian Islamic Jihad; Khaled Mishaal, from Hamas; Imad Mughniyeh of Hizbullah; and many representatives from the Muslim Brotherhood and *jihadi* groups from all over the Muslim world. The event was described by some in the Western media as a 'terrorism conference'.

I actually attended this conference; its aim was, in fact, to provide an alternative to the Arab League and a platform for all who rejected the 1991 US intervention against Iraq and opposed the Arab regimes which supported such military adventures by a foreign power.

It was in this context, then, that bin Laden consolidated his presence in Sudan and sought to establish a safe haven for young men in search of *jihad* as well as the many Arab *mujahedin* who had been refused the right to return to their homelands after the Afghan war.

Bin Laden was very proud of the fact that he was resisting the US even through his agricultural projects. He boasted to me that he had managed to grow sunflowers of such enormous record-breaking proportions that the US, despite its advanced agricultural technology, would never be able to match him.

Meanwhile, although his activities inside Sudan were essentially political, bin Laden decided to attack the US military in two operations elsewhere. In what were to be al-Qaʿida's first attacks, it bombed US soldiers in transit at the Goldmohur Hotel in Aden, Yemen, in 1992, killing three people and wounding five, and in 1993 two Black Hawk helicopters were brought down in attacks in Mogadishu (later recreated for the Hollywood film *Black Hawk Down*). The Mogadishu attack was headed by Abu Ubaydah al-Banshiri, al-Qaʿida's military commander, who drowned in a 1996 ferry accident on Lake Victoria. The US swiftly withdrew its troops from Somalia, something bin Laden later told me he greatly regretted, for he had been planning to force a war of attrition against them (something now apparently well under way in Iraq).

Under increasing pressure from Egypt, Saudi Arabia and the US, by 1994 the Sudanese government started to search for a means of ridding itself of the increasingly dangerous bin Laden. By now he had escaped several assassination attempts, the most bloody carried out by three people led by a Libyan national, who stormed into the mosque where bin Laden worshipped and opened fire. When they discovered that he was neither among the dead nor among the survivors, they continued to search for him at the offices of his company in Khartoum and then at his house in the al-Riyadh district of East Khartoum. It was rumoured at the time that the assassination attempt was either directly or indirectly orchestrated by elements within the Sudanese government.

Muhammad Atef (aka Abu Hafs al-Misri) told me that bin Laden began to feel very hemmed in at this stage. In 1994 Sudan was clearly unhappy about his presence, and the Saudis had revoked his citizenship. Bin Laden felt he now faced two clear options: he could return to Saudi Arabia to spend the rest of his life either in detention or under house arrest, or he could begin a full-on military campaign against his enemies, which he would continue until he was captured or killed.

From then on, according to Atef, bin Laden's focus shifted from political activism. He began to concentrate on building a considerable military organization to carry out operations against US military, administrative and business targets, initially on the Arabian Peninsula.

A series of meetings between bin Laden and the leaders of the Egyptian Islamic Jihad and Jama'at Islamiyah groups (Dr Ayman al-Zawahiri and Rifa'i Ahmed Taha, respectively) also strengthened his resolve to turn to extreme violence.

Al-Zawahiri has had an enormous influence on bin Laden, which shall be examined more fully later in this book. His ideology was unique at that time in that it combined a Salafi-*jihadi* outlook with pan-Arab radicalism – something which is emerging now as a major force in the Iraqi insurgency. Al-Zawahiri encouraged bin Laden to shift focus from local Islamic causes such as those in Bosnia, Chechnya, Albania, Kosovo, the Philippines and Thailand, to the central Islamic causes especially in Palestine and Iraq. As his relationship with al-Zawahiri strengthened, bin Laden's strategy widened to include any arena or circumstance where he could damage the US or its interests. The idea of global *jihad*, which now informs al-Qa'ida's strategy, has its origins here.

The 1995 al-Qa'ida bombings in Riyadh which killed five, including three American military experts at a Saudi National Guard base, resulted in increased pressure on Sudan to expel bin Laden. When he heard that negotiations were taking place between Sudanese and Saudi officials, he realized there was a very real possibility he might be surrendered to Riyadh, and began looking for a viable exit strategy.

Bin Laden became increasingly suspicious and bitter, no longer certain whom he could trust. Al-Turabi had lost bin Laden's confidence when he played a leading role in the capture of the notorious international terrorist 'Carlos the Jackal' in Sudan in 1994. Bin Laden was now very wary of the Sudanese government. However, he categorically refused to level any blame at them publicly. He even requested that I edit out a section of my interview with him in which he complained of being betrayed and accused the Sudanese government and President Omar al-Bashir of stabbing him in the back.

In 1996 bin Laden had a private meeting with al-Bashir, who assured him that he was still welcome in Sudan and that no deportation orders would be served. However, al-Bashir also told him that the Sudanese government was unable to protect him from assassination attempts. Bin Laden understood this delicately put message and decided to leave the country voluntarily. He contacted old friends among the Afghan *mujahedin* such as Sheikh Yunis Khalis and Brigadier Jalaluddin Haqqani, who exerted considerable influence in the Jalalabad region. This was prior to the extension of Taliban influence beyond the Kandahar region; at that time different Afghan regions were ruled by different factions.

Back to Afghanistan

Bin Laden eventually left Sudan for Jalalabad in May 1996 on board a privately owned, twelve-passenger chartered plane piloted by a Russian who didn't speak a word of Arabic and had no inkling of just who he was transporting. Those travelling with bin Laden included his personal bodyguard Humud al-Zubayr (killed in the 2001 US invasion of Afghanistan), Sayf al-Adl al-Misri and two of bin Laden's sons, Saad and Omar.

Sayf al-Adl had no trust in the pilot: he didn't tell him their route in advance and only disclosed their destination when they were nearly in Afghan airspace. He sat close beside him in the front seat throughout the entire journey, his gun across his lap, scouring maps and checking the navigation instruments. The other al-Qa'ida men were also armed. (Bin Laden related this adventure with some humour during my visit to Tora Bora; I can only imagine that the pilot must have been terrified.)

The operation was highly secret and only President al-Bashir and the head of his intelligence service knew the departure time from Khartoum airport. Coordination on the other side was the responsibility of Engineer Mahmood from the Afghan Islamist group Hezb-e-Islami whose leader, Yunis Khalis, was at the airport to receive these guests personally.

Following his exit from Sudan, bin Laden received three catastrophic financial blows. The first was a decision by the Saudi government to freeze all his known assets; they had been incensed when bin Laden praised the 1996 Khobar Towers bombing, and now insisted they would accept nothing less than his return home in full repentance. It is estimated that the assets frozen by the authorities ranged, on the day they were placed under the control of an official agency, from $200–300 million. Prince Turki al-Faisal, the former head of the Saudi intelligence service, estimates that bin Laden still controls around $50 million in the form of currency held in secret bank accounts.

Bin Laden told me that he had later received a message, delivered to him by his mother and uncle who visited him in Kandahar, in which the Saudi government offered to unfreeze his assets and double their value to half a billion dollars, under certain conditions. In order to repossess the $200–300 million, he was to return to the kingdom and announce upon arrival, at the airport, that the Saudi royal family was indeed implementing *shari'ah*, and that the Saudi monarch was a faithful Muslim who abided by the teachings of his religion. The reason for this strange demand was that bin Laden had very publicly accused the House of Al Saud of apostasy and blasphemy, charges punishable by death. In *shari'ah* terms it would have been permissible to shed the blood of those in charge of the regime. Additionally, dethroning the king or overthrowing the royal family would become a religious duty.

The second financial blow bin Laden received was the Sudanese government's inability to pay back the costs of the projects he undertook for them, including the 'Defiance Highway' linking Port Sudan and Khartoum. Bin Laden told me he lost about $165 million in these projects, and that he managed to recover no more than about 10 per cent of his investments. He added that when he consulted al-Bashir about recovering his money he was told the Sudanese treasury was empty and that they could only pay him in wheat, corn, gum or cattle, which he could sell to other countries to recoup his debts. (Hence bin Laden's ironic comment to me in Tora Bora about the likelihood of anyone buying such commodities from a notorious fugitive; Dr Muhammad al-Masari, a Saudi dissident living in London and a specialist on al-Qa'ida's ideology, told me that he did indeed remember an al-Qa'ida delegation arriving from Afghanistan on a mission from bin Laden to sell grain in 1996.)

The third blow was the loss of a number of businesses that had been closed down because their connection to bin Laden was leaked to the Saudi government. The source was a relative, the husband of one of bin Laden's nieces and formerly a resident of London, who surrendered himself to Saudi intelligence. He then moved to the United Arab Emirates and from there to Riyadh, where he disclosed some of al-Qa'ida's financial secrets in order to pave the way for his return home.

What pained bin Laden most was Sudan's apparent ingratitude. It aggrieved him that they betrayed him in exchange for nothing, rather than negotiating some benefit for doing so.

The bombing of Khobar Towers was a major turning point for al-Qa'ida. Bin Laden did not immediately claim responsibility for the attack, and the Saudi government was keen to assert that it was the work of Shi'ite terrorist groups. The Saudi government refused to cooperate with the subsequent American investigation and withheld permission to interrogate a number of detainees suspected of plotting the attack.

A source close to al-Qaʻida said at the time that the attack on the National Guard quarters in Riyadh had been in retaliation for the persecution of one of al-Qaʻida's leaders. The attack on Khobar Towers, however, was in revenge for the execution of four men who were accused of the Riyadh bombing and forced to confess on television, while in reality they had nothing do with the attack.

A short while after the Khobar bombing, in August 1996, bin Laden faxed *al-Quds al-Arabi* his 'Declaration of *Jihad* Against the Americans Occupying the Land of the Two Sacred Places'. That communiqué was not issued in the name of the Advice and Reform Committee, as all previous statements condemning the situation in Saudi Arabia had been when he was in Sudan. The twelve-page document was signed personally by bin Laden.

The Saudi ambassador in Islamabad exercised considerable pressure on Sheikh Yunis Khalis (who held a Saudi passport and had a good relationship with the royal family) and Jalaluddin Haqqani to hand over bin Laden, but they refused. They issued a joint statement: 'If an animal sought refuge with us we would have had no choice but to protect it. How, then, about a man who has given himself and his wealth in the cause of Allah and in the cause of *jihad* in Afghanistan?'

Bin Laden had initially been wary of the Taliban, but established a good relationship with them after his first meeting with their *emir* ('prince' or 'leader'), Mullah Omar, in the summer of 1996. The latter expressed great admiration for his Arab guest's neutral observations and refusal to side with any of the *mujahedin* factions that were deadlocked in the struggle for power. Bin Laden decided to give his *bayat* (pledge of allegiance) to Mullah Omar. He ordered his own followers to fight under the banner of the *emir* and despatched a group of 300 strong and hardy Arab *mujahedin* to the Tajik areas in order to fight the anti-Taliban Northern Alliance. (Bin Laden would later relate with great sadness that many of these men died on the way from the cold, unable to endure the harsh conditions of those regions.) However, though it has been asserted that a relationship by marriage was established between Mullah Omar and bin Laden, through the former marrying the latter's daughter, such talk is completely unfounded.

The Saudi government tried to win the Taliban movement over when they saw them gaining power. When Kabul fell, Saudi Arabia recognized the Taliban as the legitimate rulers of Afghanistan. They sent pilgrimage invitations to every cabinet member, and Sheikh Muhammad Rabbani, the Taliban prime minister, accepted.

Once the relationship between Mullah Omar and bin Laden was consolidated, and al-Qa'ida's security in Afghanistan assured, bin Laden decided to take definitive action against the US. In early 1998 he obtained a *fatwa* signed by forty Afghan and Pakistani scholars supporting his earlier communiqué in which he demanded the expulsion of US troops from the Arabian Peninsula. In February 1998 he and al-Zawahiri announced the formation of the World Islamic Front for Jihad Against the Jews and Crusaders. This was, in effect, an umbrella group for various *jihadi* organizations including Egyptian Islamic Jihad (led by al-Zawahiri), Egyptian Jama'at Islamiyah (led by Rifa'i Taha) and several others from Kashmir and Pakistan. Bin Laden's focus widened to encompass other politically and ideologically similar networks and, crucially, to target the US and its allies globally, everywhere and anywhere he could.

All of this coincided with the escalation of the US military threat against Iraq after Saddam Hussein expelled the United Nations weapons inspection teams. As a US attack on Iraq became imminent, bin Laden sought to harness Arab and Islamic resentment. Establishing himself as a popular Islamic hero who dared issue a *fatwa* inciting attacks on the US would enable him to use this position to mobilize the masses for battle. However, the US managed to contain the crisis, and Saddam Hussein agreed to let the inspectors back in.

The bombings of the American embassies in Nairobi and Dar-es-Salaam using two explosives-laden trucks on 7 August 1998 were the first attacks by the World Islamic Front. Statements issued by al-Qa'ida explained that these cities had been chosen because they each housed a large US military presence and because both the Kenyan and Tanzanian governments backed US aggression against Iraq and had close links with Israel.

The US administration responded to these attacks by bombarding al-Qa'ida positions in Afghanistan. Their targets included bin Laden's quarters in Kandahar – a disused Soviet airbase – but, with the uncanny 'sixth sense' he has often exhibited in such circumstances, he and his family had left the place two days before the bombardment.

On 21 August 1998, in the wake of the US bombardment, Muhammad Atef (then al-Qa'ida's military chief) telephoned me at the paper to declare that the US bombardment had failed to accomplish its objectives: Osama bin Laden was still alive, and so were all the leaders of al-Qa'ida. The bombardment had resulted in the martyrdom of five fighters, he said, two from Yemen, two from Saudi Arabia and one from Egypt. He promised to send the photographs of the five men by post, and did indeed do so a while later. He then added that Sheikh Osama bin Laden wished to send this message to US President Bill Clinton: that he would avenge this attack in a spectacular way and would deal a blow to America that would shake it to its very foundations, a blow it had never experienced before. It would seem that this revenge was delivered by means of the attacks on the World Trade Center and Pentagon on 11 September 2001, and shows that preparations for 11 September may have been well under way at the time the two US embassies in Africa were bombed.

Under immense pressure from the US to put bin Laden out of commission, Prince Turki of Saudi intelligence flew to Kandahar in September 1998. He travelled in a private jet accompanied by Sheikh Abdullah al-Turki, who was at the time the Saudi minister of Islamic affairs, and Salman al-Omari, the Saudi *chargé d'affaires* in Kabul.

The Syrian radical Islamist Abu Mus'ab al-Suri was present at this meeting, and gave me a very detailed account by telephone afterwards. The Saudi delegation asked Mullah Omar to cede bin Laden to the US because he was a terrorist. Mullah Omar was enraged by this request, that a Muslim government would seek to deliver a fellow Muslim to an 'infidel state'. He said to the Saudi prince: 'If you speak in the name of America, do not blame me for speaking in the name of bin Laden.' Prince Turki claimed Mullah Omar had previously promised to hand over bin Laden, but Mullah Omar categorically denied this. He spoke rather harshly to Prince Turki, but the interpreter refused to translate everything he said. Mullah Omar insisted that his exact words be communicated to the prince, who was then so angry that he threatened to withdraw Saudi recognition of the Taliban government; bearing in mind that only three countries ever had acknowledged its legitimacy, this was a very serious matter. Mullah Omar heatedly ordered the prince to leave and take the *chargé d'affaires* with him. Soon afterwards, the Saudi government severed diplomatic relations with the Taliban.

Bin Laden: A Portrait

Bin Laden's reputation as a warrior amongst those alongside whom he has fought is marked by deep admiration for his courage and for the fact that he displays no fear of death. He has frequently expressed regret that he has not yet been 'martyred' like so many of his comrades in Afghanistan. During the Afghan *jihad* he came under heavy bombardment more than forty times. On at least three of these occasions, witnesses say, gruesome carnage ensued, with flesh and body parts flying in the air, but no trace of fear was visible in bin Laden. One of the *mujahedin* who fought in Afghanistan told me that once a Scud missile exploded less than twenty yards from bin Laden, who didn't flinch. He was hospitalized several times after being wounded in battle. Once he was nearly killed by poison gas from a chemical weapons attack, and still suffers throat pain as a result.

Osama bin Laden was the twenty-first of twenty-nine brothers, yet he always had immense authority and influence within the family, especially after he was fêted as a hero during the Afghan war. In any family feuds – which are inevitable in such a large clan – he would be brought in as an arbiter. The claim that his brothers disowned him after 11 September is not entirely true. A statement that they disowned him was indeed published in the Saudi press, but I have been told that this was under duress in response to enormous pressure from various authorities. Many family members have dissociated themselves from that statement in private, and I have met several of his siblings personally who express great admiration for their brother as a person and as a Muslim. However, I do not believe they approve of his violent acts, which seem to have taken them completely by surprise, and they have indeed been at pains to distance themselves from these attacks.

While researching this book, my meetings with bin Laden's brothers and sisters took me to several European capitals. They have requested that their names not be mentioned for fear of repercussions. Two of bin Laden's younger sisters were particularly eager to meet me. They hadn't seen their brother for many years and wanted to know every detail of my meeting with him – how his health was, what he ate, what he drank, how he walked and so on.

Contrary to what many believe or claim, bin Laden does not have any special or personal relationship with the Saudi royal family. Certainly he would have met some of them when he lived in Saudi Arabia, as many of his brothers are close to them, but when I met him he expressed a very deep-rooted contempt for the Al Saud, which he described as consisting of 'corrupt infidels' who had 'stolen the wealth of the nation and deviated from Islam'. He may also have a more personal reason to bear a grudge against the royal family: according to his brother and eldest of the male siblings, Ali bin Laden, who now lives in Paris, the royal family had appointed a Council of Guardians to administer the bin Ladens' father's estate after his death, and that Osama was often infuriated by the council's incompetence.

Bin Laden harbours an absolutely malicious hatred for the US. This probably dates back to its treatment of the Afghan and Arab *mujahedin* during the war against the Soviet Union in Afghanistan. As he describes it, they used the fighters for their own ends, exploiting their Islamic fervour to rid a Muslim land of 'infidel' occupiers and then, once the Soviets had been defeated, simply tossed them aside like discarded tissues. Then, bin Laden says, the US did exactly as the Soviets had done, occupying a Muslim land themselves by sending troops to the Arabian Peninsula in 1990. There are many assertions that bin Laden had been connected to the CIA or other foreign intelligence agencies; in Prince Turki's view, expressed during an interview with the Arab satellite channel MBC: 'We have no knowledge of any communications between him and foreign government agencies save for the Pakistani government.' Indeed, it is probably due to his connections with the Pakistani intelligence services that bin Laden was able to slip away through the back door, as it were, when the US bombed Tora Bora in November 2001.

Bin Laden sees the US as the root of all evil – theologically, politically and morally – and the source of all the misfortunes that have befallen the *umma* (Muslim world). He has said that he hates the US for supporting such corrupt and oppressive Arab regimes as Saudi Arabia, and for its unquestioning backing of Israel.

Bin Laden's popularity among many of the world's 1.3 billion Muslims might well be accounted for by the fact that he is perceived as giving voice to feelings of frustration, alienation and neglect. Muslims in favour of bin Laden feel he is a powerful person who fights in their corner.

It is my experience that bin Laden enjoys wide popularity on the Arabian Peninsula especially, and particularly, in Saudi Arabia and Yemen. In Yemen – where his father came from – people appear very proud of their infamous compatriot and hang his portrait on their walls. A large percentage of his followers and all his bodyguards are Yemenis or come from the Assir region of southern Saudi Arabia, which historically was part of Yemen. Bin Laden trusts his sixteen personal bodyguards absolutely, not only because of the connection with his father but because Yemenis are renowned in the Arab world for gallantry, bravery, sincerity and loyalty.

The Western media has also played a part in elevating bin Laden to the status of folk hero in the Muslim world, as whoever is portrayed as an enemy of the US tends to be celebrated.

One measure of the level of admiration for bin Laden in the Muslim world is the sudden popularity of the name 'Osama'. In northern Nigeria, which is predominantly Muslim, 70 per cent of baby boys born in the months following 11 September were named after him.[2] It has also become popular in Mali, Pakistan, Senegal, Palestine, southern Philippines and Thailand. When I was in Turkey I noticed a great demand for cigarette lighters bearing his image, and a shopkeeper there told me bin Laden was his hero, that he had his photo on the wall at home. T-shirts with pictures of bin Laden on the front are now popular not only in the Muslim world but also in Central and South America.

Bin Laden conducts himself with a certain humility. He is never aloof, eats with his men and dresses as they do. He encourages his wives and children to live the same austere, ascetic lifestyle that he himself has chosen, despite being from one of the wealthiest families in the world. I am sure this also contributes to his popularity. Saad al-Faqih, a Saudi dissident living in London, told me that when bin Laden was in Sudan he had air conditioning in his quarters but, even when the temperature reached 50 degrees Celsius, never turned it on. He also reported that bin Laden fasts for two days in every week, in summer and winter.[3]

Abu Jandal (real name: Nasir al-Bahri) was one of bin Laden's bodyguards, with whom we conducted lengthy interviews for *al-Quds al-Arabi*.[4] He recalls that upon the discovery of a plot to assassinate bin Laden, Mullah Omar asked him to move from Jalalabad to Kandahar, where he would be safer. He gave him two choices of accommodation – either the electric company compound which had all amenities, or a disused Soviet airbase that had none.

Bin Laden chose the latter, where he and his family lived without running water, electricity or even a toilet. He said he wanted to live the way the Prophet's companions and the early Muslims lived.

The principles behind such austerity are as strategic as they are ascetic. Bin Laden often talked about military organizations that fail because of the extravagance of the leadership and the inability of their soldiers to endure hardship.

Abu Jandal reported that bin Laden had a bitter argument with his eldest son Abdullah about his lifestyle when they were living in Khartoum. Abdullah reasoned that God had blessed the family with wealth and that they should therefore enjoy it. He later returned to Saudi Arabia with the help of his uncles and the blessing of the royal family, joined the family business and started to lead a life of luxury. (Ironically, this disagreement saved bin Laden from an attempt on his life. It delayed his return to his office by a few minutes, so he wasn't there when a hit squad burst in and opened fire on everyone inside.)

Bin Laden married four women after his Syrian cousin Najua. Three of his other wives are from Saudi Arabia, and the fifth from Yemen. Najua left Sudan with her son Abdullah and returned to Saudi Arabia, where she is still living. His second wife, Umm Ali, was divorced in Sudan, and also returned to Saudi Arabia with her son and daughter. She now lives in Jeddah.

Bin Laden married for a fifth time in July 2000, this time to a seventeen-year-old Yemeni woman named Amal al-Sadah. He paid a dowry of $5,000. The marriage was arranged by Abu Jandal, who says the al-Qa'ida leader threw a fabulous party to celebrate the wedding, attended by a group of his followers. By all accounts his wives have coexisted happily under one roof for many years, and bin Laden tolerates no disputes among them.

Bin Laden's eleven sons and thirteen daughters have all lived with him in Afghanistan except for his eldest son, Abdullah, and another son and a daughter by his second wife, Umm Ali. When Abdullah returned to Saudi Arabia to live a more affluent lifestyle, he dealt bin Laden a heavy blow. Bin Laden considered his behaviour disobedient and disrespectful, and never mentions his name. Umm Ali rebelled against him while in Sudan and asked for a divorce. Like Abdullah, she could not endure the life of harsh austerity that was forced upon them.

His wives Umm Hamzah and Umm Khaled are both from well-known Saudi families. The former has a doctorate in Arabic language studies and the latter a doctorate in *shari'ah*. Umm Khaled comes from the renowned al-Sharif family; she is the sister of one of bin Laden's comrades from the Afghan *jihad*. These two wives may still be with bin Laden, although sources close to al-Qa'ida have told me that he travels alone with just one bodyguard now that he is constantly on the run.

His Yemeni wife Amal was smuggled out of Afghanistan with her baby daughter two months after 11 September. In early 2002 she returned to Yemen, having been in hiding in Pakistan. She was detained and interrogated before being placed under house arrest in her father's compound. Later that year she, her father and her brother were all arrested after a gun battle at the compound; nobody is sure where they are now. When she first returned to Yemen I tried to contact her for an interview, but the Yemeni government had banned the whole family from speaking to the media.

Bin Laden used to enjoy the rural life, and loves horse riding. He often organized trips to the desert for the family and trained his wives and children in the use of firearms. He also enjoyed sport, especially volleyball – because he is 6 feet 3 inches tall, he had an advantage over his rivals. In Afghanistan he would captain one team and Abu Hafs al-Misri the other; people who were there at the time report that these matches were watched by a large crowd of al-Qa'ida *mujahedin*, and were very competitive and spirited.

There have been reports that bin Laden suffers from serious illnesses. Some fanciful accounts even had him requiring kidney dialysis – often on the same page as another story which had him fleeing US bombardments on horseback through the mountains. I had heard that he has some form of mild diabetes, but when I spent three days with him and slept in the same cave, I didn't notice him taking any medication or showing any signs of ill health at all. We walked for more than two hours in the snow-covered mountains, and he seemed fit and well.

I know that he was hit in the left shoulder by shrapnel during the bombardment of Tora Bora in 2001. This was evident in his first television recording following the attack in January 2002, when he wanted to prove to the world that he was still alive. It could be seen that his left shoulder was larger than his right, and his left arm seemed completely paralyzed; he didn't move it at all despite being left-handed. In a subsequent television appearance later the same year he deliberately moved his left shoulder and arm in order to prove that he was well. It is believed that al-Zawahiri, who is a qualified surgeon, performed an operation to remove the shrapnel.

Bin Laden has been the object of several assassination attempts. On one occasion the Saudi government is alleged to have sent an eighteen-year-old Tajik man to Kandahar to carry out the mission, having promised him Saudi citizenship and 1 million Saudi *riyals* – the equivalent of $250,000. However, the young man was caught before the act, admitted his guilt and broke down weeping. When bin Laden confronted him face-to-face, he asked if he had thought it likely he would escape alive after carrying out the assassination. The young man was so terrified he couldn't speak through his sobs. Bin Laden pardoned him and ordered his guards to let him go.

Abu Jandal disclosed that one night prior to the bombardment of Kandahar in August 1998, bin Laden left for Khost to tour its training camps. An Afghan cook working for the CIA told its agents where bin Laden was headed. With his 'sixth sense' mentioned earlier, bin Laden suddenly changed his mind halfway along the journey and went to Kabul instead. The following day, US warplanes raided the al-Qa'ida camps in Khost, killing five.

Bin Laden didn't like to use the term 'salaries' and called the money he paid al-Qa'ida members 'monthly sponsorship'. The sponsorships were offered only to those who were married and ranged from $50 to $120 per month, depending on the size of the family and the rank of its breadwinner. Unmarried members did not receive any monthly stipends. They would eat in the camps or bases, where meals were prepared and served three times daily.

After 11 September and the retaliatory attacks on Tora Bora, bin Laden has been on the run. Little is known about his personal life since November 2001.

I am always being asked: 'What does bin Laden want?' I do not believe that the world's most dangerous man has any particular personal ambitions – he does not, as is often claimed, wish to become the Muslims' *caliph*. According to the dissident Saad al-Faqih, bin Laden could not, in any case, ever be *caliph*: 'He is from Hadramaut, and his tribe is not from Quraish. Islamic prophecies state that he who will re-establish the caliphate will originate from Quraish and be a descendant of the Prophet.'

Life for bin Laden is a test designed by the Creator to examine his faith, steadfastness and obedience. He used to say that he only aspired to Paradise, and the quickest way to that destination was martyrdom fighting for the cause of Allah.

Bin Laden has constantly changed his tactics and strategies, exhibiting extraordinary flexibility. The man who wishes to die has nevertheless contrived to remain alive to be the bane of the US. Having expended $337 billion on the wars in Afghanistan and Iraq with the aim, in large measure, of finishing off al-Qa'ida, the Bush administration has succeeded only in providing the network with a safe haven at the heart of the Arab world and enabling bin Laden to consolidate a reputation amongst millions of people as the most famous Muslim warrior of our times.

2

Holy Warrior

> Terrorizing you while you are carrying arms in our land
> is a legitimate duty we are morally obliged to fulfil . . .
> in order to re-establish the greatness of the *umma* and to
> liberate the occupied sacred places . . . Our youths are
> different from your soldiers. Your problem will be how
> to convince your troops to fight, while our problem
> will be how to restrain our youths.
>
> 'Declaration of *Jihad* Against the Americans Occupying
> the Land of the Two Sacred Places', Osama bin Laden,
> *fatwa*, 1996

Thus, in typically dramatic style, did Osama bin Laden declare
war on the world's greatest superpower from a cave in the Afghan
mountains.

No serious study of bin Laden and al-Qa'ida can ignore the
Islamic background and history from which they have emerged. A
very specific interpretation of the faith, refined and politicized over
the centuries, informs their identity and assures their status in the
Muslim world. Without Islam there would be no al-Qa'ida.

Some Western commentators have responded to bin Laden's
fatwas[1] with less than complete understanding, even derision. People
in the West do not often fully understand the deep connection
many Muslims feel with their past, and how bitterly many lament
the lost glory of the *umma*. This sense of historical loss is all too

often combined with a contemporary experience that is often defined by disappointment and humiliation.

For centuries, Muslim civilizations were the greatest military powers on Earth. Their armies invaded Europe, Africa, India and China. They also led the world in terms of economic power and arts and sciences. Bin Laden's archaic form of rhetoric recalls and celebrates a time when the *umma* was in the ascendant and, coupled with his aggressive assertion that a global caliphate can be re-established, is undeniably part of the charismatic appeal and influence he exerts in the Muslim world. He has become a figurehead for a resurgent Muslim identity which is at once political and inextricably linked with a Salafi interpretation of Islam.

Of course, not all Muslims, nor even all those who follow bin Laden are Salafis. But Islam is the defining feature of the daily lives of most of the world's Muslims, and the significance of this devotion must be understood. Islam informs every aspect of Muslims' existence: behaviour, education, clothes, eating habits and personal relationships. This is why the call to *jihad* (which can, of course, mean several kinds of struggle and does not refer uniquely to military combat) should never be underestimated. Under certain circumstances it becomes a Muslim's sacred duty, which cannot be shaken off lightly.

For centuries Muslim scholars have developed theological and ideological arguments around the concept of *jihad*. In our times this debate impacts on the future security of the whole world. In the Middle East, Asia and Africa the *jihadi* argument against the US – most potently embodied in al-Qa'ida's ideology and even, arguably, in the person of Osama bin Laden – appears to be rapidly gaining ground.

The concept of *jihad* is an intrinsic part of Islam. The model of the *mujahed* (one who undertakes *jihad*) was provided by the Prophet Muhammad himself and has a range of applications, from exercising restraint (morally and, indeed, from acts of violence) to offering oneself as a sacrifice for a noble cause.

The Model of the Prophet

For the first thirteen years of his mission Muhammad enjoined his followers not to respond to persecution with violence in any form. In exchange for their patience, they were told, they would be rewarded with eternal life in Paradise.

After more than a decade of perseverance, Muhammad and his followers were driven from Mecca and dispossessed. The oppressive elders of Quraish had been plotting to murder Muhammad, but he escaped in the middle of the night and sought refuge in Medina. There the Arab tribes of Aws and Khazraj all converted to Islam, while Medina's three Jewish tribes retained their own religion. This is a key moment in the history of Islam, marking the creation of the Muslim political community. Indeed, the Islamic calendar begins with the day of Muhammad's *hijra* (migration) from Mecca to Medina.

Shortly after his arrival, Muhammad was officially recognized as the political head of a new, mixed community in Medina, composed of the Arab inhabitants who had embraced Islam as a faith and a way of life and the Jewish residents who accepted Islam as a political system. It was then that the concept of *jihad* acquired an additional dimension as, it was believed, Allah gave Muslims the right to fight – it could now also signify exerting oneself in combat for victory or martyrdom. (The *shari'ah* is very clear on the subject of *jihad* which does not, incidentally, only mean 'holy war'. The Arabic word for war is *al-harb*, and for combat, *al-qital*. *Jihad* as defined in the *shari'ah* means literally to 'strive', 'struggle', 'persevere' or 'labour', and can also mean the moral battle a person undergoes in resisting sin and temptation.)

The unity of the Muslims in *hijra* demonstrated that Islam was a stronger bond than blood or feudal ties. For this reason *hijra* is a key concept in al-Qa'ida's recruitment strategy, inspiring young men to leave their families and homes and join the *jihad* wherever it may be.

The first major battle in the history of Islam was in 624 CE. The polytheist Meccans sent an army of about 800 to attack the Muslims at Badr. Numbering just 300, the Muslims won the battle with very few casualties. This victory continues to inspire young Muslims, and is celebrated every year during the month of Ramadan.

In 630, Muhammad returned to Mecca in triumph, marching on the city with an army of 10,000 Muslims. The Meccans surrendered almost immediately, and the majority of the city's inhabitants voluntarily converted to Islam.

Town after town and province after province, Arabia fell to the Muslims, and Arabs embraced the new creed in their thousands. Only those who campaigned militarily against the Prophet and his followers were fought and forced to surrender. The claim that Islam was forced on people or that it was spread by means of the sword are entirely baseless.

For several generations, the Muslim nation expanded geographically and demographically. These first generations of Muslims are known as the Salaf. The incredibly rapid spread of Islam throughout the Arabian Peninsula and way beyond is often held to be due to the fact that the model they presented was superior in moral values and respect for humanity than any other in existence elsewhere at the time.

Not surprisingly, the continuing decline of Muslim fortunes the world over since the 'Golden Age' has been blamed on rulers and peoples deviating from the true path of Allah. Calls for a return to the 'true faith', as practised in the time of Muhammad and those who came immediately after him, have recurred frequently throughout the history of the Muslim world, exemplified by the Salafis (who do not embody a specific ideology; 'Salafism' is more of a generic term embracing a wide spectrum of conviction from the very mild and moderate to the most extreme and violent).

Jihad

Muslims strive to live their lives by the book – literally. It is to the book or books that we must turn in trying to understand the concept of *jihad* or religiously inspired struggle. In this case we are not talking about the personal *jihad* in which the believer struggles spiritually, but *jihad* in the sense of combat.

There are two main sources in Islam: the Qur'an – believed to be the eternally true and trustworthy Word of Allah as revealed to Muhammad – and the Hadith. *Hadiths* are texts recording either actual sayings of the Prophet or descriptions of his actions as reported by his companions. They were mostly written down after the Prophet's death, since he did not want people to confuse the revealed words of Allah with his own. For Muslims, the Hadith texts are indispensable, as they explain or complement the Qur'an.

Unfortunately there was a tendency among some unscrupulous political and ideological groups to fabricate *hadiths* for their own ends; Muslim scholars, especially at the beginning of the second century of Islam, embarked on the exacting task of extrapolating the authentic material from the huge body of texts attributed to the Prophet.

There are six main collections of the Hadith canon which vary in reliability. Only two collections are accepted by the majority of Sunni Muslims as 100 per cent authentic: those written by al-Bukhari and Muslim ibn al-Hajjaj.

There is no clergy as such in Islam, but the interpretation and application of the Qur'an and the Hadith is a crucial role fulfilled by Islamic scholars, known as the *ulama* ('learned ones').

Shari'ah is a set of guidelines drawn from both the Qur'an and the Hadith. The Islamic state established by the Taliban from 1996–2001 was governed by *shari'ah*. Commentators such as Dr Azzam Tamimi, director of the London-based Institute of Islamic Political Thought, deny that *shari'ah* is championed and applied solely by groups such as the Taliban and al-Qa'ida. He suggests that one of the main reasons al-Qa'ida's rhetoric abounds with terms such as *jihad* and *shari'ah* is precisely because they are so important to the average Muslim. Al-Qa'ida, he argues, is reflecting a longing that is already in the hearts of Muslims, and this is why its message is so enormously appealing.

It is a completely alien cultural concept for many in the West that a religion might not only sanction killing but enjoin its followers to kill as a religious duty. In certain circumstances Islam does just this.

According to the Qur'an, Allah gave the Muslims permission for *jihad* in the second year of *hijra* to defend themselves and deter their enemies from attacking them. The Qur'an very clearly states: 'Fight in the cause of Allah those who fight you and do not transgress, for Allah loves not the aggressors' (2:190). However, peace may be made with those who give up hostilities: 'But if they desist let there be no hostility except against the wrongdoers' (2:193).

Anticipating reluctance to undertake *jihad* the Qur'an acknowledges: 'Combat is ordained for you, though it is hateful unto you; but it may happen that you hate a thing which is good for you, and it may happen that you love a thing which is bad for you. And Allah knows, but you do not' (2:216).

Perhaps these quotations can help us understand how the apparently mild-mannered, soft-spoken Osama bin Laden became the terror of the Western world.

Jihad as combat is perceived as having two expressions – offensive and defensive. The aim of offensive *jihad* is to come to the rescue of the oppressed and deter tyrants who might contemplate attacking Muslims. This form of *jihad* is characterized as *fard kifayah*, meaning that if some capable Muslims are engaged in accomplishing the mission others are exempt from the duty.

Defensive *jihad* is considered *fard 'ayn*, meaning obligatory for every single Muslim at the time and place concerned. Many Muslims concur that such invaders as colonizers or occupying forces are cause for defensive *jihad*. Some (certainly bin Laden and al-Zawahiri) would add that struggle against an oppressive regime is a legitimate expression of defensive *jihad*. It is worth mentioning here that defensive *jihad* is not restricted to physical fighting. A devout Muslim, according to Islam, can contribute in one of three ways: become a fighter, with the attendant guarantee of immediate access to Paradise in the event of martyrdom; support *jihad* financially (bin Laden has also done this in abundance); or support it morally, by believing in the just cause and, if required, taking care of the family of a person who has left for the battlefield.

Defensive *jihad* is the absolute religious duty of every able-bodied Muslim man, and if asked to participate by a 'just and pious leader' he must not refuse. The emphasis on the calibre of leadership here is very important, and gives us some insight into why bin Laden is so careful about his image. His piety and austere lifestyle have become legendary in the Muslim world.

Offensive *jihad* can only be called for by the *caliph*, the head of the *umma*. The question of which Muslim authority, if any, may declare offensive and defensive *jihad* has been particularly problematic since 3 March 1924, when Kemal Atatürk abolished the *de facto* caliphate, which the Ottoman sultans had held since 1517, and the empire collapsed into nearly fifty different nation-states divided according to racial, ethnic, linguistic, political, geographical and historical differences.

The absence of a caliph is seen by some Muslims as a violation of the *shari'ah*, and restoring it a crucial first step in reversing their fortunes. One of al-Qa'ida's declared aims is to restore the caliphate and, by implication, the former glory of the *umma*.

The Rise of Political Islam

Whole books have been devoted to this topic alone. I intend here to limit my observations to the scholars and ideologues who have most directly influenced bin Laden and al-Zawahiri in the development of their own *jihadi* tenets.

Bin Laden has been influenced and informed by a variety of Islamic schools of thought that can be collectively characterized as Salafi. He has personally encountered many of the most esteemed contemporary Islamic scholars and ideologues, but is believed to have been most influenced first by Abdullah Azzam and then by al-Zawahiri, later his deputy in al-Qa'ida.

Salafis' belief that only the first three generations of Muslims followed the correct path refers to the Prophet Muhammad's saying, reported in a *hadith*: 'The best of people is my generation, then those that come after them, then those that come after them.'

Taqi al-Din ibn Taymiyyah (1262–1328) was probably the first Salafi. He began his intellectual career at a very young age and is considered one of the greatest Islamic scholars ever to have lived. He was based (mainly) in Damascus at a time of immense political and religious upheaval in the Muslim world. In 1258 the unthinkable happened: the invading Mongol armies defeated the Abbasid Empire, the caliphate, and ransacked its capital, Baghdad. Ibn Taymiyyah sought an explanation for this calamity and concluded that Muslims were no longer following the true faith and were neglecting their religious duties. He reminded his contemporaries of the Prophet's promise to the first Muslims just before his death: 'I leave with you two things, you shall never go wrong so long as you adhere to them: the Book of Allah and my Sunnah.' (The Sunnah refers to the traditions of the Prophet.)

Ibn Taymiyyah was particularly outspoken in his condemnation of Muslim leaders for not upholding and encouraging true Islamic faith and *shari'ah*. Naturally, this made him many powerful enemies, and he was imprisoned several times both in his native Syria and in Egypt. His popularity among the masses, however, grew throughout his life, and when he died 200,000 people mourned him in the streets.

Bin Laden and al-Zawahiri are not alone in admiring Ibn Taymiyyah, who some consider an ideological guru and role model. Reputed to have been a warrior of dauntless courage, Ibn Taymiyyah was also known for his great piety and sense of justice. Intellectually brilliant with a prodigious memory and encyclopaedic knowledge, he was also a great orator.

He virulently condemned those converts to Islam, in particular the Mongols, who wanted to incorporate traces of their previous beliefs into their new faith. The Mongols had by then converted to

Islam but failed to adopt the *shari'ah*, holding instead to the *yasa* codes of law brought to them by Genghis Khan. Ibn Taymiyyah issued a *fatwa* against the Mongols – establishing a precedent of *jihad* against the *kafir* (infidels) even if they happen to be rulers.

Bin Laden refers to Ibn Taymiyyah in his 1996 'Declaration of *Jihad* Against the Americans . . .', stating that true believers will incite the *umma* against its enemies just as their ancestor scholars like Ibn Taymiyyah did.

Wahhabism, the Saudis' own branch of Islam which originated in the eighteenth century, is addressed in some detail later. Here I wish only to draw attention to the role of *jihad* in establishing Wahhabism – at that time considered the true faith – in the region. By 1811, through an alliance with the warrior Ibn Saud, the Wahhabis managed to unite much of the Peninsula under their umbrella. In the early part of the twentieth century, a group of followers of Ibn Abd al-Wahhab known as the Ikhwan ('Brothers') emerged from among the Bedouin; up to 100,000 of these very ferocious *mujahedin* were based in camps called *hijra* (in homage to Muhammad's flight from Mecca). Their aim was to fight 'deviant' Muslims as well as non-Muslims as part of their project to bring the Peninsula back to what they considered to be 'the true path'.

It is interesting to note that the Saudi authorities refer to al-Qa'ida as a 'deviant group' in direct reference to this earlier history – a state of affairs not without irony, as al-Qa'ida has openly accused the Al Saud of being *kafir* themselves.

Wahhabism is one of the two main trends that influenced the thinking of al-Qa'ida leaders, the other being Qutbism, based on the thoughts and writings of the Egyptian Sayyid Qutb (1906–66).

The two years Qutb spent studying in the US in 1948–50 turned him against Western liberalism and, once back in Egypt, he set about warning his countrymen against the dangers of Western lifestyles. He joined the Muslim Brotherhood (MB), becoming one of its most vociferous champions. The MB was founded in 1928 by the Egyptian Hassan al-Banna on the following principles: 'Allah is our objective, the Prophet is our leader, the Qur'an is our constitution, *jihad* is our way and dying in the way of Allah is our highest hope.'

The MB spread at an astonishing rate through the 1930s, and now has branches in seventy countries. Most manifestations of Islamism have been influenced by it to some extent. Except in the case of occupation by a foreign power where they condone armed resistance (as in Palestine and Iraq), the MB's agenda nowadays is to find peaceful means to achieve reform and to participate wherever possible in the political process. Many of the more violent *jihadi* organizations, including al-Qa'ida, condemn this approach as a form of compromise.

Qutb's writings have been adopted by groups like al-Qa'ida to confirm and establish certain core precepts concerning governance, most significantly that the oneness and sovereignty of God preclude human rule, which should be violently overturned if necessary; that the only legitimate form of government over Muslims is an Islamic state headed by a *caliph*. Qutb borrowed the term *jahilyya* from the Indian-born scholar al-Mawdudi – this is the bestial state of ignorance man is believed to have lived in before the arrival of Islam; bin Laden often refers to it.

Qutb was arrested and imprisoned for an alleged attempt to assassinate Nasser in 1954. He spent most of the rest of his life in prison, where he wrote some of the most influential Islamic texts of the modern age. These include *In the Shade of the Qur'an* and a manifesto of political Islam, *Milestones*. His writing sprang from his own radicalization, having witnessed and experienced barbarous violence and torture in prison, and his rejection of what he considered to be the utterly illegitimate regime of Nasser. Offered the opportunity of release if he would beg Nasser for a pardon, he uttered these famous words: 'The index finger that testifies to the oneness of God in every prayer refuses to request a pardon from a tyrant.' He was executed in 1966.

Another scholar closely associated with the genesis of al-Qa'ida is

Abdullah Azzam, bin Laden's mentor from his university days. A Palestinian from the West Bank who fled to Jordan during the Six-Day War, Azzam was influenced by Qutb's teachings. He asserted the necessity of _jihad_ to liberate Muslim lands from foreign occupation, but did not believe that violence should be used against Muslim regimes no matter how far they appeared to have deviated from _shari'ah_ principles.

Five years after the Soviets invaded Afghanistan, in 1984, Azzam issued 'Defence of the Muslim Lands, the First Obligation After Faith', a _fatwa_ declaring that _jihad_ in Palestine and Afghanistan was _fard 'ayn_ (obligatory) for all Muslims. This _fatwa_ was supported by the Grand Mufti of Saudi Arabia, Sheikh Abdul Aziz bin Bazz, whose 1990 _fatwa_ welcoming US troops on Saudi soil would later constitute a remarkable volte-face.

Azzam moved to Peshawar in 1980, playing a key role in mobilizing the Afghan Arabs, organizing travel, accommodation and military training at camps he established for the purpose. In much of this he was aided by bin Laden and the two men became very close, establishing an organization called Makhtab al-Khidamat (MAK). Azzam joined the battle himself and fought regularly with both Afghan and Arab _mujahedin_ units, becoming an inspirational figure for many Muslims worldwide.

Azzam identified the incitement of other Muslims as a religious duty. It is not unusual nowadays to hear Muslim clerics urging young men to join _jihads_ in Palestine, Iraq or any other country where resistance against an occupation is under way.

Islamic movements had typically been focused on local, national struggles, but Azzam pointed out that many of the so-called national boundaries had actually been imposed upon the _umma_ by European colonizers: 'Unfortunately, when we think about Islam we think nationally. We fail to let our vision pass beyond geographic borders that have been drawn up for us by the _kafir_.' This was the first ideological step towards the global _jihad_ that would characterize the al-Qa'ida project.

Azzam and his two sons were assassinated in 1989. There had been a breach between him and bin Laden, who had been drawing closer to al-Zawahiri. The latter arrived in Peshawar in the mid-1980s and stayed in a camp that brought together members of Islamic Jihad – a group opposed to the Muslim Brotherhood. Azzam was often accused of compromise by al-Zawahiri and his colleagues because he objected to their ideology of *takfir* (accusing fellow Muslims of apostasy), and to their strategic goal of toppling existing regimes by force.

There is little basis, however, for the suggestion that bin Laden authorized Azzam's murder. Other suspects have included the ISI (Pakistani intelligence), the CIA and Mossad (Israeli intelligence), which feared Azzam's often declared intention to direct his attentions and *mujahedin* to the liberation of Palestine once the Afghan *jihad* was over. (In 1979 Azzam had issued a highly provocative *fatwa* declaring: 'If only the Muslims would apply Allah's command and implement the laws of *shariʻah* concerning the General March[2] for just one week in Palestine, the Jews would be removed from Palestine.')

In an interesting departure from what most commentators believe, Azzam Tamimi of the Institute of Islamic Political Thought has said that in his opinion the extent of Abdullah Azzam's influence on the formation of al-Qaʻida has been greatly exaggerated. He notes: 'Rather than blame al-Qaʻida on an assumed continuity of ideology and ambition that goes right back to the very foundation of Islam, the real roots of this phenomenon should instead be traced to the profound political crisis that plagues the Muslim world. It is this crisis which propels today's Muslim youths towards al-Qaʻida, which offers an opportunity for nationhood, pride and victory to a generation brought up on demoralization, defeat and humiliation.'

Merging Paths: bin Laden and al-Zawahiri

The development of bin Laden's and al-Qaʻida's ideology – perhaps best described as Salafi-*jihadi* – is inextricably linked with that of al-Zawahiri. Although the two men did not officially join forces under al-Qaʻidaʼs banner until 1998, they certainly met and exerted increasing influence on each other throughout the preceding decade. In particular, al-Zawahiri is thought to have been very instrumental in persuading bin Laden to adopt more violent methods. It is interesting to compare their respective careers during this period.

That bin Laden was not a born warrior seems clear from accounts of his early years, which speak of a mild-mannered man. When he first went to Afghanistan in the early 1980s his initial role was to support the *mujahedin* in financial and administrative ways. He did not remain in the country full-time, but jetted back and forth from Saudi Arabia. There he was active in the family construction company and in contact with the Saudi royal family, which channelled funds to the *mujahedin.* The US was also funding the campaign against the Soviets and championed, trained and armed the *mujahedin* – whose numbers comprised, in large part, the same men who today perpetrate acts of terror worldwide.

Al-Zawahiri (born 1951 in Egypt) is six years bin Ladenʼs senior. He had joined the Muslim Brotherhood at fourteen and adhered to the teachings of Sayyid Qutb, often quoting his saying: ʻBrother, push ahead, for your path is soaked in blood. Do not turn your head right or left but look only up to Heaven.ʼ In one of many paradoxes, al-Zawahiriʼs chosen profession was medicine, and he became a surgeon. By 1979 he had joined the much more radical Islamic Jihad group, which had the overthrow of the Egyptian state at the top of its agenda.

Islamic Jihad reacted to President Anwar Sadatʼs 1979 peace treaty with Israel by assassinating him in 1981. Al-Zawahiri was implicated in the assassination, sent to jail and tortured, despite the lack of evidence against him. It seems to have been whilst in prison that he became leader of Islamic Jihad in Egypt, which he relaunched when he was released in 1984. He travelled to Pakistan and Afghanistan in 1985 to support the *jihad* against the Soviet Union.

In 1986 bin Laden began befriending Egyptian radicals including al-Zawahiri and Abu Hafs al-Misri. At this time the *mujahedin* were under immense military pressure and bin Laden made his debut on the battlefield as a commander. He fought in several battles during the remaining three years of the conflict. There are many (possibly apocryphal) tales from this time. One tells of bin Laden's men crying because they had survived a battle and not been martyred; another, of the battle at Jaji when, under ferocious bombardment by the Soviets, bin Laden entered the state of *seqina* (tranquillity), a spiritual calm, fell asleep and escaped entirely unharmed. (Bin Laden related the latter story to both the British journalist Robert Fisk and to me.)

An embryonic al-Qa'ida first emerged in 1988. It was composed of an 'inner' circle giving their *bayat* (oath of allegiance) to bin Laden, the *emir* or leader, and an 'outer' circle whose numbers and commitment would fluctuate. At this time bin Laden's deputy was Abu Hafs al-Misri, who had been part of Islamic Jihad and was close to al-Zawahiri. It seems to be at this point that bin Laden's and al-Zawahiri's paths came to merge, although they would separate again with the end of the Afghan *jihad* a year later.

Shortly afterwards, following that defining moment in 1990 when the Saudis ignored his offer of *mujahedin* forces against Iraq and turned to the US instead, bin Laden settled in Sudan. Road-building and agricultural projects in Sudan kept him engaged for the next few years, but behind this façade he was evolving his *jihadi* ideology and strategy. Like Azzam, his concept of *jihad* was global rather than local, and in 1992 he was ready to strike at the US. In Aden, al-Qa'ida operatives bombed US servicemen on their way to Somalia; a year later they struck again, launching the Mogadishu attack on three US helicopters.

Al-Zawahiri, meanwhile, returned to Egypt, advocating ever more daring and violent operations by Islamic Jihad. Unlike bin Laden, his agenda at this time was purely local, and his target was the Egyptian government. He also managed to visit the US twice during the early 1990s. His purpose is not clear, but some have suggested he was fundraising for Islamic Jihad. Other sources have indicated that funds were also available at this time for Islamic Jihad from al-Qa'ida.

A very well-placed source has indicated that the failed assassination attempt on Egyptian president Hosni Mubarak in 1995 was funded by al-Qa'ida via Abu Hafs al-Misri and al-Zawahiri. Bin Laden launched his first attack on his other great enemy – the Saudi regime – in 1995 when an al-Qa'ida cell in the kingdom bombed a housing compound for foreign workers in Riyadh. In 1996 the US army was attacked at Khobar and bin Laden issued his 'Declaration of *Jihad* Against the Americans Occupying the Land of the Two Sacred Places', urging Muslims to join him in this fight.

In 1997 al-Zawahiri was implicated in the gruesome massacre of fifty-eight tourists and four Egyptians at Luxor, which he later heralded as a 'major event . . . in the offensive against the enemies of Islam'. The Egyptian public did not agree with this assessment, and whatever popularity *jihadi* groups had enjoyed there swiftly evaporated. In 1998 leaders of several radical groups announced a ceasefire with the government. Al-Zawahiri defiantly rejected this call for peace with the *takfir* (apostate) government and headed for Afghanistan, where he made a definitive alliance with bin Laden, becoming his right-hand man and theoretician. In 1999 he was sentenced to death *in absentia* by the Egyptian authorities.

The World Islamic Front

Insiders assert that bin Laden and al-Zawahiri exerted equal amounts of influence over each other, but in different ways. The increased daring and violence of al-Qa'ida actions together with the manipulation of the media and the development of a psychological strategy came from al-Zawahiri. Al-Zawahiri had been critical of bin Laden's 1996 twelve-page declaration of *jihad* on the US. According to Saad al-Faqih, 'al-Zawahiri told bin Laden that the US would never take him seriously as long as his complaints were reasonable. Wanting to get US troops out of Saudi Arabia is something even the average American citizen can understand and might sympathize with, so this is not going to make the headlines and if it doesn't get the exposure it's not going to help with recruitment'. He also pointed out the impracticality of copying and distributing such a long document. These were days, prior to the Internet, when making photocopies was difficult and expensive.

Instead, al-Zawahiri told bin Laden: 'Let the Americans become your personal media agents – they've got the biggest PR machine in the whole world.' He urged bin Laden to issue a short and to-the-point *fatwa* targeting 'all Americans and all Jews' wherever they are – at home or abroad – and then translate this into action. According to al-Faqih, 'bin Laden was not happy with this idea. He couldn't accept that every American was his enemy. "This is not for the purpose of killing Americans," al-Zawahiri told him. "This is for the purpose of driving them crazy. They are cowboys and will react without thinking."'

On 23 February 1998 bin Laden and al-Zawahiri announced the formation of the World Islamic Front for Jihad against the Jews and Crusaders, which brought together Islamic Jihad, the Egyptian Islamic Group and Pakistani and Bangladeshi militant groups under one umbrella for the first time. The unification of diverse groups was very much part of al-Zawahiri's vision and the concept of globalizing *jihad* had moved to the forefront of the evolving al-Qa'ida ideology.

In their statement, which was sent by fax to me at *al-Quds al-Arabi,* they call upon 'every Muslim who believes in Allah to do Allah's will by killing Americans and stealing their money wherever and whenever possible'.

The American reaction was as predicted by al-Zawahiri. First Sandy Berger (then head of the US National Security Council) announced that he believed bin Laden really did have both the intention and the capability to harm American citizens. The declaration was followed by the simultaneous bombings of US embassies in Nairobi and Dar-es-Salaam in 1998, in which 213 and 11 people were killed respectively.

Bin Laden was now officially Public Enemy Number One in the West. Al-Zawahiri's strategy was a master stroke of propaganda; bin Laden's face was flashed around the globe. He was world-famous in seconds, and in the Muslim world his popularity soared. He had proved he was a credible antagonist to America and, unlike Saddam Hussein (who had also issued a challenge to the superpower), he wasn't an oppressor who owned sixty palaces. Here was someone many Muslims perceived as having been faithful to his cause, living a personal life of quiet austerity.

The US responded with a series of attacks on seven targets in Afghanistan and Sudan, which resulted in public-relations damage both at home and abroad. At a cost of more than $56,250,000 (the price alone of the seventy-five Tomahawk missiles deployed at $750,000 each) the US struck, among other targets, the al-Shifa pharmaceutical plant in Sudan, which was deemed a nerve-gas factory owned by bin Laden. In fact, it produced 50 per cent of the impoverished nation's medicines. The strike inflamed Muslims the world over, and motivated many to join al-Qa'ida in the Afghan Kush.

The bombing of the destroyer USS Cole by two al-Qa'ida suicide bombers in a little skiff in 2000 added to the David-versus-Goliath view of al-Qa'ida – a compelling one for many Muslims who have long felt cowed by the vastly superior military hardware and financial resources of the West.

The Taliban

The Taliban had an enormous impact on world perception of *jihad*. It had emerged from the Afghan *mujahedin* whose heroism the US had lauded for the better part of the 1980s. By the time the US realized what kind of creature it had helped to create, it was too late.

The Taliban was uniquely successful in Islamist terms in that they actually managed to establish the kind of austere, puritanical *shari'ah*-based theocracy that al-Qa'ida and other Salafi-*jihadi* groups long for. Despite the fact that it was only recognized as a legitimate state entity by three countries – Pakistan, Saudi Arabia and the UAE all accepted the credentials of Taliban ambassadors in 1997 – the mini-caliphate under Mullah Omar was left alone to pursue its experiment from 1996–2001.

The Taliban provided al-Qa'ida with a safe haven and sheltered the training camps that would mass-produce *mujahedin* for the coming global *jihad* against what they regarded as the Muslim world's new enemy, the US. Other *jihadi* and guerrilla groups had also set up camps there, but al-Qa'ida's widely broadcast anti-US agenda and preference for 'martyrdom operations' attracted the most zealous and audacious recruits.

Bin Laden told me that when he landed in Jalalabad from Sudan on 18 May 1996 he was under the protection of Sheikh Yunis Khalis, a *mujahedin* leader who was at odds with the Taliban. Initially wary of the Taliban himself, bin Laden soon realized that if they seized control of the whole country, as looked increasingly likely, it might be difficult for him to stay if he didn't form links with them.

The Taliban had emerged in Kandahar, which was being torn apart by warring tribal leaders. Initially an obscure student movement based in local *madrassas* (*taliban* means 'Islamic student'), they were sponsored from the outset by the Pakistani ISI. When one of the warlords abducted and raped a local girl in 1994, the Taliban rose up and started a successful revolt against the tribal leaders, which was quickly joined by the local people.

The Taliban immediately imposed *shari'ah* law on Kandahar, bringing order to bear on utter chaos. As other towns and villages followed suit and rose up against the warlords, it is said that they asked the Taliban for help. Crucially, the ISI turned against Prime Minister Rabbani's government in Kabul and started to support and arm the Taliban.

By the time bin Laden arrived in May 1996, the Taliban had strongholds in many parts of the country. He told me that he spent some time assessing the situation and approved of the Taliban: they appeared to be free of corruption and had faithfully implemented *shari'ah* law. Accordingly, he established contact with them in June 1996, and slowly developed a good relationship with them. When they took over Jalalabad on 11 September 1996, bin Laden was already on their side; Sheikh Yunis Khalis reluctantly submitted to their rule and was allowed to stay in his compound.

Bin Laden told me that he had been instrumental in the Taliban's final victory in Kabul on 27 September 1996. He had persuaded Rabbani's minister for justice, Jalaluddin Haqqani, who still wielded enormous military influence, to defect to the Taliban, taking with him several commanders and military units. The Taliban was totally lacking in military expertise and had no idea how to deploy or operate the vast range of modern military hardware, including warplanes and missiles, which they had at their disposal – some captured from the Afghan government, some provided by Pakistan and Saudi Arabia. Now Haqqani and his men stepped in to train them.

Bin Laden also told me that when the Taliban consolidated its position after the fall of Kabul and established what was to all intents and purposes a caliphate in the whole of Afghanistan, he gave his *bayat* to Mullah Omar – the only person to whom he has ever given this oath of allegiance. Another indication of how close al-Qa'ida had become to the Taliban was the 'defection' of Abu Mus'ab al-Suri, who became Mullah Omar's media advisor and established an Arabic-language radio station to broadcast throughout the region.

In April 2001 a source close to al-Qa'ida in Kandahar contacted me to ask if I would like to interview Mullah Omar. They were eager to gain some objective coverage in the Arab press, where they felt they were being misrepresented despite the fact that their government had been recognized as legitimate by Saudi Arabia and the UAE as well as Pakistan; I was very interested in another trip to Afghanistan and even harboured hopes of a second meeting with bin

Laden. I got a visa from the Pakistani embassy, but at the last minute
I changed my mind. I felt it was almost certain that I would be followed by any number of intelligence agents. It would have been
much more dangerous for me, for bin Laden and Mullah Omar
than my first trip to Afghanistan back in 1996. I decided against it.

Under the Prophet's Banner

In December 2001 al-Zawahiri, now al-Qa'ida's second-in-command,
published a book called *Knights Under the Prophet's Banner* (a deliberate reference to the 'knights of the holy tomb', as those who fought
against the Crusaders in the Middle Ages were called). By this time
al-Zawahiri was the undisputed main theoretician and strategist of
al-Qa'ida. It is believed that most of the book was written before the
attacks on America on 11 September.

It is safe to assume that the contents of this very revealing
document reflect not only al-Zawahiri's but also bin Laden's
evolving *jihadi* ideas and tactics. It also provides an insight into
how they envisage al-Qa'ida – and the *jihad* movement in
general – developing.

Al-Zawahiri urges unity of diverse *jihadi* groups, developing the
concept of allegiance which Muhammad al-Masari, the Saudi dissident expert, identifies as key to the future of the *jihadi* movement.
Al-Masari believes that the Taliban and al-Qa'ida have recently overcome whatever ideological differences they might once have had
and can now be 'considered as one'.

Speaking of the globalization of the 'enemies' of Islam, al-
Zawahiri asserts in the document that the *jihadi* movement must
itself form a 'coalition': 'The Western forces that are hostile to Islam
have clearly identified their enemy. They refer to it as Islamic fundamentalism. They are joined in this by their old enemy, Russia . . .
The *jihad* movement must realize that half the road to victory is
attained through unity.'

The long-term ambitions of al-Qa'ida are carefully outlined.

First, an Islamic state based on *shari'ah* law must be created in the region as a base from which to regain the caliphate and 'lost glory' for the *umma*. Al-Zawahiri refers to the days of Saladin, describing how this founder of the Ayyubid dynasty regained Muslim lands little by little in the twelfth century; 'when Jerusalem was added to that, only then did the cycle of history turn against the Crusaders'. Although al-Qa'ida has not, to date, been active in Palestine, the leadership frequently refers to the necessity to liberate the al-Aqsa mosque in Jerusalem as a pre-requisite to re-establishing the caliphate. The Crusader, the enemy, is firmly identified as the 'Americans and Jews'.

The idea of targeting 'the enemy' at home is mooted in this document for the first time, anticipating 11 September 2001, which we now know was in the planning since 1998. 'We must move the battle to the enemy's grounds to burn the hands of those who ignite fire in our countries,' al-Zawahiri declares, adding ominously, 'small groups could bring frightening horror to the Americans.'

In keeping with his past record, al-Zawahiri speaks candidly of his belief in the legitimacy of using extreme violence. Justifying his stance, he affirms that other methods have been tried – bin Laden organized boycotts of American goods, for example, and in Algeria the Islamic Salvation Front tried to operate within the framework of democracy: 'They thought the gates of rule had been opened for them but instead they were pushed towards the gates of detention camps and prisons and into the cells of the New World Order.'

Discussing tactics, al-Zawahiri states: 'The West, led by the US, which is under the influence of the Jews, does not know the language of ethics, morality and legitimate rights. They only know the language of interests backed by brute military force. Therefore if we wish to have a dialogue with them and make them aware of our rights we must talk to them in a language they understand.'

He advocates the use of human bombs to 'inflict maximum casualties on the enemy at the least cost in terms of casualties for the *mujahedin*'. He argues for targeting the American people, perhaps addressing the initial doubts bin Laden had expressed on this matter in 1998. American citizens, he says, 'make free choices. It is true they may be largely influenced by media bias and distortion but in the end they cast their votes in the elections to choose the governments they want . . . these people have willingly called for, supported and backed the establishment and survival of the state of Israel'.

When bin Laden addressed the American people in a video four days prior to the November 2004 presidential elections he said: 'Your security is not in the hands of [John] Kerry or Bush or al-Qaʻida. Your security is in your own hands. Any nation that does not attack us will not be attacked.' Al-Qaʻida's long-term tactic is to turn Western peoples against their leaders, holding the latter to blame for attacks on their soil which are portrayed as the inevitable outcome of their misguided policies in the Middle East. In a video broadcast on al-Jazeera on 4 August 2005, in the wake of the 7 July London bombings, al-Zawahiri addressed the British people: 'Blair has brought you destruction to the heart of London, and he will bring more destruction, God willing.' If the people can be provoked into rebellion, the reasoning goes, Western societies will implode and fall.

Another interesting aspect of al-Zawahiri's document is a clearly delineated psychological strategy for winning the approbation and participation of the Muslim people in general. He recommends that 'the *jihad* movement dedicate one of its wings to work with the masses through all available avenues for charity and educational work . . . we must win the people's respect, confidence and affection. The people will not love us unless they feel that we love them, care about them and are ready to defend them'. Perhaps mindful of the public outrage and consequent loss of support for *jihadi* groups in Egypt after the horrifying massacre at Luxor in 1997, al-Zawahiri recognizes that al-Qaʻida 'wins over the *umma* when we choose a target that it favours, one that means it can sympathize with those who hit it . . . it has responded favourably to the call for *jihad* against the Americans'.

Popular causes such as 'liberating the *umma* from its external enemies' and championing the Palestinians gain even more appeal 'when portrayed as a battle of Islam against heresy and infidels', according to al-Zawahiri. The development of good PR and a psychological strategy for recruitment and incitement is also part of the long-term al-Qa'ida agenda: 'In order for the masses to move they need a leadership they can trust, follow and understand, a clear enemy to strike at, and the shackles of fear and the impediment of spiritual weakness must be broken.'

If the battle is deemed a defensive *jihad*, it is *fard 'ayn* for every Muslim and 'if asked by a just and pious leader he cannot refuse'. The quality of leadership, then, takes on an immense military significance: 'Any leadership flaw,' al-Zawahiri asserts, 'could lead to an historic catastrophe for the entire *umma*.' So long as bin Laden and al-Zawahiri are viewed as 'just and pious', the reasoning goes, no true Muslim can deny their call to *jihad*.

Engaged in a conflict as asymmetric as their battle with America, the only way al-Qa'ida considers it can make any military impact is with an endless supply of *mujahedin* prepared to die for their cause.

After 11 September

The events of 11 September 2001 made an indelible mark on the world. Al-Qa'ida became uniquely dangerous in the history of guerrilla warfare as the first group to explicitly advocate and encourage the mass murder of civilians, a direction it has continued to pursue with horrifying atrocities like the bombings in Bali, Madrid and London, among others.

For the *jihadi* movement, however, 11 September was a day of undreamed-of victory; the day that defined al-Qa'ida as a global military force to be reckoned with and bin Laden as a figurehead for the resurgence of the Muslim nation. They had struck at the heart of the enemy and, symbolically, at all it holds dear – the World Trade Center represented financial power; the Pentagon, military might;

and had the third plane reached its intended target, the White House, the seat of American democracy would also have been demolished.

Western viewers cringed at a video of bin Laden laughingly describing the collapse of the Twin Towers and celebrating his victory, but from the *jihadi* perspective this was a great military triumph.

A significant number of ordinary Muslims, perhaps despite themselves, also felt a sense of victory that a blow had been struck at America. A young Yemeni female journalist, Rahma Hugira, was interviewed on the US television network CBS shortly after 11 September, and said:

> I didn't used to think that I could support violence. When I saw the World Trade Center and the Pentagon burn, I cried, I fainted with joy. And I prayed that God would help al-Qa'ida . . . if I have nothing else to offer, my last resort is to raise two or three children to become Sheikh Osama bin Laden's. What we all see in Osama bin Laden is the man who was able to take our revenge, to wipe the tears that have been falling for a long time for our brethren in Palestine and Iraq. Through him divine justice was achieved when America was shaken on 11 September.

Recruitment soared, as did the credibility of al-Qa'ida. For millions of Muslims, bin Laden was now perceived as a leader who could deliver.

The events of 11 September marked a shift in the relationship between al-Qa'ida and the general public in Western nations. Through the cruel directness of mass killing, al-Qa'ida began a dialogue with the people rather then their governments.

Since 11 September al-Qa'ida has had a huge impact on the internal affairs of some Western countries. In Spain, for example, the Madrid transport system bombings of 11 March 2004, which killed

200 people, forced a change of government: in the subsequent general election voters chose the Socialist Party leader José Luis Rodríguez Zapatero, who had promised to withdraw Spanish troops from Iraq. The people of Spain evidently made a direct connection between their country's support for the invasion of Iraq and al-Qa'ida's attack on them (by contrast Tony Blair, following the London bombings, has refused to do so). Bin Laden responded by offering the Spanish people a truce.

In Britain and the US, al-Qa'ida's activities have resulted in the imposition of draconian legislation. Claiming to protect the population from 'terror' the Bush and Blair governments have effectively chipped away at their civil liberties. Ironically, this feeds into al-Qa'ida's strategy, which explicitly aims to foment insurrection among increasingly oppressed and disaffected Western citizens.

The Sheikh of the Holy Warriors

Militarily, al-Qa'ida has been exhibiting an increasingly hardline approach since the emergence of the ferocious *emir* of 'al-Qa'ida in the Land of the Two Rivers' (i.e. Iraq), the late Abu Mus'ab al-Zarqawi. Any doubts that bin Laden and al-Zawahiri might have had about the legitimacy of targeting Shi'i Muslims or the collateral deaths of Iraqi citizens were swept away in the relentless flood of bloody attacks unleashed by al-Zarqawi and continued by his successor, Abu Hamza al-Muhajir (whose last name means 'the immigrant').

Al-Qa'ida's global presence and impact have dramatically widened as the organization transforms into a network of loosely affiliated franchises operating more or less independently of a leadership on the run. Al-Qa'ida's ideology, long-term strategy, training materials and justification of *jihad* are freely available on the Internet, enabling any independent cell or group to operate within its framework. There is no longer a need for the kind of centralized base they enjoyed in Afghanistan and few *mujahedin* now have any form of personal contact with the inner core of leaders. However, that is not to say that the significance of bin Laden for some Muslims is in any way diminished.

Muslim people have sought iconic leaders throughout history, finding inspiration in diverse figures from Saladin to Nasser. The desire for spiritual comfort and nurturing is expressed in pilgrimages to the shrines and graves of even relatively obscure holy men. Osama bin Laden is the latest in a line of figureheads, for many, in keeping with Muslim tradition.

Al-Zarqawi referred to him as 'the Sheikh of the Holy Warriors', and it is the iconic (some of his followers have even used the word 'messianic') status of bin Laden that confirms al-Qaʻida's identity and ensures its continued existence and growth. Even if he were killed (he has sworn he will never be captured alive), bin Laden's image would still adorn posters, banners, T-shirts and mugs across the Muslim world. He would still be the figurehead of a worldwide movement, embodying the political aspirations of a significant proportion of the Muslim nation, aspirations which are inextricably bound up with their faith.

However, al-Zawahiri issued a caveat on this matter, warning against the excessive elevation of one man's status: 'If loyalty to the leadership reaches the point of declaring it holy . . . the movement will suffer from methodological blindness', he wrote in 2001.

3

Human Bombs and the Concept of Martyrdom

> What people in the West simply don't understand is that we love death even more than they love life. It is my biggest regret that I have not been martyred yet, for this life is rotten.
>
> Osama bin Laden, November 1996

When I met bin Laden, he spoke movingly of fellow *mujahedin* who had died in the course of battle. I soon realized that the tears welling up in his eyes were not because he mourned them, but because he was happy to think of them in Paradise.

We are used to people striving for an end which they hope to see fulfilled in their lifetime. Most soldiers, whilst risking their lives for something they believe in, actively seek to preserve themselves to enjoy the victory they hope for.

But many *jihadis*, including bin Laden, are more interested in dying than living, believing with unshakeable clarity and vivid detail in the afterlife. Martyrdom, they believe, brings the common goals of the *umma* closer and guarantees them an instant place in Heaven.

The attacks of 11 September, the escalating insurgency in Iraq and the bombings in London on 7 July 2005 have focused world attention on the phenomenon of the 'suicide mission'. Considered objectively, the human bomb is now the single most effective available weapon in the *jihadi* fighters' arsenal, designed to devastate and terrorize an enemy.

The suicide mission is not only a physical event. It has an enormous psychological and ideological impact. The suicide bomber, as well as deploying him or herself as a very efficient weapon, is also demonstrating willingness to die for a cause. The logic of social psychology infers that such a cause might, at the very least, be just. The word Muslims use for what most in the West refer to as 'suicide bombers' – though the French media has been using the term *kamikaze* – is *istish-hadi*. The term is derived from the Qur'anic word *shahid* ('martyr', or 'witness to the faith'). History tells of many martyrs through the centuries; people who have died for what they believe or to save others. In Christianity they are usually made saints. The modern phenomenon of the *istish-hadi* is different in that the *shahid* willingly gives up his or her life but inflicts death and misery on others in the process.

That the *mujahedin* are prepared to die for their cause is very much in contrast with the life-preserving approach of their main enemy – the American military. Bin Laden has often mockingly referred to the 'cowardice' of American soldiers, comparing them unfavourably with the Soviet troops he fought in Afghanistan. The reluctance of US military personnel to die for their cause, or rather for the cause of their superiors, is perceived as a moral and military weakness by the *jihadis*.

There is little anyone can do in the face of an assailant who is not only willing to die but is actively seeking death. It is frighteningly unreasonable behaviour that no form of threatened punishment can deter and few interventions can thwart.

History of Martyrdom Operations

Contrary to popular belief, the concept of the suicide attack is not a modern phenomenon. The late Dr Zaki Badawi, who was Chair of the Council of Imams and Mosques and a leading voice among what he described as the 'mainstream' Muslims of Britain, points out that probably the first reference to an attack of this nature is the Biblical story of Samson's destruction of the Philistines' temple, which killed them and also him. Two Jewish groups, the Sicarii and the Zealots, terrorized the Romans in 66 CE in their efforts to liberate Judea. Because they were almost always captured and promptly crucified or burnt alive, death was an accepted part of the mission.

Probably the most famous of the early suicide warriors were the Ismaili Assassins, a radical Shi'ite Muslim sect established by the 'old man of the mountains', Hassan ibn Sabah. Based in the remote Elburtz mountains in northwestern Persia, the group sustained a systematic terror campaign against the (mainly Sunni) local sultans and Christian Crusaders for over two centuries. Armed only with daggers, their fierce and fearless assaults on well-armed and guarded targets inevitably ended in their own deaths. It was a successful tactic, and the much-feared Assassins despatched many victims between 1034–1255 CE, eventually establishing their own territorial state and taking over castles in the region.

The sect became strong through shared beliefs and practices. They pledged their allegiance to each other and to their leaders in rituals and ceremonies. Shrewdly ensuring maximum publicity for their attacks, they typically chose a public place, preferably during a holiday period. Their reputation as suicide killers gave them power completely out of proportion to their numbers and weaponry, compelling militarily stronger adversaries to abandon campaigns against them, often making enormous concessions to establish long-term peace settlements.

Like today's suicide bombers, they eagerly sought death. The first successful Assassin is reputed to have cried, 'the killing of this devil is the beginning of bliss' as he fatally stabbed the vizier of the Shah of Persia in 1092. Some Sunni historians suggest that these early martyrdom operations were fuelled by excesses of *hashish* – this is the root of the word 'assassin' (*hashishiyun*) – rather than religious zeal alone.

There are obvious comparisons to be made with al-Qaʿida here, in the emphasis on and power of allegiance and the desire for and effective use of martyrdom as a weapon, in an asymmetric war.

Suicide attack is not, historically, uniquely a Muslim tactic, but Muslims have had the longest and most sustained record of using it in conflicts with Western powers. According to Stephen Dale, throughout the eighteenth, nineteenth and early twentieth centuries Muslims engaged in suicidal *jihads* against the European colonial powers, particularly in Asia in southwestern India, northern Sumatra and the South Philippines.[1] Lacking the military capacity to effectively engage their enemy in traditional combat, the early suicide attackers would simply charge in a dedicated frenzy into the heart of enemy troops, killing as many as possible with whatever weapons they had to hand before inevitably being killed themselves.

European anarchists conducted many daring attacks and high-profile assassinations from 1870 through to the end of World War One. With dynamite entering the equation for the first time it is tempting to describe them as the first suicide bombers, except that they all tried to escape and only paid with their lives as a result of having been subjected to the judicial process. Japanese *kamikaze* pilots in the latter stages of World War Two (1943–5) hold the record for the largest number of suicide missions in history, with over 3,000 in the period. The Japanese did not limit themselves to airplanes – they also trained suicide gliders, suicide submariners and suicide motorboat captains. Japanese suicide missions in their various guises accounted for around 5,000 US naval deaths.

With the development of higher-tech explosive devices it became as effective to plant a bomb and detonate it from a place of safety, and suicide missions became less common. During the 1950s, 1960s and 1970s hijacking planes became frequent – there were more than 200 in these three decades with a peak of almost one hijacking per week from 1968–72. When airport security tightened, the terrorist organizations had to think again and the reintroduction of suicide attacks was part of the adapted strategy.

The notable exception to this lull in suicide attacks were the Viet Cong. During the Vietnam War they regularly employed suicide bombers, who rode motorcycles or drove stolen jeeps straight into the target before detonating explosives strapped around their own bodies. Suicide bombers were put to particularly spectacular use during the so-called Tet Offensive at the end of January 1968 (Tet is a public holiday to celebrate the lunar New Year). A series of attacks rocked Saigon, killing 232 US soldiers among other heavy casualties. A squad of nineteen suicide bombers blew itself up in the US embassy; suicide attackers also hit the US airbase at Bien Hoa, a power station at Thu Due and a large crowd of US military person-nel, among other high-profile targets. The Viet Cong had several trained 'special forces' designated for suicide attacks, which included men and women; many had the slogan 'Born in the North to die in the South' tattooed in Chinese letters on their forearms. In the Middle East, suicide missions began again in earnest in the early 1980s. On 15 December 1981 a car packed with explosives crashed into the Iraqi embassy in Beirut, killing sixty-one people. Amal (a pro-Syrian Shi'ite organization) claimed responsibility. In the Iran-Iraq war at the beginning of the 1980s Iran deployed so-called 'human waves' of teenage martyrs who would deliberately detonate land mines, taking the force of the blast themselves so that troops could advance unscathed.

Hizbullah's use of suicide bombers against occupation forces in Lebanon forced the complete withdrawal of American and French troops in 1983 and the partial withdrawal of the Israelis in 1985. The Shi'ite organization's operatives had been trained by Iranian Revolutionary Guards sent by Tehran specifically for this purpose.

The Liberation Tigers of Tamil Eelam (aka the Tamil Tigers) car-ried out its first suicide attack in Sri Lanka in 1987. As innovative as the Japanese *kamikaze*, they have produced such strange destructive hybrids as the suicide cyclist and even the suicide scuba diver.

From the 1990s onwards, several organizations have turned to suicide missions, including al-Qa'ida. Their trademark trucks loaded with explosives, which were used in the US embassy bombings in Nairobi and Dar-es-Salaam, were replaced with four passenger planes on 11 September 2001. On that day nineteen suicide attackers killed nearly 3,000 people.

Hamas was the first Palestinian organization to use human bombs, starting in 1994. Now suicide operations are commonplace in the Occupied Territories. According to Abdul Aziz al-Rantisi, one of the leaders of Hamas (who was assassinated by Israel on 17 April 2004), this tactic was adopted by the Palestinian movement, 'prompted by a deep sense of vulnerability and helplessness in the face of the armed-to-the-teeth Israeli army and settler militias'. It was the 25 February 1994 massacre of Palestinian worshippers at Hebron's al-Ibrahimi mosque which provoked Palestinian Islamists into sending suicide bombers – 'in the hope of compelling the Israelis to agree to a truce agreement of some sort', according to al-Rantisi.

The US-led invasion of Iraq has unleashed an unprecedented (in the Middle East) tidal wave of suicide bombings. Since March 2003, at least 500 suicide attacks have taken place at the time of this writing.

Suicide and Martyrdom

Committing suicide is considered a sin in Islam, as in Christianity and Judaism. If anything, suicide is even less acceptable in Muslim culture than it is in the West. Statistics suggest that Islam reduces the likelihood of suicide, as suicide rates in Muslim countries are among the lowest in the world. In recent years the global average suicide rate has ranged between eleven and fifteen per 100,000 population. The highest rate is seventy per 100,000 in Russia and Lithuania. Palestine is the only Muslim country with a high suicide rate at twenty-nine per 100,000 – surveys say that 50 per cent of Palestinian citizens suffer from psychological trauma serious enough to require treatment. By contrast, Jordan, Egypt, Iran and Syria have a suicide rate of less than one per 100,000. Kuwait, Turkey, Azerbaijan, Albania and Bahrain have fewer than five per 100,000.

There is no cultural predisposition for suicide among Muslims, nor is there any correlation between national suicide rates and the number of suicide bombers originating from Muslim nations, except in the case of Palestine.

Suicide in the usual sense of the word is defined by socio-psychologists as 'egoistic suicide'. It is usually the result of an unhappy, perhaps traumatized individual who is excessively isolated from society and sees no purpose in his or her continued existence. The final act of self-destruction is usually solitary and private, with the very rare exception of suicide pacts, which account for no more than 1 per cent of all suicides.

Suicide attacks, on the other hand, are usually carried out by groups of people acting together. Apart from its operations inside Iraq, al-Qaʻida has used squads of two or more suicide bombers in 89 per cent of its attacks. Even when it is a solo attack, suicide bombing typically involves many individuals with a variety of preparatory and logistical tasks, working together as a team, involving extensive social interaction and shared purpose.

'Egoistic suicide' is looked down upon in most societies. Conversely, and this is difficult for many to digest, suicide bombings are widely admired and applauded in the social group that has produced the bomber. This approbation is certainly one of the motives for a would-be *shahid*. In some countries (Palestine, for example) children aspire to martyrdom as Western children aspire to be pop stars or footballers. Approbation also implies that the act is useful and benefits his or her society.

The essential difference between suicide and martyrdom is that the one is prompted by concern for oneself, and the latter is, essentially, altruistic (as it is perceived by the perpetrator). Lastly, unlike suicide, martyrdom is usually a religious and always a deeply political act.

The following quote from 'Confessions of a Human Bomb' was

posted on the Free Arab Voice website by a young Palestinian woman going by the name of 'Hujayra al-Arabi' who was about to undertake a suicide attack against Israelis:

> The human bomb provides an example of that selflessness, demonstrating unequivocally that no life can be considered more valuable than the future of our people. The human bomb acts for all, not for himself or herself. 'Use me as a weapon of your will,' the human bomb declares. 'Let my life be sacrificed for the future of all our people.' This is emphatically not the act of someone committing suicide! Suicide is a selfish act, the act of someone who repudiates life and embraces death as a solution. The human bomb does not repudiate life at all. The human bomb embraces death as a comrade in arms, acting as a weapon for the cause of justice and freedom from Occupation.

Martyrdom and Islam

Some prominent Muslim scholars have stated that 'martyrdom operations' are, in fact, suicide and therefore prohibited. In August 2005, Abu Nasir al-Tartusi, the Syrian theorist, issued a *fatwa* that 'suicide missions do mean that a person is committing suicide, which contradicts tens of valid and correctly interpreted religious texts which prohibit suicide, whatever the incentive. Allah says: "Give generously for the sake of Allah and do not with your own hands cast yourselves into destruction" (Qur'an 2:195), and the Prophet says, in the verified Prophetic saying: "Whoever commits suicide with an item in this world would be tortured with it on Judgement Day."'

Azzam Tamimi has a different point of view: 'Suicide is unacceptable in Muslim societies and therefore it is very important for the would-be martyr or *shahid* to be convinced that his or her act is not suicide but an act of self-sacrifice for a noble cause in a legitimate *jihad.*' He points out that the Prophet Muhammad and his followers displayed a willingness to die for the cause of Islam. 'The Qur'anic injunction to fulfil *jihad* under certain circumstances is key to understanding martyrdom operations,' he says.

In *jihadi* ideology, the highest expression of *jihad* is martyrdom – either through a suicide mission or being killed by the enemy. This is the only form of *jihad* that guarantees eternal life. To quote the Qur'an (3:169): 'Think not of those who are slain in the way of Allah as dead. Nay, they are living. With their Lord they have provision.'

Other forms of *jihad*, in descending order of 'worthiness', are: supporting *mujahedin* financially; recruiting support and fighters for *jihad* (done mostly in mosques and through the media); and stating support for and belief in *jihad* without actually contributing either financially or as a fighter.

For al-Zawahiri, the *umma* is under attack from several corners at once. In his book *Knights Under the Prophet's Banner* he identifies what he (and presumably also bin Laden) consider to be the different manifestations of the enemy, legitimizing them as 'targets' for suicide or other attack:

> The Western forces have adopted a number of tools to fight Islam including:
> 1. the United Nations
> 2. friendly rulers of the Muslim people
> 3. multinational corporations
> 4. the international communications and data exchange system
> 5. international news agencies
> 6. international relief agencies, which are used for espionage, proselytizing, coup planning and the transfer of weapons.

Today, more than four years after writing this and with the opportunities afforded by the US-led invasion of Iraq, al-Zawahiri could tick every box on this macabre 'wish-list'.

According to al-Zawahiri, other methods for resisting the 'new Crusades' have been tried, from the boycott of Israeli goods called for by bin Laden in 1987, through attempts at peaceful negotiations and international appeals for justice. According to al-Zawahiri these have irredeemably failed, and now 'there is no solution without *jihad*'. This is the position adopted by most radical clerics, including those based in Britain, and most clearly outlined in bin Laden's 1998 '*Fatwa* Against the Jews and Christians', in which all 'Crusaders' are deemed legitimate targets.

The Sunni community is divided when it comes to the theological aspect of *jihad*. According to Zaki Badawi, the unofficial leader of what he describes as the 'mainstream' Muslims of Britain: 'The form of Islam espoused by al-Qaʿida is nonsense. The killing of civilians is against the *shariʿah* . They use force where reason would suffice. Osama bin Laden is not a religious authority and he has no right either to issue *fatwas* or to declare *jihad* against America on behalf of the whole *umma*.'[2]

However, when it comes to the political aspect of suicide bombing the gap between radicals and conservatives narrows significantly. 'People sacrificing themselves in battle is not uncommon,' says Badawi. 'In Palestine and Iraq they are fighters in a very difficult situation with huge forces gathered against them and oppressing them. These people must be looked upon with respect for the great sacrifice they are making.' This point of view is not uncommon even among moderate Muslims. In many Muslim countries a significant element within the population supports and admires martyrdom operations precisely because they are perceived as the only weapons available in the face of immense military superiority. The first *intifada* in Palestine, for example, was the *intifada* of stones. The second is the *intifada* of the *shahid*.

Muslim scholar Sheikh Yusef Qaradawi, who is considered so radical he is no longer permitted entry to the UK, has a similar understanding: 'Allah is just. Through his infinite wisdom, he has given the weak what the strong do not possess and that is the ability to turn their bodies into bombs as Palestinians do.'

Military Impact

The sustained use of suicide missions in Lebanon by Hizbullah in 1983 forced the complete withdrawal of American and French forces. A similar campaign in 1985 saw the Israelis, heavily supported by the US, leave much of Lebanon. In 1994 and 1995 a suicide campaign by Hamas secured Israeli withdrawal from Gaza and part of the West Bank. The suicide mission is apparently a successful coercive tactic, and one that is almost impossible to resist. In an asymmetric war, where one side is so much stronger militarily than the other, it is seen as an effective strategy.

In his 'Declaration of *Jihad* against the Americans . . .' bin Laden warns: 'Due to the imbalance of power between our armed forces and the enemy forces, a suitable means of fighting must be adopted . . . [our] youths' only intention is to enter Paradise by killing you.'

Suicide bombing has several distinct military advantages. The first is the element of surprise: however frequently we hear reports of these attacks, they remain incomprehensible to most human beings who are governed by a strong instinct for survival, and so we are less likely to detect or anticipate a suicide bombing. A suicide bomber has the same ease of access as a non-combatant individual and can easily penetrate a target, be it a Shi'ite mosque, Iraqi army recruitment centre or Israeli checkpoint. Suicide bombing can be extremely precise, all the attacker has to do is stop beside the intended target and detonate.

Perhaps the greatest military advantage is identified by al-Zawahiri, who speaks with grim pragmatism of 'martyrdom operations' as 'the most successful way of inflicting damage against the opponent and the least costly to the *mujahedin* in terms of casualties. In general, suicide attacks claim ten to fifteen times the casualties of conventional bombings and ambushes'.

Al-Qa'ida consistently inflicts the maximum number of casualties with the minimum loss to itself. The attacks of 11 September 2001 had the highest bomber:casualty ratio, with nineteen suicide attackers claiming 2,955 lives – an average 155.5 victims per attacker.

Up-to-date statistics are hard to come by in Iraq, but a report in the *Boston Globe* on 10 June 2005 quoted Pentagon officials (who asked to remain anonymous) who stated that over 50 per cent of the seventy insurgency attacks per day (on average) are now carried out by suicide bombers. Casualty levels fluctuate wildly but average around twelve deaths per suicide attack, with exceptional attacks creating statistical blips: in July 2005, for example, one suicide bomber blew himself up under a tank of liquid igniting a massive fireball that killed over 100 people.

In terms of logistics, the suicide bomber typically pilots a vehicle laden with explosives into the target or detonates bombs carried on his own body, sometimes in a bag or rucksack (as in the London bombings) or, more commonly, in a suicide belt or vest. A suicide belt is easily manufactured, and several websites give step-by-step instructions in how to customize a strip of strong fabric with pockets to hold the explosives and detonators. Worn underneath the bomber's normal clothing, it is very difficult to detect. The suicide belt was pioneered by the Tamil Tigers in 1991. A young woman named Dhanu assassinated Indian Prime Minister Rajiv Gandhi, approaching him with a garland of flowers. Instead of placing it round his neck she blew herself up along with him. Just as al-Zarqawi's al-Qa'ida in the Land of the Two Rivers would do twelve years later, the Tamil Tigers made sure such attacks were captured on film for recruitment and review purposes.

In Iraq the majority of suicide attacks originate from al-Qa'ida in the Land of the Two Rivers and are carried out in the main not by Iraqis but by zealous recruits from all over the Muslim world who are flooding to Iraq in their hundreds with only one aim in mind – martyrdom. Often these young men have had no military training and cannot even handle a gun.

The Salafi-*jihadi* umbrella group Jaish Ansar al-Sunnah (JAS) has also carried out several suicide attacks and the Shiʻi cleric Moqtada al-Sadr's Mahdi Army has been known to carry out suicide missions, but only *in extremis* and when a similar result cannot be obtained by more conventional means.

The majority of the insurgents are secular ex-Baʻth or army members, who are opposed to suicide bombings and prefer conventional means of attack – usually with snipers, ambushes or RPG bombardments. On 9 November 2005, however, three Iraqi nationals believed to have been sent by al-Qaʻida in Iraq carried out suicide attacks on three hotels in Amman, Jordan. Two of the bombers were just twenty-three years old, pointing to a new phenomenon – the 'sanctions generation', home-grown Iraqi suicide bomber. These are young people who grew up under the severe hardships inflicted by US sanctions following the first Gulf War. They were more familiar with Islam than their parents due to Saddam Hussein's policy in the 1990s allowing Islam to exert more influence in everyday life. 'This generation are more open to *jihadi* persuasions,' Dr Haitham Zubaidi, an Iraqi academic now living in London, explains: 'They have tasted the humiliation of US oppression and listened to the calls for revenge often voiced in mosques.'

Most suicide attacks pre-11 September were aimed at military, financial or administrative targets – so-called 'hard targets'. Targeting civilians in housing compounds, restaurants, nightclubs, mosques, etc – 'soft targets' – has been shown to weaken popular support for al-Qaʻida (this was most evident in Saudi Arabia in 2003 and 2004). However, al-Qaʻida in the Land of the Two Rivers has a different, much more ruthless presence, first imposed by the late al-Zarqwi, and demonstrates total indifference to 'collateral damage'. Sometimes a suicide bomber seemingly aiming for a military target detonates prematurely or inaccurately, suggesting that the suicide bomber's personal desire for martyrdom is more compelling than the intended strategic impact of his or her action. More recently in Iraq, however, al-Qaʻida has adopted a new policy – that of widening the scope of targets it considers legitimate to include Shi'is, thus greatly increasing the chances of a sectarian civil war. Initially bin Laden was opposed to attacks on Shi'is and urged al-Zarqawi to avoid civilian deaths. Their differences ended with a public declaration of alliance and the creation of al-Qa'ida in the Land of the Two Rivers at the end of 2004. Bin Laden had apparently changed his mind, and was now convinced al-Zarqawi's strategy in Iraq was correct. It is difficult to assess the level of support and cooperation between the secular insurgents and al-Qa'ida. It seems they do not hinder each other, in any case.

In Palestine most resistance organizations now have a suicide wing. The most active since the outbreak of the second *intifada* have been Hamas, the Al-Aqsa Martyrs' Brigade (part of Fatah) and Palestinian Islamic Jihad (PIJ). Even when an organization is secular, the religious aspect of martyrdom is key in the 'suicide wing'. Within this wing there are separate cells: one for selecting suitable recruits from among the many volunteers; one for the training and preparation of the 'living martyrs' (as those who are about to undertake a suicide attack are called) and one for locating 'targets'.

The organizational structure seems to be similar in Palestine, Iraq and al-Qa'ida. Each cell has a commander who does not usually undertake martyrdom operations himself but prepares the path for recruits; his expertise and experience are considered to be of more use than his death. The most notable exception to this was Mohammed Atta, the team leader of the 11 September attack, who piloted the first plane into the World Trade Center.

Who Are They?

The young fighters who flock to Iraq are overwhelmingly from the US's closest allies in the Muslim world, and not from the US State Department's list of 'state sponsors of terror'. The majority of al-Qa'ida's membership has been and remains from Saudi Arabia, perhaps the US's greatest friend in the region. The US is seen as an invading and occupying force, a veiled colonizer which also happens to be Christian. This notion has an immense emotional and political resonance. Those who respond to al-Qaʻidaʼs rallying cry do so on the basis of repelling what they see as a foreign infidel invader.

Because individual Muslim nations are not strong enough to repel the US military, the notion of a coalition of the *umma* to counter the ʻinvadersʼ has an enormous appeal for those who feel humiliated by history and frustrated at being ʻunderdogsʼ. The use of suicide attack combined with religious unity of purpose feeds into the sense that victory is, after all, possible in this asymmetric war.

Websites listing martyrs who have died in Iraq testify to the wide range of countries they come from including Yemen, Algeria, Syria, Jordan, Pakistan, Saudi Arabia and Kuwait. Sources agree that there are significant numbers of ʻblue-eyed, blonde-hairedʼ recruits. An American terrorism expert[3] has described Iraq as a ʻmecca for terrorists since the US invasion has turned it into a weak state with lax security, creating a perfect environment for extremists.ʼ Training camps have sprung up in the mountains to the north of the country and in the western desert.

An enemy who has no fear of death, no concern for his own safety and whose only aim is to destroy you is the stuff of Hollywood nightmares. The idea that the suicide attacker might be ʻnormalʼ, and not the psychopath of common perception and media portrayal, is hard for many to countenance. Two often-quoted psychological profiles of suicide bombers have been a couple of gloomy reports produced in the 1980s and 1990s. Ariel Merari, an Israeli psychologist, came to the conclusion that ʻterrorist suicide . . . is basically an individual act rather than a group phenomenon: it is done by people who wish to die for personal reasonsʼ. Professor Jerrold Post of George Washington University diagnosed ʻparanoiaʼ.[4] Both men portrayed the typical suicide bomber as uneducated, unemployed, socially isolated and unmarried – in other words, the type of ʻoutsiderʼ, ʻlonerʼ or ʻloserʼ associated frequently with serial killers in Western countries. This characterization reflects a need to present suicide bombings as irrational 'illnesses'.

Sexual frustration is also often cited as motivating suicide bombers, hence the obsession with the seventy-two 'virgins', the *houris*, apparently promised to each male *shahid* when he attains Paradise. The Qur'an, of course, promises many wonderful things in Paradise, as do the scriptures of all religions. ('Therein are rivers unpolluted, and rivers of milk whereof the flavour changes not, and rivers of wine delicious to the drinker, and rivers of clear-run honey' [47:15].) The *houris*, however, are not mentioned in every description of Paradise in the Qur'an, and when they are it is thus: '. . . and with them are those of modest gaze, with lovely eyes . . .' (37:48). These are 'loving companions', idealized wives.

The Qur'an makes no mention of how many *houris* live in Paradise, nor how they are to be apportioned. If a would-be suicide bomber is sexually frustrated, there is no reason why he could not get married rather than blow himself to bits – indeed, Islam permits him four wives. Moreover, how can this reward motivate increasing numbers of actual and potential female suicide bombers in Palestine and Iraq?

Ramadan Abdullah Shallah, leader of the PIJ, points out that some Sunnah texts do indeed refer to seventy-two *houris* but cautions: 'this is part of the reward allocated for a person who gives his life for what he believes to be a noble cause defending truth and justice. In other words, it is the perception of a lack of justice or dominance of falsehood that incites and it is not the reward that attracts'.

One psychological factor that many people find difficult to understand is that life and death have come to have different relative values in situations where killing is commonplace. In Palestine and Iraq, murder is not exceptional as it is in, say, Europe – rather, it is everywhere, and highly visible. It would be difficult to find a Palestinian in the Gaza Strip (or, indeed, an Israeli in Jerusalem) who has not witnessed the slaying of someone close to them. In these extreme circumstances it is not surprising if some young people see an individual life not as something to cherish but as a disposable minor detail in the vast, chaotic battle going on all around them.

Suicide bombers do not come from any one type of social background – they are as likely to come from the well-educated elite of Saudi Arabia as the illiterate poverty-stricken ghettos of Pakistan. Nasra Hassan, a UN relief worker in the Gaza Strip, interviewed 250 aspiring Palestinian suicide bombers and found that 'none were uneducated, desperately poor, simple-minded, suicidal or depressed'.[5]

Psychological profiles show that there are as many different types of suicide bombers as there are types of people. Robert A. Pape, in his study of suicide terrorism *Dying to Win*, conducted extensive research into the demographics of suicide bombers. He concluded that, psychologically, they are likely to be completely normal, though some (particularly Palestinians) may have suffered trauma. He found that the average age of attackers varied across the groups. Pape's findings do not substantiate the all too common portrayal of suicide bombers as young people in their teens (hence easily manipulated). Hizbullah *shahids* were the youngest, averaging just 21.1 years; Palestinians, at 22.5 years; al-Qa'ida's operatives were the second most mature at 26.7 years; the average age for Chechens was 29.8 years. In general, female suicide bombers tend to be older than their male counterparts – typically in their mid-twenties and upward.

In terms of education and income, Pape found that suicide attackers were likely to be better educated and less likely to be impoverished than the average person in their country – more than 50 per cent have post-secondary education. Nearly 80 per cent are working- or middle-class, with under 20 per cent being described as low-income or unemployed. By comparison, in the general Palestinian population under 50 per cent of people are working- or middle-class and 30 per cent are low-income.

Suicide bombers are not uniquely drawn from among civilians. Recently there have been several incidences of suicide bombers from within the security forces in Saudi Arabia and in Pakistan, where three policemen blew themselves up in attacks on the Shi'ite mosques in Karachi (7 May 2004) and Quetta (4 July 2004). A Palestinian policeman carried out a suicide bombing in 2004.

Most organizations have strict criteria regarding selection for suicide missions. When it was based in Afghanistan, al-Qa'ida would choose the most suitable candidates on the recommendation of training camp commanders. Conversations with Hamas leaders and the PIJ leader Shallah reveal that they expect the following attributes:

1. religious zeal, which gives the *shahid* moral conviction, steels him for the task and assures him of the life hereafter;
2. courage (preferably tested in a combat situation);
3. mental stability;
4. a clean criminal record, as this lessens the likelihood of surveillance;
5. a minimum age of eighteen;
6. no spouse (in addition to the preference for single people, in Palestine people without siblings are usually refused as are those who are likewise a family's sole breadwinner).

All the organizations report that 'hundreds' of young men (and, increasingly, women) have been volunteering for martyrdom operations.

There is little need for active recruitment in Palestine. Commanders say that after every Israeli incursion or assassination, hordes of young people present themselves to be taken as *shahids*. Basim Abdul-Khaleq, a secondary school teacher in Gaza, notes the following:

> Teenagers have posters of the latest *shahid* on their bedroom walls instead of Eminem, and smaller children write his or

her name with a pen on their arms. When asked what they would like to do when they grow up, children who in the past might have hoped to be a doctor or a teacher now reply, 'I want to be a *shahid.*' In the playground, rather than playing with Game Boys or whatever the latest craze might be, primary school children re-enact *shahid* ceremonies hon-ouring the martyr, squabbling over who will play the key role.[6]

Many of those who flock to Iraq and other al-Qa'ida bases are well-educated and have abandoned families and careers. Moreover, 'graduates' of the al-Qa'ida training camps in Afghanistan, particularly those from Pakistan and Algeria, are believed to be actively recruiting young *mujahedin* in their homelands.[7]

A growing trend is the recruitment of *jihadis* in Europe. In Italy in 2003, Tunisian *imam* Mourad Trabelsi was wire-tapped and recorded making arrangements to send North African and Kurdish immigrants to Ansar al-Islam in Northern Iraq. Algerian Abderazzak Mahdjoub is currently on trial, also in Italy, for helping to send nearly 200 *jihadis* from Europe to al-Zarqawi in Iraq. Al-Zarqawi and Abu Mus'ab al-Suri (al-Qa'ida strategist and, it is believed, recruiter) actively cultivated European connections, as did al-Zawahiri, who was personally involved in the conduct and training of the London bombers.

These international recruits often speak of the enormous influence bin Laden has had on them, citing his words as the ultimate inspiration to undertake *jihad.* Lebanese journalist Hala Jaber told of one young man who had travelled to Iraq to join al-Zarqawi's group in 2005, and who described a feeling of 'being changed', eerily echoing Christian fundamentalist vocabulary, and of 'becom-ing one of Osama's'. Initially stirred by one of bin Laden's taped speeches, he tracked down everything he could find on the Internet about and by 'the Sheikh' before deciding to offer himself as a martyr.

Why Do They Do It?

> O ye who believe! What is the matter with you, that, when ye
> are asked to go forth in the cause of Allah, ye cling heavily to
> the earth? Do ye prefer the life of this world to the Hereafter?
> But little is the comfort of this life, as compared with the
> Hereafter. Unless ye go forth, He will punish you with a griev-
> ous penalty, and put others in your place; but Him ye would
> not harm in the least. For Allah hath power over all things.
> (Qur'an 9:38–9)

This verse, from the Qur'anic *sura* of 'al-Tawbah' ('Repentance') is
typical of the religious exhortation employed in both bin Laden's
and al-Zarqawi's many calls to *jihad*, now most commonly published on the Internet. The power of this emphasis on honour,
religious duty, the desirability of death and the bliss of the hereafter
should not be underestimated.

Dr Eyad Serraj, a Gaza psychiatrist, reports that suicide bombers
'do not believe they are going to die – rather that they are going to
a new life, which is a better life'. This is not to suggest that suicide
bombers are acting out of personal despair – Serraj also notes that
attackers are typically the most determined members of their families – rather that they reckon their act as a positive action designed
to force change in an otherwise desperate situation, an act that will
also bring the attacker the personal reward of Paradise.

But the religious impetus is not the end of the story. Political
motivation is also crucial, with greater or lesser significance depending on the historical context. Bin Laden, in his 'Declaration of *Jihad*
against the Americans . . .' wrote: 'Terrorizing you while you are carrying arms on our land is a legitimate and morally demanded duty.'
In the cases of both Palestine and Iraq, suicide bombers are opposing an occupying power and, as noted before, bin Laden finds the
very idea that US forces are stationed on the Arabian Peninsula
utterly repugnant. The bombings in Madrid and London were

intended to drive coalition forces from Iraq, and in the case of Spain the attack was successful.

There seem to be two prevalent conditions under which suicide attack has emerged as a weapon in our times: the presence of an occupying force and radical Islam. Only the first is essential – the Tamil Tigers, after all, are not Muslim, nor were the Viet Cong. Perhaps the fact of occupation generates the phenomenon of suicide bombing; the widespread hatred of the US in many Muslim lands is not prompted by religious differences alone, but is a direct response to the evident US agenda there.

It is interesting to observe the balance between religious and political imperatives in the following 'last wills and testaments' of three suicide bombers. The first is another extract from the 'last will' of Hujayra al-Arabi, the young Palestinian suicide bomber:

> I do not want to die. I am not in love with death. I am not even 'half in love with easeful death' like the English poet. I want to live. I want to have a home filled with children, and I still want to be a doctor. From the age of about six, I dreamed of becoming a doctor, of being able to save lives. I wanted to do something real that would save the lives of my people. And yet, I see now that there are many ways of saving lives, and that taking lives can be a part of the process of saving lives. That is where I am now, preparing to take lives in order to save my people.

This is from the 'last will' of one of the 11 September hijackers, Saudi-born Ahmed al-Haznawi, made five months prior to the attack:

> The time of humiliation and slavery is over, and the time has come to kill the Americans in their home and among their children and in front of their military forces and intelligence services . . . God, I give myself to you, so accept me as a

martyr . . . accept me into the Garden of Eden . . . may we be
joined there with the prophets and the holy people and the
martyrs and the pious people. And they are the best
companions.

The religious content and rhetoric of the latter have all the hallmarks
of bin Laden and al-Qa'ida. The style and content have been even
further refined by the time suicide bomber Barwa al-Kurdi made the
following 2004 videotaped statement prior to his attack on a US
troop convoy in Iraq which killed more than thirty soldiers and
destroyed several tanks and armoured vehicles:

> I am carrying out this martyrdom operation and all Muslims
> should know that they do not have any excuse anymore for
> not confronting the infidels while we see the Muslims insulted
> and humiliated at the hands of these Crusaders under the
> command of the United States whose hands have become
> covered with the blood of thousands of Muslims. *Jihad* has
> become today the individual duty of all Muslims so as
> to restore the rule of the *shari'ah* of Allah, praise and glory be
> to Him. Let the Muslims know that the infidels are weaker
> than they think, and I hope Allah will accept this from me.

Most al-Qa'ida fighters perceive themselves as members of the
umma with a long-term goal, the re-establishment of the caliphate.
Ousting the US from Iraq is only one step on this ideological journey. The fighters who flock to Iraq are actively looking for battle; in
Palestine, they feel they have no choice.

The honours heaped on a martyr have their own allure, elevating
an ordinary youth to the status of superhero. In Palestine a whole
ceremonial culture has evolved around martyrdom despite the
inevitable Israeli retaliation, whereby tanks swiftly raze the family
home to the ground regardless of whether or not anyone is in it.
Posters of the latest *shahid* are flyposted on walls; a *shahid* tent is

erected against the family home where the 'last will and testament' and photographs of the martyr are displayed. Family, friends and fellow members of their organization gather to celebrate, rather than mourn. The tent and the food for the celebration are normally paid for by the organization the attacker was part of.

The Internet is full of videos depicting suicide missions in Iraq. These are designed to glorify the action, serve as homage to the martyr, show that the battle is being won and compel others to do likewise. The late al-Zarqawi realized the immense impact these recordings would have and even now each bomber in Iraq is despatched with up to three cameras to capture his attack from several different angles. These videos are often high-resolution, well-produced and edited and, crucially, posted on the Internet within hours of being shot.

The most common form of attack filmed in Iraq is the car or truck bomb. Typically, the soundtrack as the suicide bomber drives to the 'target' is that of rousing *jihadi* songs which are sung in harmony with no instrumental accompaniment (musical instruments are frowned upon by Salafis). Without hesitation, the bomber drives straight into his target to repeated and exalted cries from the camera crew and its companions.

Bin Laden's broadcast homage to the 11 September 'martyrs'[8] describes the nineteen suicide attackers as 'men who purged the history of the *umma*' through the 'conquests in New York and Washington.' Their sacrifice, bin Laden affirms, is 'the only way to stop the tyranny of the infidels'. Referencing early Islamic history when the *umma* was in the ascendant, extending its influence as a result of *jihad* through the centuries, bin Laden creates an epic historical imperative and a collective sense of religious and historical identity. This clearly strikes chords with many Muslims.

In the same broadcast bin Laden extols the personal qualities of the 'martyrs' in brief, poetic descriptions, further adding to their mystique by presenting them as morally, mentally and spiritually superior: 'Mohammed Atta, the destroyer of the first tower, a serious and creative man, he was honest and carried the pains of the *umma*.

We hope God will accept him as a martyr . . . Marwan al-Shehhi . . . the destroyer of the second tower, life wanted him but he ran away from it seeking what God had for him.' Others are described as 'pure', 'determined, decisive, heroic and courageous', 'humble' and 'patient', a 'lover of *jihad*'. In a rare brush with the modern world, bin Laden describes another hijacker who was a scientist, now 'freed from being hostage to their salaries'.

For bin Laden the character of the martyr is impeccably refined through religious duty and martyrdom itself, 'the great sacrifice', a two-edged sword ensuring the personal salvation of the individual whilst inflicting mortal damage on the enemy.

Within al-Qa'ida even devastating military operations are laced with mysticism. There are many reports of bin Laden's belief in the integrity of dreams, and how these are a frequent topic of conversation among his followers. One of the organizers of the 11 September operation, Ramzi Binalshibh, even claimed that the date for the attack was the result of one of Mohammed Atta's dreams: 'he saw two sticks and a line between them. A cake with a stick dangling.' Realizing this represented an 11 and a 9 the news was relayed to 'brother Abu Abdullah' (bin Laden), who received it as 'a very good tiding'.[9]

In Palestine the approach is more worldly, the aim more specific and local, the experience more immediately personal. Palestinian suicide bombers are typically motivated by anger and a sense of injustice resulting from the hardships of life under the Israelis in the Occupied Territories, constrained by checkpoints, job opportunities kept tantalizingly out of reach even for highly qualified graduates. Many *shahids* speak of the desire to 'liberate' the land and people from the Israeli 'tyrant'.

Then there is revenge. The father of nineteen-year-old Raed Zakarneh told how his son had been tortured by the Israel Defence Forces (IDF) and threatened with rape in prison. When he came out, his father says, he was 'changed beyond recognition' and shortly afterwards drove a car packed with explosives into an Israeli bus stop.

The murder of a child, spouse or friend is a common ingredient in the Molotov cocktail brewing inside a *shahid*. Israeli aggression and assassinations are invariably followed by retaliatory suicide missions.

The Western press has made much of the financial compensation offered to the families of suicide bombers; at one point, Saddam Hussein would provide them each with $20,000 following an attack. But there is little if any financial compensation available now. Since 11 September 2001, the US has been supervising all transactions and transfers of money from and to Arab banks to ensure that no such payments can be made. This action has other unintended consequences: as there is no social security system in most Muslim countries, charity is ingrained in the culture. If, for example, someone sends a charitable contribution to an impoverished student who subsequently carries out a suicide attack, the donor risks being incarcerated for financing and supporting terrorism though they would have known nothing of the student's intentions. (This exact scenario happened to Princess Haifa of Saudi Arabia, wife of the ambassador to Washington, Prince Bandar. She provided funds in response to the request of an unknown student, who later turned out to be an al-Qa'ida associate.) In any case, if a would-be human bomb was motivated by financial gain, collaboration with the security forces pays just as well and doesn't require suicide.

The truth is more complex. The men and women who become suicide bombers apparently feel that by carrying out a martyrdom operation they can fight back and reclaim lost dignity. As the father of a Palestinian suicide bomber said: 'My son wasn't a radical person, he was radicalized by the anger, by the humiliation . . . we are living in a jail.'[10]

Istish-hadiyah – *the Phenomenon of the Female Martyr*

The female martyr (Arabic: *istish-hadiyah*) is a particularly potent weapon – not only strategically (because she can go more easily undetected to the target) but also in propaganda terms.

Traditionally, and it seems by inclination, women do not generally go to war. It must be a very just cause indeed, the rationale goes, for a woman not only to kill but to sacrifice her own life in doing so.

In fact female suicide bombers are not uncommon: 30–40 per cent of all suicide attacks claimed by the Tamil Tigers are carried out by women. The Chechen rebels also use a high percentage of female fighters, known as the fearsome 'black widows'. Recent reports tell of an Uzbek widow training Pakistani women in the tribal districts in special female-only camps.[11] Until recently, however, there were few female martyrs from Palestinian organizations (though to date every Palestinian resistance organization has deployed female suicide bombers against Israeli targets).

Al-Qa'ida's leadership had remained resolutely opposed to using female suicide bombers on theological grounds; however, 28 September 2005 saw an apparent change in policy when a woman disguised in a man's robes detonated explosives strapped to her body whilst standing in line with army recruits in Baghdad, killing at least six and wounding thirty-five. Al-Qa'ida had reported a steady stream of women volunteers for such missions, and the organization was quick to claim responsibility for the attack, which it described as having been carried out by 'a blessed sister'. There has been no comment on the matter from either bin Laden or al-Zawahiri.

Female human bombs have been the cause of some controversy within the Muslim community, which expects and requires women to fulfil a nurturing role. Theologically, the matter is highly controversial.

A *hadith* reported by Ahmed bin Hanbal recounts how Aisha, Muhammad's wife, asked the Prophet if there was any *jihad* for women. He replied: 'There is *jihad* for them in which there is no fighting.' Salafi-*jihadi* groups, al-Qa'ida in particular, have maintained the position that women should support and encourage their menfolk in *jihad* but not fight themselves.

In August 2001, however, the High Islamic Court in Saudi

Arabia proclaimed that a woman could, and should, join *jihad*. Sheikh Abdullah Nimr Darwish, founder of the Islamic Movement in Israel, agreed in 2002, saying: 'Israel has signed a death warrant against the Palestinians, so it is reasonable for women to join the struggle.' Nevertheless, PIJ and Hamas demurred until 2003 and 2004, respectively.

Palestinian Islamic organizations were also divided over whether or not an *istish-hadiyah* should be accompanied by a brother or her father to protect her honour. Some Israeli commentators were quick to call the first female suicide bombers' honour into question, suggesting their acts resulted from an affair, pregnancy or other transgression.

The first female suicide bomber was sixteen-year-old Muhaidi Sana who, in 1985, drove a truck into an IDF convoy, killing two soldiers. She belonged to the secular Syrian Socialist National Party and was from a Christian family.

In January 2002 Wafa Idris, a paramedic from the Al-Aqsa Martyrs' Brigade, became the first Palestinian female suicide bomber, killing an eighty-one-year-old Israeli man and injuring more than 100, in Jerusalem. In 2003 the first PIJ *istish-hadiyah*, nineteen-year-old Hiba Daraghmeh, killed three people in an Israeli shopping mall. Perhaps the most famous Palestinian *istish-hadiyah* was Hanadi Jaradat from Jenin, a twenty-nine-year-old lawyer also with the PIJ, who blew herself up inside the Haifa Maxim restaurant in October 2003, killing twenty-one. It was not until 14 January 2004 that Hamas finally sanctioned female suicide attacks, and Reem al-Reyashi killed four Israeli soldiers at a checkpoint. She was a mother of two children, aged three and one.[12]

Obviously the only female suicide bombers who can be interviewed are those who are either in preparation or who have failed for one reason or another. Questioned about their motives, a very large proportion cited revenge. The Chechen 'black widows' include many actual widows or those who have lost loved ones in the battle for independence from Russia.

Obeida Khalil, a Palestinian, was interviewed on Australian television in February 2004 in her Hasharon prison cell in Israel. She was being held there along with seventy-five other female prisoners who had either been arrested on their way to carry out a suicide bombing or who had helped others reach their target. She described her reasons for carrying out her failed suicide mission: 'I was young during the first *intifada* but I saw how Israelis killed our little children and destroyed our houses . . . during the current *intifada* I was engaged, but four days before our wedding my fiancé was killed by the Israelis. My brother and female cousin were also *shahids*.'

Hanadi Jaradat was interviewed in *al-Arab al-Yum* four months before she blew herself up. She described how her younger brother, Fedi, due to be married three days later, had been murdered in front of the entire family by an Israeli undercover unit which had come to execute her cousin Saleh, who was also present. Jaradat had tried to protect Fedi but had been beaten by the Israelis, who then pumped his and Saleh's bodies full of bullets. 'Since the day I saw my brother's blood,' Jaradat said, 'I have determined to play a part in liberating Palestine. That goal is bigger and more important than my private pain.'

In December 2003 Hala Jaber interviewed nine trainee female suicide bombers. They had changed their names to Thawra ('Revolution'), Jihad, Tahereer ('Liberation') and Nur ('Light') among others, 'to prepare for death'. Some were mothers (one had five children) and others teenage girls. What frightened them most was not the thought of pressing the button on the detonator but the fear that their families would find out what they were training to do and prevent them from carrying out their missions.[13]

Istish-hadiyahs have fired the popular imagination across the Muslim world; they are acclaimed as Islamic versions of Joan of Arc, and lauded in poems. Ghazi al-Qusaibi, then the Saudi ambassador to London, offended many in Britain in August 2001 when he published a poem in praise of a Palestinian female suicide bomber, Ayat al-Ahras, in the newspaper *al-Hayat*. He was duly removed from his post, though he was subsequently 'kicked upstairs' on his return to Riyadh, when he was made minister of a department created specially for him – the Ministry of Water. Here are some of the offending lines:

> Ayat the fair
> kissed her death
> while smiling with good tidings

Preparation

Following a series of discussions and interviews I have established the following key facts concerning preparation for suicide missions both by al-Qaʻida and Palestinian groups.

Those who are selected by resistance commanders for suicide attacks undergo training in the practicalities of their mission as well as psychological and religious preparation for ending their own lives and those of others. It seems that, as in any war, discipline and a sense of duty are crucial, that there is no room for empathy or compassion in a battle to the death. The collective derogatory term *kafir* (infidel) effectively dehumanizes the enemy and strips him or her of the individuality that might prompt an emotional engagement with the victim.

Where there are actual training camps, a rigid discipline informs the structure of each day which begins with early-morning prayers followed by demanding physical training. Afternoons are spent learning how to dismantle, clean and fire guns, RPGs and other light weapons. Israeli security services are increasingly on the look-out for potential suicide bombers, and Palestinian attackers often have to shoot their way into heavily protected targets. If their bomb fails to detonate for any reason, the bomber is expected to shoot him- or herself to avoid being taken prisoner and interrogated. As in any army, immersion in the task, the sense of common purpose, shared beliefs and discipline ensure moral fortitude and a willingness to die for the cause.

Recently, the al-Qa'ida training website 'al-Battar' and other online training resources have widened the catchment area for recruits. It is no longer necessary for young men to physically attend the camps. A pattern seems to be emerging of groups of like-minded youths forming a 'cell' locally, procuring weapons and explosives and training themselves using al-Qa'ida manuals.

Recruits practise carrying the 20–30 kg of explosives they will have distributed around the body or packed in suicide belts or vests. Such a heavy weight can alter the way someone walks and thus raise the alarm. They learn how to handle explosives and link them up before simulating the moment when they will blast themselves to bits at the push of a button on the detonator. There are two buttons, in case one fails.

Videos of previous operations provide inspiration and instruction. The logistics of the attacks are mapped out and analysed with real and potential obstacles considered and dealt with hypothetically.

Typically recruits are not told they have been selected for a mission until a few days before. This is to avoid the possibility of the 'living martyr' (as those who are being prepared are known) getting cold feet or telling their families, who might restrain them. In the only known case where a 'living martyr' (nineteen-year-old Palestinian Muhammad Farhat) told his mother he was about to carry out a martyrdom operation, she gave him her blessing and some final advice: 'do not hesitate, my boy, remember Allah in every move you make . . . and strike as harshly as you can against the enemy'. This woman, Umm Nidal, had already seen two other sons die as human bombs.

Much of the information that follows concerns Palestinian organizations, but it is likely that al-Qa'ida uses similar methods where time allows. In Iraq, the relentlessness of the human tidal wave of suicide bombers suggests that little time is given to preparation, and that recruits arrive already more or less ready to die.

In Palestine the 'living martyr' spends many hours in one-to-one conversation with a commander discussing what is about to happen and reading from the Qur'an. The recruit is reassured that whilst suicide is considered a great sin in Islam, their mission is not suicide but martyrdom, using the body as a weapon. Much discussion and reading centres on the reward a martyr can expect in Paradise.

At some point during their preparations the 'living martyr' will make a videotape of their 'last will and testament'. Apart from urging their families and friends not to grieve for them, these videotapes ensure a further supply of inspired recruits . . . and make it rather difficult for the 'living martyr' to back out should he or she want to.

If the 'living martyr' is judged committed, steady and prepared, they enter the final phase of preparation which can last anything from a few hours to days, retreating with the Qur'an for solitary contemplation. It is said that they achieve a spiritual peak of utter faith and belief that cannot be shaken, and which enables them to detonate the bomb they carry or drive a vehicle packed with explosives into its target without hesitation. These preparation techniques date back to Hizbullah's practices in the early 1980s, when it was established that spiritual and psychological readiness through religion was key.

A separate cell within the suicide wing is responsible for reconnaissance. Commanders keep a list of potential targets and sometimes recruits have their own ideas, for example, a target where someone in their family or they themselves have been hurt or humiliated. Usually a target will have political significance or be linked to an event for which retaliation is sought.

When the 'living martyr' is ready, s/he is informed of the target location and told how to enter it, usually with the help of photographs, pictures or diagrams. Once inside it is up to the attacker to determine when and where detonating their bomb will cause maximum impact. Success is reckoned in numbers killed and these are never personalized or categorized into men, women or children, as this might cause remorse. Death is instantaneous and very grisly, usually resulting in the decapitation of the bomber.

There are occasions when a suicide mission fails. If this is due to the malfunction of equipment or arrest by security forces, the failed suicide bomber is treated with as much respect and honour as if he or she was indeed a *shahid*.

If, however, the would-be suicide bomber panics or loses their nerve at the last minute, it is a different matter. In the rare cases where this has happened the failed suicide bomber has been driven out of his native town, village or refugee camp. Shunned by his community, his failure brings shame on the entire family.

The phenomenon of suicide bombers is becoming more commonplace, yet it remains baffling, disturbing and above all, frightening. The concept of the human bomb reverses all the norms in our experience of the world, whatever our culture or history. It is usual to love life and seek to preserve it, but the suicide bomber loves and welcomes death. The alien nature of this value set contributes to the fear the phenomenon generates.

It has been observed that suicide bombers are the product of an asymmetric military balance of power in the context of an occupation. Recent events in Madrid and London – which were in response to the occupation of Iraq – point to a geographical expansion, even globalization of this form of protest and attack. The harsh reality is that as long as the US and its allies pursue a foreign policy which includes and recommends military occupation, the current escalation of suicide attacks is unlikely to abate.

Cyber-*Jihad*

Entering the Fray

The day of 11 March 2004 was an ordinary one at the *al-Quds al-Arabi* offices, with financial difficulties top of the agenda. Suddenly news came in of massive bomb attacks in Madrid. More than 200 people had been killed, and up to 1,500 injured. I was immediately certain that this was the work of al-Qa'ida and that it was not unrelated to the forthcoming Spanish general election on 14 March. The Spanish government had backed the US invasion of Iraq, and this was a clear message to the people that they should vote to have their soldiers brought home.

The Spanish, British and American governments set about finding an alternative culprit and pointed the finger at the Basque separatist group ETA.[1] This was the version carried by all mainstream media channels; meanwhile the facts were freely available on the Internet, which was rapidly becoming the best source for independent information.

At the time al-Qa'ida was in the habit of sending emails to our newspaper, claiming responsibility for attacks. Nowadays it simply posts a communiqué on any one of a number of *jihadi* websites ensuring it will be read by millions of people around the world within seconds.

The first al-Qa'ida email we received was back in October 2002. A small boat had been blown up next to a French tanker in Yemen, blasting a massive crater in its side; in November 2003 al-Qa'ida emailed us again claiming responsibility for the attacks in Istanbul on the London-based HSBC bank and the British consulate.

I was therefore expecting to hear from al-Qa'ida on 11 March. I asked my staff to monitor all communications very carefully, and in the early evening I received a mysterious telephone call from somewhere in the Gulf informing me that I should look out for a special email at 7.30 PM – just half an hour before we send the newspaper to press. I decided to hold the front page.

On the dot, an email arrived, and I could see immediately that it was a genuine al-Qa'ida communiqué. This was clear from the rhetorical style and the way the information was framed. It claimed responsibility for the Madrid bombings and was signed by the Abu-Hafs al-Misri Brigade.

Describing Spain as 'one of the pillars of the Crusader alliance', the five-page email asserted, 'this is part of settling old accounts with Spain, the Crusader, and America's ally in its war against Islam'. This was our front-page story, and I immediately passed the email to all the news networks and wire services. It was the next day's headlines across the globe.

A conflict broke out between me, as editor of *al-Quds al-Arabi*, and American, British and Spanish government spin doctors who still wished the bombings to be passed off as the work of ETA. We were accused on television and in newspapers of being an untrustworthy source. Our integrity was challenged before millions of people, and the email dismissed as a fake.

Nevertheless, within half an hour of passing the email on to the wires, our offices were raided by the British security services and police. They had a warrant to search the premises, and they took the hard drive of the computer which had received the al-Qa'ida email. Armed police stood guard outside our offices all night while officers copied the contents of all our computers onto discs. Evidently the security forces wished to trace the origins of the email from al-Qa'ida, while simultaneously insisting it was a hoax.

This was an historic email for many reasons: it effectively brought down the government of José María Aznar, who was voted out of office, and ensured the withdrawal of Spanish troops from Iraq as promised by the Socialist Party victor, José Luis Rodríguez Zapatero. It also contained al-Qaʻida's first-ever offer of a truce to a member of the 'Crusader-alliance'.

My paper had unwittingly joined the fray in the latest theatre of the Islamist-American conflict – the Internet.

Islamism and the Internet

Hamid Mir, the Pakistani journalist and bin Laden biographer, described how he watched al-Qaʻida men fleeing US bombardments of their training camps in November 2001: 'Every second al-Qaʻida member [was] carrying a laptop computer along with his Kalashnikov,' he reported.

At first glance it is enormously paradoxical that an organization such as al-Qaʻida, which has pitted itself so vehemently against the modern world should increasingly rely on the ultra-hi-tech electronic facilities offered by the Internet to operate, expand, develop and survive.

Radical Islamist organizations first started debating the matter in the 1980s, and some of the Wahhabi groups in Afghanistan were opposed to using any kind of technology that was of largely Western origin or innovation. Sheikh Abdullah Azzam, however, who would have an immense influence on the young Osama bin Laden (see Chapter Three), immediately saw its possibilities; by the mid-1980s he was encouraging *mujahedin* groups to exploit the potential of evolving electronic technologies.

The Internet has become a key element in al-Qaʻida training, planning and logistics, and cyberspace a legitimate field of battle. Some commentators have gone so far as to declare that al-Qaʻida is the first web-directed guerrilla network.

In 2003 a writer calling himself 'al-Salem' published a document on the 'al-Farouq' website (a known Saudi-based al-Qa'ida domain) called 'al-Qa'ida: The 39 Principles of *Jihad*'. No. 34 extols 'performing electronic *jihad*' as a 'sacred duty': believers are called upon to join the *jihad* by participating in Internet forums to defend Islam and to explain and recommend the 'duty' of *jihad* to all Muslims; al-Salem adds that the Internet offers the opportunity to respond instantly to false allegations and to reach millions of people in seconds; those who have Internet skills are urged to use them to support the *jihad* by hacking into and destroying 'enemy' (i.e. American and Israeli) websites as well as 'morally corrupt' ones (such as pornographic sites).

Sheikh Omar Bakri Muhammad, founder of the radical Islamic group al-Mahajiroun, referred to 'thousands of bin Laden supporters currently studying computer science as a way to support the cause', averring that 'all types of technical means, including the Internet, are examined now in the light of their application in the large-scale war against the West'.

Nowadays *jihadi* groups require four essential ingredients: members, a leader, a religious guide and information technology specialists.

Perhaps the paradoxical combination of radical Islam and hi-tech expertise is rendered a little less strange if we look behind the electronic aspect of the Internet and forget about the satellites in space that enable its communications. Then we are left with two areas in which the Arab world excels – cryptography and secrecy. These are also two crucial aspects of any type of warfare: as the fourth-century Chinese military philosopher Sun Tzu observed, 'all warfare is based on deception'.

Nor should we overlook the immense importance to the al-Qa'ida network of this uncensored, unmediated communications platform. For the time being this is a revolution in media terms and one that the *jihadis* have been exploiting to the full. For the first time in history, those who are opposed to the system can broadcast their news and opinions independently and to mass audiences throughout the world. It is no exaggeration to say that the Internet is the single most important factor in transforming largely local *jihadi* concerns and activities into the truly global network that al-Qa'ida has become today.

This is particularly relevant in the case of Abu Mus'ab al-Zarqawi. Prior to his death, his status within al-Qa'ida rivalled that of bin Laden, almost entirely due to his masterful use of the Internet. Al-Qa'ida in the Land of the Two Rivers has averaged nine online communications a day; at least 180 statements appeared in the first three weeks of July 2005. No al-Qa'ida operation in Iraq occurs without being filmed, and the videos are uploaded immediately. With such worldwide exposure, al-Zarqawi has become a household name.

In a guerrilla first, al-Zarqawi released a highly professional forty-six-minute film called *All Religion Will be for Allah* via the Internet on 29 June 2005. This slick production condensed many operations, including suicide bombings and ambushes, into one gory celebration. The distribution was as professional as the production, handled via a specially designed web page with dozens of links to the video. Al-Zarqawi's 'information wing' offered the film in several formats – a high-resolution version for those with broadband and a smaller file for those with dial-up connections, and it was even possible to download it onto a mobile phone. In the case of al-Zarqawi, real-time war and what has come to be known as 'cyber-*jihad*' are inextricably linked. Operations seem to be as strategically valuable in cyberspace as they are on the ground. Al-Zarqawi is the new face of al-Qa'ida in this respect, which explains his great appeal for the new-technology generation of today.

The Internet is a multipurpose tool and weapon. It can be used to communicate one-to-one or to millions; it can be used to convey hidden information, instructions or plans; and since computers control the majority of the developed world's infrastructure, it is a chink in the West's armour, easily penetrated by dedicated hackers. Cyber-attacks can create enormous damage at very little cost to the *jihadis*, a principle they value and which we have already seen applied with devastating results in al-Qaʻidaʼs preference for suicide missions over armed combat.

Al-Qaʻida has put the Internet to many and varied uses. Increased surveillance might currently restrict its range of online activities, but it is important to consider past as well as potential future aspects of cyber-*jihad*.

Secrets and Spies

Cryptography, as defined in the *Cambridge Encyclopaedia*, is ʻthe alteration of the form of a message by codes and ciphers to conceal its meaningʼ. So-called crypto-systems are at the heart of cyber-warfare. Messages are concealed, embedded or coded, hidden from the enemy (in a multitude of ways, some of which we will consider below) yet easily accessed by an ally.

But cryptography is nothing new: Muslims have successfully been using it since the tenth-century ʻGolden Ageʼ of Islam, when the Abbasid *caliphs* used encryption to securely communicate state secrets. Books from this period such as the *Adabal Kuttab* (ʻThe Secretariesʼ Manualʼ) had sections dedicated to cryptography.

In terms of technological innovation, Arabs were actually not that far behind the West. IBM launched the first personal computer in 1981, but only one year later an IT company called Sakhr was set up in Kuwait and developed a personal computer with its own operator interface; as Microsoft swiftly monopolized the market, however, Sakhrʼs position was no longer tenable. (Today it is still the biggest Arab IT company.)

There may well be a cultural aspect to the skill and enthusiasm with which the Muslim world has taken to cyberspace, in particular Islamists in waging cyber-*jihad*. Secrecy and the necessity for secrecy, or at least discretion for survival, has historically been part of the Arab experience, as is the ability to undermine an enemy with a patient watchfulness that will discover his secrets.

Logging On

More than 50 per cent of *jihadis* come from the Gulf, where well-educated people are sufficiently affluent to have owned personal computers since the late 1980s and are extremely adept at using the Internet and exploiting its capabilities. They are also good at finding ways around the interventions of officialdom.

It was not until 1999 that Saudi Arabia officially allowed use of the Internet, and even now has only one Internet service provider (ISP), which is state-controlled, closely monitored and censored. It is routed through the King Abdulaziz City for Science and Technology. All traffic is channelled through a filter where it is subject to censorship. The kingdom long withstood domestic and external pressure to allow Internet access because, as the Saudi dissident al-Masari explains: 'It meant breaking the rigid monopoly over influencing minds. It meant the kingdom of silence would no longer be the kingdom of silence.' Censorship of the Internet is draconian, with millions of pages banned periodically. Not surprising, then, that Islamists have dubbed King Abdulaziz City the 'City of Darkness'.

In reality, Saudis have been online since the late 1980s, using international dial-up to access overseas ISPs they subscribe to whilst abroad or using software secretly brought into the kingdom. The central-filter censorship is actually very easily circumvented for people with even limited know-how.

The situation in Iraq was even more backward, as the Internet was entirely banned under Saddam's regime. Following the invasion, however, the US provided Iraqis with the very latest online technology, including satellite Internet. Having applied themselves assiduously to getting to grips with the new technology, the Iraqi insurgents and their allies daily upload myriad images, videos and written accounts of their military successes against the invading US army. These are now known to be key recruiting tools, inspiring thousands to join the *jihad* in Iraq and still others to commit the kind of atrocities we recently witnessed in London on 7 July 2005.

Home Page

Experts state that there are now in excess of 4,500 overtly *jihadi* websites which help al-Qaʻida maintain itself as a global ideological movement bringing together like-minded people from all over the world.

Islamist and *jihadi* groups started using email lists to disseminate information from 1995 onwards, including the Advice and Reform Committee established by bin Laden in London, which was headed by Khaled al-Fawwaz. It would not be unreasonable to surmise that bin Laden and al-Fawwaz communicated with each other in this way. Internet surveillance was in its infancy at the time, as they would no doubt have been aware.

According to Albrecht Hofheinz, a leading researcher on the use of new technology in the Arab-Islamic world, the term 'cyber-*jihad*' was first coined by Muslim students living in the US who started up Islamic websites in the mid-1990s. The first overtly *jihadi* website was probably one belonging to Chechen rebels which appeared in 1999, called 'kavkaz.org' (not to be confused with 'kavkaz.com', the Chechen government site). The site made international headlines when it urged readers to financially support the Taliban and gave details of how and where to hand over the money.

The first al-Qaʻida website is believed to have been 'maalemaljihad.com' ('Milestones of Holy War'). It was set up in February 2000 by an Egyptian Islamic Jihad sympathizer, 'Mr Muhammad Ali', who travelled to southern China for the purpose. Presumably China was chosen not only for its technological expertise but because the web designers 'Mr Ali' worked with had no idea what he was writing about: 'The Arabic letters just looked like earthworms to us,' Chen Rongbin, who worked for the ISP, told the *Wall Street Journal* in November 2002. In more recent times cyber-*jihadis* are believed to have been using Japanese servers and even chat forums for the same reason.

The 'maalemaljihad.com' home page displayed al-Qa'ida's symbol, two swords joined to form a winged missile – a suitable metaphor for the contents of the site, which merged fundamentalist Islamic theology with modern technology. A mirror site was established in Pakistan a few months later (a mirror site is a failsafe: if a server shuts one down, the other remains up and running).

The content was provided many miles away in Afghanistan: statements by bin Laden and al-Zawahiri, the newsletter *al-Mujahidun*, news digests, a gallery of 'martyrs' and a forty-five-page theological endorsement of the legitimacy of 'martyrdom operations'. Uploading was also a global enterprise with information being sent out on discs and posted on the website from various computers across Europe.

'Maalemaljihad.com' crashed in China in February 2001 when 'Mr Ali' forgot to pay the renewal subscription on time – a low-tech mistake for such a high-tech venture. The Pakistan-based twin site crashed in the summer of 2001.

In 2001, sources close to al-Qa'ida say, the organization was desperately seeking a secure private server in London, a clear indication of how crucial the Internet was to their operations at a time when preparations for the 11 September attacks were in full swing. Having spent £4,000 (then approximately $5,750) on what it was looking for, it found its new server blocked and destroyed by the security services after just a few days. After several more failed attempts al-Qa'ida decided to avoid using servers based in the UK or the US, although many al-Qa'ida-affiliated sites continue to use US-based servers.

After 11 September there was a proliferation of *jihadi* and Islamist sites carrying pictures of the 'nineteen martyrs'. Webmasters became increasingly insolent: the owner of the al-Qa'ida-affiliated 'jihad-online' registered the site in the name of Abdel Rahman al-Rashid – the former editor of the Saudi daily *al-Sharq al-Aswat*, who is now in charge of the Western-controlled satellite channel al-Arabiya. Al-Rashid was mortified when he found out.

The regional franchises of al-Qa'ida have their own websites and online magazines. Established in late 2003 by its then-leader Yusef al-Ayeri (killed later that year), al-Qa'ida in Saudi Arabia's 'al-Battar' was still flourishing at the time of this writing. Incorporating extremely explicit military training instructions, the over 100 editions of 'al-Battar' could equip anyone to run their own guerrilla army and military campaign.

'Al-Battar' also published poetry praising *jihad* and martyrdom. This extract is by Hamad al-Aslami:

> Why shouldn't I die as a martyr?
> The martyr's spirit will soar so high
> . . .
> he'll be flying with the birds of paradise,
> humming over palaces
> . . .
> you'll receive such comfort in the grave
> and enjoy the resurrection.
> You'll be crowned with honour and
> people everywhere will respect you.

A similar website, 'thurwat al-sinam', produced by al-Zarqawi's al-Qa'ida in the Land of the Two Rivers, details operations carried out in Iraq, and posts eulogies of martyrs and exhortations from al-Zarqawi himself to young Muslims to join the *jihad*. In a recent edition, al-Zarqawi posted an open letter to the Arab media asking it to portray the insurgents' activities in a more sympathetic light. Very detailed military techniques, including how to manufacture explosives and poison, are also available on this site.

The International Media Front of Islam (IMFI) is bin Laden's cyber-presence. Constantly mutating, it is always delivered in a different form and at the end of a series of links from and through other sites. Over 200 sites have links to IMFI sites. In September 2005, with typical audacity, the IMFI launched its own news programme. 'Voice of the Caliphate' has regularly appeared since then, bringing viewers on the site up to date on the Iraqi insurgency and al-Qa'ida's ideology, and even advertising for volunteers to contribute to this latest broadcasting endeavour.

Each al-Qa'ida franchise has its own 'information department' which takes care of Internet postings. Often inner-circle al-Qa'ida leaders record a communiqué on a disk, which is then sent by messenger to a minor operative who uploads the material using a computer at a cyber-café. Operatives working in this way may be observed behaving suspiciously in Internet cafés or caught on CCTV, and several have been arrested. The Pakistani group which kidnapped reporter Daniel Pearl (who was eventually killed) sent pictures of its hostage from an Internet café in Karachi. US intelligence agents located it through the IP address, seized the owner's CCTV footage and identified the culprits – though it was too late to prevent the murder of the victim.

The inner-circle al-Qa'ida leadership no longer uses the Internet because of the risk of being tracked. Bin Laden and al-Zawahiri are kept up to date with Internet activity, however; relevant material is downloaded onto disk or printed and then delivered to their hiding places by trusted messengers.

The successful use of the Internet in cyber-*jihad* depends entirely on secrecy and deception on the one side and vigilance and intelligence on the other. We are going to consider the main aspects of the game of hide-and-seek that is cyber-*jihad* before looking at the different ways in which online battle is joined.

Hide . . .

The Internet is impossible to police, and secret *jihadi* organizations were swift to realize the opportunities the medium presented. 'Nine hundred million people use the Internet annually,' says Dr

Muhammad al-Masari, the London-based Saudi dissident, physicist and IT expert. 'It is impossible to keep it under random surveillance.' Even for those who are well-known to intelligence services, there are many ways of concealing the secret messages they wish to send through cyberspace.

As in conventional warfare, intercepting crucial messages is key to a defence strategy, and finding ways to conceal the meaning of such messages essential for the attacker. A prime historical example is the cracking of the Enigma code at Bletchley Park during World War Two which enabled Britain to foil Luftwaffe attacks and undoubtedly contributed to the Allied victory.

It is widely believed that al-Qa'ida used the Internet – to a greater or lesser extent – to orchestrate all its major attacks since the two US embassy bombings in Nairobi and Dar-es-Salaam in 1998.

Seven months before 11 September 2001, FBI investigators were becoming increasingly alarmed about bin Laden's Internet capabilities. In February 2001 *USA Today* reported that bin Laden and others 'are hiding maps and photographs of terrorist targets and posting instructions . . . on sports chat rooms, pornographic bulletin boards and other websites'.

US intelligence officers seized the computer of Abu Zubaydah – believed to have masterminded the 11 September attacks – and claimed to have found a large number of encoded emails, the last one dated 9 September 2001.

The most common and easily accessed way of concealing an electronic message is encryption. An encryption programme uses mathematical 'keys' to scramble and unscramble a message. Anybody can download the software to do this free of charge from the Internet, although many commercial programmes nowadays have a built-in 'back door' allowing government agencies to access the 'keys', intercept and eavesdrop. In order to enter into an encrypted communication both parties set up and exchange passwords and 'keys'. In theory only they can then decrypt the message. The problem is that the 'keys' are sent via the Internet. The most reliable form of encryption is when the 'keys' are passed non-electronically, as from person to person or in a letter. It is believed that encryption setups like this are widely used by al-Qa'ida operatives – to contact or establish sleeper cells, for example.

Experts point out that any terrorist or criminal organization with a lot of secrets and a modicum of programming know-how can produce its own extremely secure and secret encryption software.[2] There is no reason to imagine that al-Qa'ida – with many young IT specialists in its ranks – would be lagging behind in this aspect of cyber-*jihad* where the latest technical innovations may hold the keys to victory. Once developed, tailor-made encryption software has to be passed between members of the communications group in total secrecy.

Another method that has historically been very important to al-Qa'ida is steganography. Using this software, a message – often itself encrypted – is hidden within a seemingly normal picture, video, sound file or even the IP address of a site or email. Using steganography a secret message is passed, completely invisible and largely undetectable to anyone who doesn't know it is there. For the informed recipient, a simple password will reveal the message.

Spam email is often used as a mailbox flag. This may appear as a link to a sex site where a pornographic image is posted containing a steganographic message. Each time the spam email appears it is a signal for the intended recipient that a new message has been sent. For the rest of the unsuspecting address list it is simply a commonplace nuisance. (Islamists have no problem with using pornographic images for the purpose of concealing messages: 'There is a state of war,' says al-Masari, 'and in war it is permissible even to use offensive material to cover up traces.')

It is fairly easy for an interceptor to discover that there is a steganograph in a file – and there are special steganalysis programmes which reveal the presence of a hidden message – but it is extremely difficult to extract it without the password.

Quite how the FBI knew what was being passed between

al-Qaʻida operatives in February 2001 in encrypted messages hidden within steganographic files is not, then, immediately obvious – it was probably an educated guess, and probably correct. How else could the plot have revolved around so many geographically disparate locations – Germany, Afghanistan and the US?

It is believed that steganography is not used as much nowadays because of the increased use of cyber-cafés by al-Qaʻida operatives. Cyber-cafés are unlikely to have the software to open, let alone create, steganographed messages.

Cyber-*jihadis* are favouring increasingly low-tech solutions in a bid to outwit intelligence organizations which naturally imagine them to be using the latest cryptographic software. One of the safest and simplest ways to convey a message without fear of interception is widely used by all sorts of clandestine and activist groups: an email account is established and the password shared between those who are going to communicate; any one of them can then write an email and save it to the drafts folder, which can be accessed by anyone who has the password from any computer anywhere in the world – because the email has not actually been sent, it cannot be intercepted or read by anyone else.

One-time-use email accounts are another *jihadi* favourite. Using Yahoo or Hotmail, a new address is created on the spot in a cyber-café, used once to send a message, and then destroyed. According to Dr al-Faqih, the al-Qaʻida expert, this method is also favoured by the Mafia and other criminal organizations: 'It's a very simple, low-tech means of deception. How will the person be able to reply? Because they will have agreed a code in advance – preferably at a physical meeting – so that if one uses an email address beginning with 'W', the other will know which address will be set up next to receive his reply.'

Short-life websites are another popular method of communicating information. Information is uploaded onto a temporary website, and members of the group alerted to the address through an encrypted email. They can then access the site and download what is on there before intelligence services become aware of it. The site is then swiftly destroyed. This method is commonly used by the Iraqi *mujahedin* to post videos of their operations, using servers in Iran, Syria or Turkey so that they can avoid being physically located by intelligence officers tracking the IP address.

A common tactic, complete with its own dry humour, is to hijack websites belonging to other individuals or organizations. *Jihad* videos were discovered on servers belonging to the Arkansas Department of Highways and Transportation in 2004. A fan who started a website celebrating the work of fantasy writer Clive Barker was dismayed when it was pointed out to him (in October 2002) that a message from bin Laden had been hidden in a concealed folder on the site. Internet security expert Mike Sweeney explains how this is easily done: 'You break into a website, you get permission to create a folder, you add a file and cover your tracks . . . it looks ordinary but if you know the path you can find it.' The hidden file can only be accessed with the correct code, which will have been furnished in advance to intended recipients along with a link to the relevant file on the website.

Tracking by surveillance authorities can be done very simply via the IP address – this is provided when an Internet account is registered and, if genuine, contains the information necessary to identify and geographically locate individual machines being used for online activity. Cyber-*jihadis* became aware of this, and nowadays change their IP addresses and servers frequently.

Another way to avoid detection via the IP address is by using a proxy server. Essentially this is a computer that sits between the user and the Internet. When a cyber-*jihadi* requests a file it passes through the proxy, which strips all the user's IP information and replaces it with its own. Proxy servers are also used to bypass the blocks that security services can put on site access from a specific country. For example, Saudi Arabia blocks access from the kingdom to al-Masari's website 'tajeed.com'. 'To access our site users go through a proxy server,' he explains. 'When we set up a new website and change the IP address, we simply send out the new details to subscribers and regular visitors.'

IP details can be used to put intelligence services on the wrong track as well as concealing the user's own identity through a service called 'Find-Not'. This removes the original IP details and provides fake ones – in China, say. Popular with cyber-*jihadis*, Find-Not has servers on several continents, so they cannot be closed down. They also offer an email service which, combined with encryption, provides very high-level security. Another software package changes the visible (though not actual) IP address every second, making physical tracking impossible.

Intelligence services in the US claim that most of al-Qa'ida's financial transactions are done via email. This is disputed by most Islamist commentators I consulted, who maintain that such communications are too risky and have become a thing of the past. They say that cash is still the preferred medium, sent in bags by messengers. However, some transactions do occur electronically using the new 'pay-as-you-go'-style credit card. This is charged with funds by purchasing vouchers. As al-Masari explains: 'Supposing someone wished to support al-Zarqawi's *jihad* in Iraq; al-Zarqawi would have a pay-as-you-go credit card account set up, in any name – it could be a donkey in the Far East – and you can buy vouchers and email him the reference numbers, which he uses to charge the credit card. He can then use the card to buy whatever he likes.'

In the past al-Qa'ida-linked sites like 'al-neda.com' contained encrypted links to more secure sites. The cat-and-mouse game of links is still commonplace when a new al-Qa'ida site is posted although these are not always encrypted, and rely instead on something like a sixth sense in the zealous visitor. The interpreters working for intelligence services might be excellent speakers of Arabic, but they will not likely understand the cryptic cultural, Islamic, geographic or *jihadi* references that give the clues as to which link will be the signpost.

When there is a new posting, it takes an experienced cyber-*jihadi* five minutes to follow the links to the latest al-Qaʻida site. Experts say that US and British intelligence need twenty-four to forty-eight hours to arrive at the site by more conventional routes, by which time al-Qaʻida will already have closed it down.

The starting point is almost invariably the chat forum on one or other of the main *jihadi* websites. These are genuine chat forums and are buzzing with interaction, information and planning – often of an extremely violent nature. However, the trained eye will spot the 'thread' (an online discussion) that leads somewhere else. The dedicated visitor will know which 'signpost' links to click and embark on an odyssey through many sites before finally being delivered to the one he is after. A new software package, allowing immediate access to the latest communiqués by automatically redirecting the online visitor, was recently tailor-made by sympathetic IT specialists and distributed to selected contacts by *jihadi* websites. As soon as the new web address becomes common knowledge, it will be hacked or closed down.

Some *jihadi* websites manage to survive by dint of extreme secrecy, sharing the password, which is changed every few days, with only a very small group of trusted visitors. 'Al-Ansar', for example, one of the websites belonging to al-Qaʻida in the Land of the Two Rivers appears to have been hacked when you try to enter it by normal means; yet people with the current password can still access it. The 'al-Firdus' website (which posts operations in Iraq linked to 'Jaish Ansar al-Sunnah') changes its server every few days and only sends details of the new address in encrypted emails to a selected few – including some journalists.

Al-Faqih points out that physical protection can be crucial in cyber-*jihad*: '*Jihadis* in the Sunni Triangle [in Iraq] are protected by the sheer number of insurgents there. Supposing the US or Iraqi intelligence services do find out the exact cyber-café or telephone line used in email or Internet communications . . . so what? They are hardly going to be able to launch a raid there.' On the other hand, anybody logging onto *jihadi* sites at a cyber-café in Baghdad is likely to be arrested as vigilant café owners have direct lines to the security services. The main reason bin Laden and other fugitive al-Qa'ida leaders cannot take the risk of using the Internet is that they no longer have the physical protection of a sympathetic state, as they did in Afghanistan.

. . . and Seek

Most of the effective surveillance work tracking *jihadi* sites is being done not by the FBI or MI6, but by private groups. The best-known and most successful of these are Haganah (of which more below), SITE (run by Rita Katz, whose fee-based clients include the FBI and various media outlets around the world) and Jihad-watch. Not as effective or famous, but interesting for a different reason, is 'itshappening.com', a website run by an ex-pornography baron, Jon Messner, who trained his sights on *jihadi* websites after 11 September 2001. He is best known for his attack on 'al-neda.com', the al-Qa'ida-related website. He hacked it so that visitors were redirected to the FBI's 'most wanted' pages. (*Jihadis* had the last laugh, however – they began using his chat forum and posted the address for the 'al-neda.com' replacement site there. This war, it seems, is not without humour, albeit rather bitter.)

Haganah, a US-based pro-Zionist website (*haganah* means 'defence' in Hebrew) run by Aaron Weisburd, tracks down *jihadi* sites and informs their ISPs that they are hosting a 'terrorist' site, which usually ensures it is closed down immediately. Some observers believe Haganah also hacks into and destroys *jihadi* sites. Utah Indymedia, a US-based media collective which believes it has been a victim of a Haganah hacking attack, has denounced Weisburd as being motivated by 'racial hatred' and a dislike of any form of independent thought. Often a zealous *jihadi* will enter the address of his favourite site only to find it has been replaced with an online US shopping site or something equally ironic.

Weisburd says he is two weeks ahead of law enforcement and

intelligence services in terms of tracking the sites and discovering who their webmasters are. To date Haganah has shut down more than 700 *jihadi* sites. Weisburd has been the victim of hackers himself, however, and when they managed to trace his home address it was posted on pro-*jihadi* websites. Weisburd says he constantly receives death threats.

During the 1990s exporting encryption packages from the US was restricted, and some programmes were even classified as weapons.[3] After the events of 11 September there was a bid by elements in the US and UK administrations to crack down on Internet cryptography. One idea mooted in late 2001 was to enforce 'key escrow', whereby the keys needed to encrypt and decrypt messages are made available to a third party for use, if required, by government agencies. While human rights agencies such as Privacy International objected on the grounds that this infringed civil liberties, the financial argument proved more persuasive: it was pointed out that this would jeopardize the security of online credit card transactions, with the result that people would stop shopping on the Internet. The idea was quietly dropped.

Nevertheless, it is certain that many commercially available encryption packages do indeed have a 'back door' whereby surveillance authorities can gain access to the keys. The irony is that nobody with anything to hide would buy such insecure software in the first place; they would either develop their own or invest in the very latest technology offering encryption at levels up to 2048-bit (to put this into perspective, encryption started out at 40 bits and that was considered difficult to crack) and guaranteeing no 'back doors'.

Laptops captured along with al-Qa'ida operatives are invaluable sources of information for security services. Cyber-forensic experts can download information, identify which websites have been visited, track correspondence, learn exactly which software the *jihadis* are using and see which strategies al-Qa'ida is currently adopting in the real and virtual worlds.

According to al-Faqih, the US is believed to have provided Saudi authorities with extremely sophisticated monitoring software, because the majority of cyber-*jihadis* (up to 70 per cent) are based in the kingdom. Inevitably this software was used not only against al-Qa'ida but also against anyone expressing dissident views.

It seems likely that the Egyptian authorities have a cyber-squad. According to the Islamist Yasser al-Sirri, whose own sites have repeatedly been hacked, crashed and demolished, Egyptian security's favourite method is to destroy sites by triggering Denial of Service (DOS) – an online attack where a network is crashed by flooding it with useless traffic using specially designed software. Most security measures that we take in good faith are actually useless in the face of a determined hacker. Software for discovering passwords will enable a spy to learn your (under eight-character) password in seconds. For the more complicated password, a software application called 'key-tracker' will simply communicate it to the spy as you enter it.

Most *jihadi* websites are shut down either by hackers or by the owners themselves within weeks. Those that remain are either protected by very strong multilayered software or have been allowed to stay live for surveillance purposes.

If a site has a very well-established and populated chat forum, it may well have more intelligence value live than shut down; on the other hand, some apparently *jihadi* sites are actually fake sites put up by intelligence services to trick naive militants into revealing their identities or their intentions. This deception is usually obvious to experienced users, who will quickly observe that the site is too slick, too expensive or too 'Western' in some way, perhaps because it includes advertisements or products for sale. A glance at those who have contributed to the bulletin boards is another means of assessing how authentic a site is – one recurring name is 'the Tunisian admirer of the two *sheikhs*'.

As in actual war, espionage is a crucial part of cyber-warfare. Intelligence services spy on *jihadi* websites in a variety of ways. The most common is to enter the chat forums pretending to be an eager young Muslim who wishes to find out how to join the *jihad*. The intention is to entrap recruiters, discover whether an operation is being planned or simply to trap an over-zealous fellow guest into revealing his identity. Unfortunately these endeavours are more Inspector Clouseau than James Bond, and online visitors joke that *jihadi* chat rooms are bursting with bungling Saudi secret police agents who are paid to chat online all day. Amusing tales abound of how faked religious zeal, inappropriate language or simply an uncontrolled outburst of the undercover agent's real point of view have betrayed the impostor.

However, while this subterfuge is obvious to the experienced eye, the novice is more easily trapped. Once intelligence information has led to an arrest, the secret police frequently take over the detained person's online identity and password in a bid to entrap further unwitting visitors.

Nowadays genuine *jihadis* would be very careful about saying too much on chat forums, except under very exclusive circumstances when a password is given to very few trusted individuals or when a discussion progresses off-site and takes the form of encrypted emails between individuals.

Western governments are still working on ways to control the Internet without damaging its vast potential and range of commercial applications. In the US, legislation has been introduced which should make ISPs more cautious. If an ISP hosts a guerrilla site the owner can be charged with conspiracy and aiding and abetting terrorism.

Babar Ahmed, who was based in London, stands indicted for conspiracy in the US on the grounds that from 1997–2004 he 'provided, through the creation and use of various Internet websites, email communication . . . expert advice and assistance, communications equipment, military items, currency . . . and personnel designed to recruit and assist the Chechen *mujahidin* and the Taleban and raise funds for violent *jihad*'. Ahmed denies all these charges.

Online Umma

Albrecht Hofheinz points out that 'in worldwide terms the Arab-language sites are unique in that out of the top 100 most popular sites, ten have a decidedly Islamic orientation'. Unlike Western Internet users with their myriad interests, we can identify that uniquely Muslim confluence of culture and religion even in the virtual universe of the Internet.

By logging on to a site or joining a chat room, a Muslim anywhere in the world can immediately feel part of the *umma*. *Jihadi* websites enable the Muslim cyber-community to engage in ideological as well as physical battles, and this is a key factor in the development and continued existence of al-Qa'ida.

Al-Qa'ida's problem is not finding trained fighters – thousands of new *jihadis* and those returned from the physical battlegrounds of Afghanistan, Bosnia, Chechnya and Iraq are willing to fight – but the central coordination and deployment of these troops-in-waiting. The Internet is providing the solution for this erstwhile problem by allowing would-be fighters to identify where the battle can be joined and keep up-to-date with operations as they occur.

Most *jihadi* sites have several sections. The most important and largest is usually the 'religion' section, which contains *fatwas* explaining who can be targeted legitimately, Qur'anic references to *jihad*, the different ways *jihad* can be expressed, and aspects of martyrdom. Online doctrinal consultations with religious *sheikhs* are often provided, with a wide range of questions posted – from the propriety of telephone conversations with one's betrothed to whether or not it is acceptable to behead a hostage with a saw rather than a knife or sword (both are genuine questions posted on websites found by researchers at *al-Quds al-Arabi*).

In the '*jihad*' section of a site, would-be recruits are encouraged to join the battle. Some general advice is given, for example, the best routes into Iraq and even the names and locations of sympathetic mosques in neighbouring countries – although no risks are taken with sensitive information. Galleries of martyr portraits are accompanied by their last wills and testaments – often in the form of a video.

Most sites have an 'IT section' where contributors are urged to share their knowledge and develop new ways of using cyberspace to further the cause of *jihad*. These challenges are enthusiastically met by a younger generation who increasingly function as much in cyberspace as they do in real-time.

The bulletin boards or chat rooms are by far the most popular forums on *jihadi* websites. Visitors can add comments or reply to ongoing conversations and debates. Sometimes an 'expert' is at hand to answer questions, especially on those sites which offer military training and logistics.

Many *jihadi* sites have a 'women's section' where wives and mothers are urged to support their men in *jihad* and help them in the psychological battle against what one site describes as 'that disease, the weakness which loves life and hates death'.

In May 2005 a site designed specifically for women appeared on the Internet. The Saudi-based 'al-Khansa' encourages women to support radical husbands and prepare their children to carry on the *jihad*. (Al-Khansa was an early Islamic female poet who wrote celebrations of the lives of Muslim martyrs killed in battle with 'infidels'.) 'Al-Khansa' also offers advice on physical training for women who actually want to fight, but reminds them that their primary role is to offer 'the blood of [their] husbands and the body parts of [their] children as [their] sacrificial offering'.

Beyond Censorship

The main benefit of the Internet to *jihadi* groups in the long run will almost certainly prove to be the uncensored platform it offers for the dissemination of news and information. The launch of the news programme 'Voice of the Caliphate', for instance, enables the network to circumvent external editorial decisions and frees it from its erstwhile dependence – on al-Jazeera, for one – to broadcast its messages and video footage in full.

In April 2005 al-Qa'ida published a document on the Internet by its leading strategist, the Egyptian Muhammad Makkawi. Titled 'al-Qa'ida's Strategy to the Year 2020', it outlined the organization's long-term project which began with 11 September 2001. The apparent purpose of posting this lengthy document online was to enable independent franchise cells to see how they might best contribute to the network's long-term strategy.

One of the most significant postings in recent times was made by al-Zarqawi in 2004 to announce his allegiance to bin Laden and to al-Qa'ida. As this news flashed around the globe it became an open invitation to all al-Qa'ida-supporting would-be *jihadis* to flock to Iraq – which they did.

The astonishing absence of censorship on the Internet is in itself immensely attractive to the many millions of Muslims who live under rigidly oppressive regimes. When the material is also something they feel passionately about, the combination is irresistible.

Saad al-Faqih was able to organize at least one successful demonstration against the Riyadh regime via the Internet, while based in London. The authorities were not able to prevent arrangements being made in cyberspace, although they responded with harsh policing and punishments when the actual physical events – which are banned in the kingdom – took place.

Nearly every insurgency operation in Iraq is filmed and posted on a number of sites and bulletin boards accompanied by *jihadi* songs. The bloodshed is presented as heroic and glorious, with the cameraman shouting '*Allahu akhbar!*' ('God is great!') as the bomb detonates or the snipers fire. No longer dependent on a newspaper or television editor's decision, all actions carried out by radical groups get maximum exposure and publicity. The freedom allowed by the Internet is not only in terms of content but presentation. The absence of any outside control or licence means that the *jihadi* groups can shape the way they are presented and perceived by various target audiences. Al-Qa'ida in the Land of the Two Rivers' film *All Religion Will be for Allah* is one example; it was widely and expertly distributed via the Internet. A seventeen-minute 'Top Ten' sequence depicting insurgency attacks in Iraq followed in August, and was promoted on the Internet as being for 'those who like to see American Crusader blood flowing'.

The Internet is also being exploited by *jihadis* as a weapon in psychological warfare. Not only *jihadis* and ordinary Muslims but also Westerners access images of American and European hostages being tormented and sometimes even beheaded by masked men holding Kalashnikovs. This is potent imagery, the stuff of nightmares in the West and elsewhere.

It is these ideological websites that Western intelligence services are at pains to close down. Strangely, they allow many sites with extremely detailed military content to survive. The Israeli researcher Gabriel Weimann recently wrote a report for the University of Haifa in which he described the Internet as 'the new Afghanistan for terror training, recruitment and fundraising'.

The Saudi 'al-Battar' contains an online military training course in sections called 'The Sword of Victory'. Would-be *jihadis* are urged to follow the course at home or in groups, obtain firearms ('preferably a Kalashnikov') and maintain a high level of fitness in preparation for taking steps to join the actual *mujahedin.* Topics covered include kidnapping, weapons, manufacturing and handling explosives and poisons, detailed instructions for making a suicide-bomb belt (even down to the correct thickness of the cloth), how to plant land mines, how to detonate a bomb remotely with a mobile phone, topography, orienteering (including crossing a desert at night), map reading and survival skills.

A Pakistani-based website, 'mojihedun.com', still active at the time of the London suicide bombs, contained a section called 'how to strike a European city' giving detailed instructions and suggestions for attacks.

The password-protected *jihadi* forum 'al-Firdus' provides highly detailed instructions for the preparation of explosive oils, recommending nitroglycerin because it is 'more explosive than TNT'.

Providing what is, in effect, an electronic *umma*, *jihadi* websites allow isolated young Muslims to engage with a worldwide network of like-minded people striving against what they perceive as a common enemy and with a singular unity of purpose. Local connections are easily established, and it is believed that many of the cells that characterize current al-Qa'ida activity are formed in this way.

Bulletin boards offer practical advice to those who wish to physically join the *jihad*. One young man in the US advises American Muslims who want to fight in Iraq to 'join the Marines and then, when you get there, switch sides!' Another suggests that the would-be *jihadi* log on to Syrian-based chat rooms to form a friendship with a young Syrian male preferably living in a village near the Iraqi border. 'After a while you can ask for his phone number,' it advises. 'You should then phone – but only once – and conceal your real purpose from him. Tell him you would very much like to visit him and his family.' Once invited by the gullible Syrian, the *jihadi* is told to simply slip over the border into neighbouring Iraq and join the insurgency.

The Internet can be exploited for misinformation purposes by both sides. Sometimes this becomes a highly complicated game with several layers. For example, in June 2005 al-Zarqawi posted a spoken message on a website responding to rumours that he had been wounded or killed. This was widely reported in the media as 'an announcement that al-Zarqawi is fine, that his wound was slight and that he is recovered'. However, on closer inspection the message contains a direct message to bin Laden saying: 'I sent you the plan and I am waiting for your orders.' Was al-Zarqawi trying to discreetly communicate with bin Laden, hoping the US wouldn't notice or, as seems more likely, was he banking on US intelligence scouring the message for clues and concluding that a big attack was imminent?

Cyber-Battles

Most *jihadi* websites have a section on hacking. Hacking, for those who are not well-versed in cyber-vocabulary, is when a person has such a high level of systems expertise that they can explore a site for security holes and then enter it to steal information or to leave a malicious virus or 'worm'. Hacking software is available to download for free on the Internet.

The first serious cyber-battles occurred during the Serbian conflict in 1999 when pro-Serbian hackers targeted NATO and US defence networks. In 2000, Palestinian and Israeli hackers engaged in a fierce cyber-conflict that coincided with the outbreak of the second *intifada*. Israeli hackers crashed the Hizbullah site and replaced it with the Israeli flag; they got into a Palestinian database and extracted and broadcast the private mobile telephone numbers of all the Palestinian leaders. But this was nothing compared with the damage done by pro-Palestinian hackers from the Middle East and the US who then went into overdrive and successfully attacked five times as many Israeli sites, including the Bank of Israel and the Tel Aviv stock exchange, the Israeli army site and eventually pro-Israeli sites in the US including the Washington-based lobby group American-Israeli Political Action Committee. Since the Israeli economy is highly reliant on e-commerce, this bout of destructive activity caused an 8 per cent dip on the Israeli stock exchange.

Al-Jazeera is an obvious target for those who dislike its choice of broadcast content. In March 2003 its website was crashed by systematic Domain Name System (DNS) flood attacks after it showed pictures of American soldiers taken prisoner in Iraq. This type of attack subjects the site to levels of traffic that it is incapable of dealing with, so that the server simply breaks down. A similar type of attack is the Internet Relay Chat (IRC) 'robot' or 'bot' attacks which are, in effect, a virtual sit-in with up to 20,000 computers acting as robots or 'zombies' doing their master's bidding again and again until told to stop. To carry out such attacks requires a dedicated team of cyber-warriors and considerable funding; the only form of defence – to keep expanding a website's bandwidth – is also costly.

In June 2003 a twenty-four-year-old Canadian acting alone managed to hack into the al-Jazeera Internet site. Visitors were redirected to pro-war sites praising the US troops in Iraq. He had simply contacted the site-hosting administrators and, pretending to be the al-Jazeera web administrator, asked them to set up a new password. Our own website at *al-Quds al-Arabi* has also been hacked on a number of occasions – once it was not available to readers for three days.

'Islamic Hackers' is a recent website run by an eponymous group of self-proclaimed cyber-*jihadis*, in possession of the very latest secure technology and powerful equipment. 'Islamic Hackers' hacked the Christian fundamentalist site 'Joy Junction' so thoroughly in May 2005 that the entire account was wiped off the server. Another group of cyber-*jihadis* operating a site called 'o-h-cjb.net' ran a campaign to destroy all sites that post anything negative about Islam, and invited visitors to propose targets which were then put to the vote. The 'lucky' winner, in one case a Christian missionary site in Arabic – 'al-Haqeeqa' – was then crashed using a special software programme called Webhakerz.

There are many weapons available in the cyber-arsenal, far too many to list here, including one curious homage to bin Laden: when the US invasion of Iraq appeared imminent, a cyber-*jihadi* by the name of 'Melhacker' (aka 'Kamil') developed a worm called 'Nedal' ('Laden' backwards) which he sent out to thousands of addresses in the US. Another, sent anonymously, was called 'VBS.OsamaLaden@mm' and contained a code which left a message referring to 11 September and then attempted to shut down the user's system and delete all files.[4]

Future

For all the sophisticated technology apparently at his fingertips, bin Laden's preferred means of communication is currently the foot messenger or donkey. The inner circle of al-Qaʿida, it seems, is wary of sophisticated interception technology used by the US's and other states' intelligence services.

Many key figures associated either directly or indirectly with al-Qaʿida are under a level of surveillance where a possible 'back door' into their Internet communications is a constant risk and one they are unlikely to take. In this sense the founding inner core of the organization has taken a step backwards and is currently unable to take full military advantage of the Internet.

The opposite is true where the al-Qaʿida global network in general is concerned. Al-Qaʿida in the Land of the Two Rivers is as aggressively active in cyberspace as it is on the ground. Its constant online presence provides proof that its leader is alive and well and that the insurgents' battle is being fought and, many would say, won. Many security experts believe that the recent attacks in Madrid and London were orchestrated via the Internet.

The potential for cyber-*jihad* to expand is enormous. Cyber-attacks on the American infrastructure could cause widespread damage at very little cost. If these were coupled with an actual attack, the result could be catastrophic. In a 2003 US naval intelligence cyber-defence report specialists estimated that with a budget of no more than $10 million, a well-prepared and coordinated attack by fewer than thirty hackers strategically located around the world could bring the US to its knees, closing down power grids, air-traffic-control systems, emergency services and financial institutions.

The Bush administration clearly fears the escalation of cyber-warfare.

The Department of Defense was targeted 75,000 times in 2004 alone by intruder attempts.[5] There is a designated cyber-security division within the Homeland Security Department, and in April 2005 the US military launched the Joint Functional Component Command for Network Warfare – an 'elite hacker crew' charged with defending all Department of Defense networks, and developing the highly secret mission called Computer Network Attack.[6]

However, such fears can also be exploited by politicians who wish to restrict the liberty of individuals. In 2003 the entire power supply to the east coast of the US and part of Canada was interrupted. The Beirut-based newspaper *al-Hayat* published what purported to be an email from al-Qa'ida claiming responsibility. (Al-Qa'ida was not in any way behind the power cuts, however.)

The Internet remains relatively free of control or interference, but human-rights groups such as Privacy International very much fear that it is only a matter of time before the excuse of 'terrorism' is used to restrict civil liberties in this domain as it is, increasingly, in the real world. The US has yet to find a way to restrict the activities of non-commercial enemy online presences without damaging the burgeoning free market in cyberspace.

As al-Qa'ida develops and expands horizontally in an ever-growing network of local franchises, the role of the Internet is increasingly important as a global forum for communication, ideology, recruitment, training and logistics. Just as the perpetrators of the 11 September attacks trained to fly airplanes, a whole new generation is becoming expert in information technology.

In a July 2005 presentation to US government terrorism analysts, longtime US State Department expert Dennis Pluchinsky regretfully concluded that al-Qa'ida is rapidly becoming the first web-directed guerrilla network in the world.

Al-Qaʻida in Saudi Arabia

> Governing is a contract between the *imam* and the people who will be ruled by him. This contract contains rights and obligations for both parties. It also has provisions for cancellation and making it null and void. One of the provisions which nullify the contract is betraying the *din* [religion] and the *umma*. And that is exactly what you have done [. . .] The people have awoken from their sleep and come to realize the enormity of the transgressions, corruption, and encroachment on their property and money. The Muslims in the Land of the Two Holy Mosques are determined to take back their rights no matter how high the price will be.
>
> Osama bin Laden, 'A Statement to the Saudi Rulers', 16 December 2004

Shortly after the 11 September 2001 attacks I met a close relative of the late King Fahd of Saudi Arabia. To my surprise she confided to me that she greatly admired bin Laden and the recent al-Qaʻida assault on the US. She knew that I had met bin Laden, and bombarded me with questions about the man, his companions and his environment.

This enthusiasm for bin Laden is shared by the general public of the kingdom. After 11 September a Saudi intelligence survey found that 95 per cent of a sample of educated Saudis aged twenty-five to forty-one supported bin Laden's cause.[1] In December 2004, CNN reported that a poll in the kingdom had found bin Laden's popularity exceeded that of King Fahd.[2]

To some extent the royal family has played into the hands of al-Qaʻida. The kingdom's 6,000 *umara* (princes) receive a salary from birth; they and 24,000 of their relatives and offspring enjoy lives of ostentatious wealth, which many believe are partly funded by corruption. In a television interview, Prince Bandar bin Sultan, the former Saudi ambassador to Washington, was blasé about bribery and corruption: 'It's human nature,' he said. 'If you tell me that in building this country and in spending $350 billion out of $400 billion that we misused or got corrupted with $50 billion, I'll tell you, "Yes, so what?"'

Bin Laden and radical clerics have often condemned the Saudi royals for, as they see it, stealing the oil wealth which should rightfully belong to the nation and not the ruling oligarchy. It is, according to al-Qaʻida's rhetoric, 'history's biggest robbery of the wealth of existing and future generations'. With oil revenues peaking in 2004 at $110 billion per year, the potential is there for every Saudi to enjoy a reasonable standard of living. Instead, members of the royal family wallow in grossly exaggerated luxury, complete with palaces, ocean liners and private Boeing 747s with solid gold fixtures and fittings, while income per capita in the kingdom has plummeted to $7,600.

The potential for dissent inherent in this unequal social system is obvious, and there are many additional irritations for those excluded from princely privilege. Unemployment is currently running at up to 25 per cent. With 60 per cent of the male population under the age of twenty, a new generation of bored, unemployed youths graduate from universities to disillusionment at a rate of 400,000 per year. Since the Saudi education system focuses largely on Wahhabism (see below), university degrees from the kingdom do not really qualify graduates for anything except perhaps recruitment into al-Qaʻida via certain local mosques with their emphasis on *jihad.* Liberal Saudi writer Raid Qusti wrote in 2004: 'Our educational system, which does not stress tolerance of other faiths . . . needs to be re-evaluated from top to bottom.'[3] The problem is reinforced by the absence of alternative perspectives, although this has been, to some extent, rectified by the advent of the Internet and al-Jazeera. No wonder bin Laden is popular in Saudi Arabia, when he voices and acts on the anger and overwhelming sense of injustice that the people feel but dare not express.

Condemnation

Since May 2003, a new branch of al-Qa'ida – al-Qa'ida in the Arabian Peninsula – has been active within Saudi Arabia, seeking to undermine the regime through a concerted campaign of attacks on domestic as well as foreign targets.

It appears that al-Qa'ida is planning a long, drawn-out campaign in the kingdom. On 16 December 2004 bin Laden issued the following menacing statement: 'Let it be known that the *mujahedin* in the Land of the Holy Mosques [Saudi Arabia] have not yet started the fight against the government. If they start, they will undoubtedly begin with the head of the *kafir,* the rulers of Riyadh, that is.' Many commentators believe an attack on the royal family is imminent.

Saudi Arabia is on the edge of a meltdown. The authoritarian regime of the *umara* is one under which everything is conducted behind closed doors and where even the most timid criticism is punished at the very least by public lashings and harsh prison sentences, and at worst by public beheadings.

The oil deposits under the kingdom should have made the nation wealthy, yet schools, hospitals and the infrastructure in general are crumbling. Even the most basic needs such as water and sanitation remain largely unmet, yet OPEC figures show that $1,200 billion in oil revenues have entered the Saudi coffers to date, with $150 billion rolling in in 2005 alone.[4] The ruling Al Saud family has created and maintained one of the most oppressive regimes on the planet – yet the voice of protest is not completely extinguished.

The regime faces two internal threats. The liberal opposition consists largely of those who were educated in American and European universities during the peak of oil wealth (twenty years from the late 1960s); at one point over 17,000 Saudis were conducting their undergraduate and postgraduate studies at American universities. When these young graduates returned home to find their country crumbling and the totalitarian rule of the Al Saud imposing the most rigid fundamentalist prohibitions on a silenced people they started to call for political reform and democracy. These liberal opponents expressed their demands through letters, articles and petitions.

The other opposition, the *jihadis*, demand change with guns. Having returned home victorious from their *jihad*[5] against the Soviet 'infidel', the so-called Afghan Arab fighters were incensed to find troops from that other great 'infidel', the US, mustering on their soil as the first Gulf War erupted little more than a year later. The kind of reforms they seek are very different to the liberals' demands, of course; they want a correct interpretation of *shari'ah* law implemented which, they object, the House of Al Saud and its 'compliant *ulama*'[6] are not doing, as well as the removal of all Western trends, elements and personnel from 'the Land of the Two Holy Places' (i.e. Mecca and Medina).

The climate is exactly right for al-Qa'ida to thrive in Saudi Arabia. Furthermore, it could be argued that al-Qa'ida would never have existed were it not for the kingdom in the first place. The birthplace of the Prophet and the seat of Islam have also produced the Islamic movements which evolved into al-Qa'ida.

Wahhabism, the kingdom's own branch of Islam, is fully embraced by bin Laden. The kingdom has always been al-Qa'ida's prime recruiting ground: openly encouraged by the regime, up to 45,000 Saudis joined bin Laden's *mujahedin* to expel the Soviet invaders from Afghanistan in the late 1980s. On their return to the kingdom they proved inspiring recruiters for a new generation of *jihadis*. The estimate that around 70 per cent of al-Qaʻida's membership is Saudi is borne out by the ratio of fifteen Saudi to four non-Saudi hijackers in the 11 September 2001 attacks.

It is a historical irony that the birthplace of bin Laden and al-Qaʻida should have become America's closest ally in the Gulf. While the US may have withdrawn its troops in 2003, the economic and cultural pervasion that will characterize Saudi Arabia's accession to the World Trade Organization (expected in late 2005) is sure to further enrage bin Laden and like-minded Islamic militants. The Prophet's injunction 'let there be no two religions in Arabia' is as much under threat from multinational corporations as from Christian churches.

The origins and history of the fatal breach between bin Laden and the House of Al Saud are key to understanding the present strategy and ambitions of al-Qaʻida both locally and globally.

The Wahhabi–Al Saud Connection

The Saudi regime as well as Saudi society is underpinned and legitimized by Wahhabi doctrine. Were it not for the financial support and constitutional endorsement of the House of Al Saud, the Wahhabis – originally an obscure Hanbali sect – might well have vanished without trace.

This complex interdependence of the Al Saud and Wahhabism has its roots in the very foundation of Saudi Arabia as a nation-state. Wahhabism was founded by the Sunni scholar Muhammad bin Abdul-Wahhab (1703–92) in the Najd area of what would later be called Saudi Arabia. Muhammad bin Saud, the then-ruler of Dir'iyyah – a desert oasis – embraced Abdul-Wahhab's strict new doctrine, which swept across the Arabian Peninsula. In 1745 the two men swore an oath that together they would conquer the peninsula (then part of the Ottoman Empire) and establish a Wahhabi-based kingdom there.

A series of marriages consolidated the union of the two families (political marriage-making is a strategy also employed by bin Laden who, for example, married his son to the daughter of his then-lieutenant Abu Hafs al-Misri in 2001). The early military adventures of Abdul-Wahhab, bin Saud and their descendants culminated in the capture of Mecca. By 1811 Wahhabi leaders had waged a *jihad* against other branches of Islam they considered incorrect, and succeeded in uniting much of the peninsula under their umbrella. But in 1818 combined forces from the Ottoman Empire and Egypt invaded and executed the ruling prince, bin Saud's grandson.

It is interesting to note that much of what fuelled the rise of Wahhabism through the eighteenth century is echoed in the complaints of today's militant Islamic fundamentalists: the influence of Islam was declining as European economic interests in the East (specifically India) expanded; the Wahhabis perceived Islam as being destroyed from within by those who were not following the 'true faith' and set about waging a *jihad* against them – a history all too gruesomely repeated by the Armed Islamic Group during the 1990s in Algeria and more recently in Iraq, where al-Zarqawi's men have targeted Shi'is.

In 1902 Abdul Aziz bin Abdul-Rahman Al Saud captured Riyadh. By 1926 the Al Saud dominated Najd and Hijaz, with the might of the Ikhwan (brothers), Wahhabi warriors, and declared the establishment of the Kingdom of Saudi Arabia in 1932. The vision of a Wahhabi kingdom that had inspired Abdul Aziz's forefathers now seemed to have become a reality, but bin Laden has famously declared that the kingdom was set up 'not for Islamic law but for Abdul Aziz's family'.[7]

When Abdul Aziz bin Abdul-Rahman Al Saud died in 1953, four of his sons in succession ruled a kingdom with no written constitution, no elected parliament, no independent judicial system, few civil liberties and no political parties – a state of affairs that persists today. So intrinsically was Wahhabism a part of the state that the only authority the Al Saud required in the execution of its constitutional duties was religious approval. The *ulama* – appointed by Al Saud – determine all matters, including foreign policy, based on their interpretation of the Qurʾan and *shariʿah*. The *ulama* have also, at times, been king-makers – in 1964, for example, they issued a *fatwa* that deposed King Saud, replacing him with Prince Faisal. Just as it has been from the outset of the Wahhabi/Al Saud adventure, the *ulama* legitimize and underpin the Al Saud's hold on power while the Al Saud and their ever-expanding bureaucracy ensure that Saudi society adheres to the ultra-conservative mores and practises of Wahhabism, thus upholding the *ulama*.

Not that bin Laden would take issue with the structural aspect of any of the above – he has openly stated that he opposes democracy in favour of rule by *shariʿah*. What he is certainly against is the hypocrisy of the current Saudi regime, where religion is worn as a cloak to conceal and justify all manner of ills.

The genesis of bin Laden's differences with the Al Saud can be traced back to 1933 when the Saudis signed a deal with the Standard Oil corporation of the US, giving it full exploration and development rights. In 1938 the company – and the kingdom – realized they were sitting on a liquid gold mine.

Oil, Money and the US

The US had been concerned about the depletion of its domestic oil resources since the 1920s. The new relationship with Saudi Arabia – and most of the American agenda in the region ever since – was largely based on the US's need to ensure, control and protect a ready supply of oil.

During World War Two, which saw a sharp increase in demand for oil from the Allied nations, the protection and control of Saudi oil reserves assumed great strategic importance. In 1943 President Franklin D. Roosevelt declared that the defence of Saudi Arabia was of vital interest to the US, thus making the kingdom eligible for lend-lease assistance[8] even though it was not party to the war in any way.

After the war, the US and Saudi Arabia established not only economic but defence ties. A 1945 meeting between Roosevelt and King Abdul Aziz bin Saud on board a ship in the Suez Canal saw the US promising security and technology in exchange for Saudi Arabian guarantees of reliable oil supplies at reasonable prices.

The US constructed the Dharan Air Base in the late 1940s but, in general prior to 1990, obviated the necessity for an actual US military presence to protect its oil supply by building bases, providing arms and training indigenous security forces.

The enormous increase in the fortunes of the Saudi regime after commercial production of oil began in 1945 had two completely incompatible long-term effects. On one hand the Saudi government started a programme of exporting Wahhabism throughout the Muslim world and even to Muslim populations in the West; on the other, its princes discovered the power of money, the modern world and Western materialism.

Wahhabi-sponsored schools, colleges and university posts proliferated. It is worth remembering that in many Muslim countries there is little state-funded education, and these Saudi-funded schools, or *madrassas*, provide the only education available. However, with the curriculum dominated by the Wahhabi interpretation of Islam, some of these *madrassas* – particularly in Pakistan and Saudi Arabia – have produced exactly the type of *jihadis* who now, ironically, represent the most serious threat to its survival the Saudi regime has ever encountered. Through the 1960s, 1970s and 1980s the *madrassas* promoted and upheld the strict religious principles of Wahhabism abroad; however, its interpretation was mutating at home.

From the early days of their great national good fortune, the Al Saud sought to distribute the financial benefits accrued from the nation's oil production by providing free education and health services.[9] Nevertheless, the increasing and very visible wealth of the ruling family highlighted social inequalities and planted the seeds of dissent. The royal family did not need to court public approval – they didn't need their subjects' votes to keep them in power, and didn't charge them income tax to fund the regime. However, they were aware that discontent could destabilize their dominance.

The focal point of religious teaching in the kingdom – now increasingly dictated by the political needs of the royal family rather than theology – began to focus on obedience to the king. The *ulama* became increasingly accommodating: 'They used religion to control the people,' as Saad al-Faqih puts it. 'They succeeded in making any opposition or even disagreement with the royal family a great crime.' Al-Faqih asserts that this has created an innate culture of secrecy: 'People now avoid – by nature rather than intelligence or judgement – involving themselves in politics.'

The career of King Faisal concisely demonstrates the conflicts that lie at the heart of Saudi society. A modernizer, he was also concerned about the rise of republicanism in the Arab world that threatened the future of the House of Al Saud. He tried to tread the middle ground, calling a conference in 1965 to reaffirm Islamic principles against the rising tide of technological innovation. In the same year, however, he introduced television to the kingdom, a move that so outraged conservative Wahhabi elements of the population that one of the king's own nephews led an attack on the television station and was shot dead by police. Faisal paid dearly for this – he himself was assassinated in 1975 by another of his nephews, apparently in revenge for his brother's murder by police in the TV station attack.

In 1979 Saudi Arabia experienced its first open rebellion by Wahhabis. On 20 November several hundred zealots, headed by the radical *imam* Guhiman al-Utaibi, seized the Grand Mosque in Mecca, accusing the Al Saud of decadence and corruption. It was eleven days before they could be dislodged. The Al Saud were obliged to ask for the assistance of French riot police, showing a dependence, which has persisted, on Western security forces to prevent domestic unrest. Subsequently, sixty-three of those who took part were publicly beheaded as an example to other would-be dissidents.

At the same time the Soviet Union was preparing to invade Afghanistan (on 25 December 1979), prompting a *jihad* and perhaps postponing the development of the dissent exhibited at the Grand Mosque in November.

The Saudis were immediately brought into the Afghan war by the US – not that there were many dissenting voices among the rulers. They needed the continued security support of the US and were anxious to do their bidding (they had seen how the Shah – another American ally in the region – had been abandoned in Iran). Furthermore, a genuine *jihad* would restore integrity and religious credibility to the House of Al Saud.

The Saudi regime split the cost of the Afghan war straight down the middle with the US, making a total contribution of $20 billion. Many millions more were raised from wealthy individuals throughout the Gulf to fund and arm the *mujahedin* in Afghanistan.

From Favoured Son to Deadly Foe

Bin Laden went to Pakistan shortly after the war in Afghanistan began in 1979. Initially, like many Afghan Arabs, he was involved in support work rather than the actual business of fighting. But by 1986 he had taken part in several battles and was becoming well-known in the Middle East as the millionaire-turned-heroic-*mujahedin*. Already displaying a natural instinct for publicity, bin Laden participated in documentaries which ensured the steady growth of his status and popularity.

The Saudi regime actively encouraged their young men to join the *jihad* and held bin Laden up as an inspiration. The Saudi media and mosques all over the kingdom joined in the campaign to raise money and fighters for the effort in Afghanistan. An estimated 35–45,000 Saudis were issued visas to travel to Pakistan in the late

1980s.[10] They went to the Afghan Arab bases established by Abdullah Azzam (and later, bin Laden) in eastern and southeastern Afghanistan, and Peshawar. Some intended to benefit from the military training on offer, some wished to experience *jihad* for a couple of months and others made a long-term commitment and became key members of the emerging al-Qa'ida network.

Throughout the 1980s there were many guesthouses in Saudi Arabia designed to receive wounded *mujahedin* from Afghanistan, who were then sent for treatment in Jeddah and Riyadh hospitals. These were funded by the government and by Islamic charities. The guesthouses were equipped with videos on *jihad*, as well as books on Islam. Every Saudi schoolchild was obliged to study the book *al-Tawhid* ('the Oneness of Allah') by Muhammad bin Abdul-Wahhab, considered by many as the source of militant Islamism. *Jihad* was part of the vocabulary of everyday life, and these times created a generation which was already radicalized, making recruitment easy for al-Qa'ida when it came to the kingdom a few years later.

Money from the US, the Saudi regime and private donors funded the construction of many bases in Afghanistan – training camps which, after the successful expulsion of Soviet troops in 1989, stayed in business right through the 1990s. These bases produced the *jihadis*, trained largely by al-Qa'ida, who later dispersed all over the globe to undertake their own operations and recruit from among their own countrymen. Bin Laden also imported machinery and expertise from the family construction firm in Saudi Arabia to prepare and fortify many of these camps.

The bin Laden family had long been close to the House of Al Saud with long-standing ties not only in business but of friendship: indeed when Muhammad bin Laden was killed in a crash in 1967, King Faisal told the fifty-three orphans they were all his children now.

Bin Laden, however, seems to have harboured doubts about the Al Saud quite early on. Certainly his antipathy to the US, Saudi Arabia's closest ally in the Afghan war, was growing. He was already telling fellow *jihadis* in the mid-1980s that America was the enemy of Islam, and in 1987 initiated a boycott of American and Israeli goods in support of the first Palestinian *intifada*.

The real breach between bin Laden and the Al Saud dates back to 1989. When the Afghan *jihad* was over, bin Laden found himself with a trained army and no immediate battle to fight. Many of his *mujahedin* originated from South Yemen, which was then under Communist rule. Trained and armed, these Yemenis now dreamed of reclaiming the lands the Marxist government had confiscated from them. This fitted in very well with bin Laden's own aspirations at that time – a prophecy in the Hadith tells of an Islamic army of 12,000 which will emerge from Yemen, and he became determined to violently overthrow the government.

His Yemeni fighters already installed, bin Laden provided them with arms and funding; sources mention suitcases full of money being trafficked between Riyadh and South Yemen.[11] Bin Laden had already entered favourable negotiations with tribal leaders in the country and, according to well-placed sources, intended South Yemen to be the new base for the Afghan Arabs. He told me about this time when I met him in 1996: 'I delivered a series of lectures in the Yemeni mosques, inciting Muslims to rise up against the South Yemen regime. This prompted the Saudi government to ban me from preaching.'

With the Yemen Arab Republic (YAR) to the north acting as a buffer between Saudi Arabia and South Yemen, bin Laden's ambition represented a considerable security threat to the kingdom. The US and Saudi Arabia had already intervened in Yemen during a border dispute in 1979, arming and training YAR troops. Eleven years later, when Soviet-backed communism was clearly in global decline, the US decided on a different approach and brokered the unification of Yemen in 1990. Bin Laden's Yemeni adventure was effectively scuppered.

It was during bin Laden's involvement in Yemen that the Saudi regime began to have serious doubts about him. Not only was he interfering in the affairs of a neighbouring state, he was active at home too. In a nation where criticism is tantamount to treason, bin Laden began questioning the Saudi regime. In a 1989 letter addressed to King Fahd, bin Laden urged reform and a more faithful application of *shari'ah* law in the kingdom. He also warned of the imminent danger posed by Saudi Arabia's neighbour, Iraq. The 'greedy and aggressive' Saddam Hussein, he claimed, had his eye on Kuwait and, ultimately the kingdom's own oilfields. He further upset the Saudi authorities by openly denouncing Saddam as *kafir*. The Al Saud were afraid of enraging Saddam, and with good reason. The royal family answered bin Laden with a warning: if he indulged in any further political activity, either publicly or in secret, he would be arrested. Shortly afterwards they confiscated his passport, a humiliating if gentle punishment.

Iraq invaded Kuwait in August 1990. Bin Laden swiftly despatched another letter to the Al Saud outlining his strategy for protecting the kingdom against inevitable Iraqi aggression. Bin Laden told me about this letter himself. He also offered the services of his Arab veterans, who would in turn train Saudi volunteers for war. Disregarding bin Laden's earlier remarkable prescience, the royal response was dismissive, ridiculing both the letter and its author and warning bin Laden not to interfere. The seeds of enmity were sown in this second humiliation. (Many commentators have written about a stormy face-to-face meeting between bin Laden and Prince Sultan bin Abdul Aziz Al Saud, the defence minister. I have not been able to find any sources to corroborate this information.)

With 100,000 Iraqi troops in neighbouring Kuwait and more of the country's million-strong army on its way to join them, it became obvious that the kingdom could not defend itself if Saddam decided to invade. For all its wealth, the Saudi state was militarily weak and vulnerable to attack. The US had sold it weapons and built a military infrastructure, but only 1,000 troops from Saudi Arabia's paltry 70,000-man army were stationed along its northern border with Iraq and Kuwait.

To the horror of the kingdom's *ulama* and much of the populace, the Al Saud now invited half a million American soldiers onto their soil. For bin Laden, Saudi Arabia became 'an American colony' from that moment on: 'We believe that America has committed the greatest mistake in entering a peninsula which no religion from among the non-Muslim nations has entered for fourteen centuries,' he said. 'The British and others used to respect the feelings of more than a billion Muslims and therefore did not occupy the Land of the Two Holy Places. America's interests would not have been harmed by not entering it.'

Bin Laden's perception of the events of 1990 is outlined in the poetic language of his 1996 'Declaration of *Jihad* Against the Americans . . .':

> Since God laid down the Arabian Peninsula, created its desert and surrounded it with seas, no calamity has ever befallen it like these Crusader hosts that have spread in it like locusts, crowding its soil, eating its fruits and destroying its verdure; and this at a time when the nations contend against the Muslims like diners jostling round a bowl of food.

The regime managed to extract a reluctant *fatwa* from the most senior *ulama* Abdul Aziz bin Baz, approving the temporary presence of American troops on the grounds that they were there to 'defend Islam'. The US assured the Saudi government that all troops would be removed on demand when the war was over. In fact, they retained a military presence in the kingdom until 2003 when, ironically, al-Qa'ida attacks on military bases and personnel forced the calculation that it just wasn't worth it.

The kingdom experienced a wave of unrest. Bin Laden and others gathered many of the country's Wahhabi clerics and scholars under one umbrella, urging them to speak out, and opposition to bin Baz's *fatwa* was openly voiced. Several of these men were exiled by the Saudi government but the spirit of dissent and opposition, once established, grew. When US troops did not leave following the liberation of Kuwait, a group of 109 thinkers, professors and clerics sent a forty-six-page 'Memorandum of Advice and Reform to King Fahd'. This 1992 document criticized the government for corruption and human-rights abuses as well as allowing the continued presence of US troops. King Fahd asked the seventeen-member Grand *Ulama* – the kingdom's highest body of religious authority – to denounce the document. The seven members who refused to do so were summarily dismissed by the king.

The US launched the attack on Iraq in January 1991. Despite fears of domestic terrorism, there was only one incident: two American airmen and a Saudi guard were wounded in an attack on a military bus in Jeddah.

In bin Laden's mind the House of Al Saud had committed the ultimate crime against Islam. For him, the holy land of Mecca and Medina had been defiled and was under 'dual American-Israeli occupation'. Bin Laden found plenty of other reasons to hate the Al Saud over the next decade and a half. On 16 December 2004 he asked:

> Who contributed $100 million to Arafat in order to quash the first Palestinian uprising against the Jews?
> Who was allied with the Jews against the weak in Sharm El-Sheikh in 1996?
> Who made military bases [in Saudi Arabia] available to be used in the invasion of Iraq?
> Who pledged to pay the cost of training the Iraqi police force so that they [Iraqi policemen] can fight and kill the *mujahedin* there?
> Aren't you the proud owner of the Beirut initiative in which you recognized Israel and its occupation of Palestine as legal? Were you out of your mind? Have you lost all dignity and honour as human beings?

In bin Laden's mind the House of Al Saud and the US were inextricably linked. He declared war on them both. Typically, bin Laden did not speak out publicly against the regime in 1991 even though he had resolved to bring it down, but employed characteristic patience. His restraint was interpreted as submission, and when he was granted a temporary passport to travel to Pakistan, he left and has never returned.

Revenge

Bin Laden found that relations between the Afghan warlords who had cooperated so effectively against the Soviets had descended into violent internecine clashes when he arrived back in Peshawar. Disappointed, he arranged to move to Sudan, where he expected to base his *mujahedin* without any interference. A June 1989 military coup by Colonel Omar Bashir and the Revolutionary Command Council for National Salvation had resulted in a government with strong ties to the political arm of the Muslim Brotherhood (MB) and the National Islamic Front, and which was implementing a state based on *shari'ah*.

Travelling from Pakistan in a private jet and under conditions of utmost secrecy, bin Laden moved his entourage of friends and selected *mujahedin* to Sudan. He had had the foresight to transfer large sums of money out of Saudi Arabia – he told me this amounted to $300 million – and immediately set about establishing a construction business in Khartoum to camouflage his real purpose, which was to plan and set into motion the global *jihad* against the US that he was already planning. Other militant organizations like the MB had also moved to Sudan, and training camps were swiftly established.

Although he was ostensibly exiled from his homeland, bin Laden told me that several of the major construction projects he undertook for the Sudanese government were funded by none other than the Saudi state, which appointed his company as its contractor. Bin Laden was able to transport heavy construction equipment from the family firm in Saudi Arabia as well as financing. His relationship with the Saudi government seems to have remained ambiguous for several years.

Bin Laden told me that some members of the royal family had voiced their support for al-Qa'ida and their opposition to the US military presence in Saudi Arabia, but he refused to give me their names. Determined to safeguard their privileged way of life, which is dependent on the *ulama* remaining the key architects of the social and economic structure in the kingdom, the majority of the princes (but not King Abdullah) are opposed to any changes that might be forced on them by reformers. For this reason they tolerate and sometimes actively endorse the teachings of radical Islamic clerics, and in the past this could well have extended to al-Qa'ida.

I believe there was an unwritten truce between bin Laden and the Al Saud based on the understanding that so long as al-Qa'ida did not target the royal family or Saudi nationals, the regime would shut its eyes to the organization's activities. The truce would have collapsed after 11 September 2001, when the US put enormous pressure on the ruling family to purge itself of terrorists and cut off sources of funding for their activities.

While in Sudan, bin Laden cooperated with other Islamic groups such as the MB and Islamic Jihad (in Egypt and Yemen), building a network throughout the region to be ready for action when the time was judged right.

Displaying the same prescience that had alerted him to Saddam's intentions in the Gulf – he closely tracks the news, and subscribed to several wire services before the Internet provided an instant global monitoring service – bin Laden became convinced in 1992 that the US was planning to move into Somalia. Working with other groups he set about orchestrating a series of attacks designed to get them out as soon as possible. Al-Fadli, an MB leader, was brought from London to Yemen by bin Laden; he led the 29 December 1992 attack on the Golden Moor Hotel in Aden. Another group of al-Qa'ida-affiliated fighters armed with RPGs were captured at the fence of the airstrip where US Air Force transports were parked.

(A significant number of Afghan Arabs were stranded in Yemen after these operations and were airlifted out in mid-1993 at bin Laden's personal expense; some sources say he spent $3 million doing this.)

Various intelligence services including those of Egypt, the US and Saudi Arabia now realized that Sudan had become a hotbed for militant radical Islamic and *jihadi* groups. Rather belatedly making the link between Osama bin Laden and such groups, the Saudi government cut off financing for his construction projects in Sudan. Undeterred, he invested $200 million of his own funds, an estimated 65 per cent of his entire personal wealth at that time.

In October 1993 al-Qaʻida-affiliated Afghan Arabs launched the Black Hawk helicopter attacks in Mogadishu in which eighteen US soldiers were killed, seventy-eight wounded and one captured and dragged through the streets. The US withdrew nearly all their troops from the region in March 1994 in a move bin Laden heralded as a 'great victory'.

The Saudi regime, under mounting pressure from the US, realized it had to do something about its renegade son. Speaking in the aftermath of 11 September, President Bill Clinton said that he had ordered the assassination of bin Laden back in 1994. Indeed, there were three separate attempts on his life while he was in Sudan, the most serious in 1994 when a mosque he was believed to be praying in was attacked by four gunmen and sixty-one worshippers were killed. Realizing bin Laden was not in the mosque, the attackers rushed to his company headquarters, where they shot at him and engaged his security guards in a gun battle. It was subsequently discovered that the assassins were led by a Libyan, but Sudanese security forces mysteriously killed them all before the origins and motives of the others could be ascertained. It seems perfectly feasible that they were commissioned by the CIA.

The Saudi government revoked bin Laden's citizenship in April 1994 and froze his assets inside the kingdom, which included substantial amounts in dividends from the family firm which continued to be paid into bank accounts he could no longer access.

Goading bin Laden in this manner was the latest in a long series of mistakes on the part of Al Saud, but their real problems with him were only just beginning. He told me in 1996:

> When the Saudi government clamped down on the country's *ulama* in September 1994, dismissing those who dared speak out from their posts in universities and mosques, banning distribution of their tapes, effectively banning them from speaking, I took a personal decision to start saying what was right and denouncing what was wrong. We set up the Advice and Reform Committee to speak the truth and make matters clear.

Around 200 junior and senior *ulama* were imprisoned between 1993–8, considered dissidents by the Al Saud; they had preached *jihad* and condemned the US military presence, Westernization in the kingdom and the corruption of the government. In an attempt to silence them, these men were tortured severely in prison. This backfired on the regime. When these *ulama* were released, they wanted revenge, and denounced the government as *murtadd* (apostate) – a crime punishable by death according to *shari'ah*. The majority of these tortured *ulama* joined al-Qa'ida and began to build cells within the kingdom, which would strike with such deadly effect in 1995, 1996 and 2003. Some had already had military experience, having fought in Afghanistan or Bosnia. They were also able to make inroads into the security forces. Bin Laden, meanwhile, was agitating against the Saudi regime from outside the kingdom:

> I issued statements from Sudan and when the Saudi government realized the big impact they were having, and how effective they were, it overcame all its differences with the Sudanese regime which had been trying for a long time to improve relations with Riyadh but had hitherto been rebuffed.

By 1995 bin Laden was ready to not only denounce the Saudi regime, but attack it. In August 1995 he sent an open letter to King Fahd calling for an end to the continued US military presence in the kingdom: 'Your kingdom is nothing but an American protectorate and you are under Washington's heel.' Unhappy with the response (silence), bin Laden activated a 'sleeper cell' of Afghan veterans in Saudi Arabia, which bombed the US-operated National Guard Training Center in Riyadh, killing seven. Bin Laden told me this attack was also in revenge for the torture and humiliation the *ulama* had endured.

The Al Saud and the US now started to exert enormous pressure on Sudan to hand over bin Laden. Diplomatic links at the highest level were restored, and the Saudis offered to make their peace with Sudan if it would expel bin Laden and stop him issuing communiqués. 'The highest level of the Sudanese government informed me of its difficult situation and the amount of Saudi pressure it was under,' bin Laden told me. 'That same day I started looking for an alternative land that could tolerate the truth . . . with God's help we returned to the land of Khorasan [an archaic name for Afghanistan] . . . there was always that possibility, and therefore we had kept our camps there.'

In May 1996 bin Laden and his entourage moved from Sudan to Afghanistan. As if to make the point that though they might have been chased out of Sudan by Saudi Arabia and the US they were not leaving with their tails between their legs, al-Qaʿida struck again: the June bombing of Khobar Towers. The Saudi authorities were at pains to implicate Shiʿi militants backed by Iran in this attack, since the embarrassing truth that they had their very own homegrown terrorism problem was inadmissible; they did not want to give the impression that there was domestic opposition to the deployment of US troops on Saudi soil.

Saudi Arabia then enjoyed a period of apparent calm, but some commentators including Saad al-Faqih say that during this time al-Qaʿida was very active inside the kingdom, recruiting members and setting up an infrastructure for future operations.

The 1998 embassy bombings in Nairobi and Dar-es-Salaam produced a great increase in support for al-Qa'ida in Saudi Arabia – more than 11,000 recruits headed for the training camps in Afghanistan between 1998 and 2001. Recruitment for the new cells being planned inside the kingdom was also boosted by these bombings.

After the events of 11 September 2001, the Saudis agreed to help the US launch its attack on Afghanistan. They froze the assets of suspected individuals and organizations and shut down Islamic charities that could have been financing al-Qa'ida. Furthermore, the Al Saud submitted to American demands that it change the education curriculum, removing books and resources that advocated *jihad* and promoted Wahhabism. They also dismissed more than 1,000 *imams* and preachers who were considered dissidents because of their criticism of the West and of American policies in the region.

Al-Qa'ida's popularity reached an all-time high inside the kingdom. Crucially, this popularity extended into the security forces, from the police and National Guard to the secret service. The interior ministry's security police, the *mabaheth*, was charged with countering al-Qa'ida and received help, advice and information from the FBI. There was only one problem – according to sources, 80 per cent of its staff was sympathetic to bin Laden.[12]

Fleeing the October–November 2001 US bombardment of Afghanistan, many Saudi al-Qa'ida members returned home to join the burgeoning numbers of indigenous *jihadis*. Ironically, the secrecy which had become so much part of Saudi culture due to the regime's oppressiveness now acted powerfully against it, as it seemed unable to root out the enemy within.

Al-Qa'ida Moves Back Home

Al-Qa'ida in the Arabian Peninsula had established an infrastructure of cells, safe houses, weapons and ammunition by the time the organization's first *emir*, Yusef al-Ayeri, launched a blitz within the kingdom in May 2003. The US were still engaged in Iraq (where the Saudi government had once again proved a willing ally) though President Bush had declared major combat over on 1 May.

As al-Qa'ida became established in Saudi Arabia, the first cell was headed by Turki al-Dandani; The second, by Ali Abd-al Rahman al-Fag'asi (also known as Abu Bakr al-Azdi); the third, by a Yemeni, Khaled al-Najj (considered by some as the 'real' chief of al-Qa'ida in Saudi Arabia) and the fourth by Abdul Aziz al-Muqrin, who encouraged individuals within the cell to establish their own independent networks, acting autonomously as an additional security measure. A fifth cell remained dormant, and when the others were subsequently infiltrated by security forces the leaders took refuge in this fifth cell.

The first cell was initially the strongest, best-financed and best-equipped. It was responsible for the first attack, which took place on 12 May 2003: a simultaneous mass suicide bombing by nine operatives who blew up three housing compounds for foreign workers in Riyadh, killing thirty-five people and wounding 200. A large number of Saudi nationals and other Muslims were killed in these attacks, which led to a dip in al-Qa'ida's popularity.

'Saudi people are not used to violence,' Saad al-Faqih comments. 'They cannot accept that it is easily done to kill a civilian, American or European, and they are certainly not convinced that in order to kill one American you need to kill two or three Saudis.'

In August 2003 the US made the planned transfer of most of its 7,000 military personnel and 200 warplanes from the Prince Sultan airbase in al-Kharj to Doha, Qatar. Coverage in the American press suggested that bin Laden had hastened the move, which had been agreed at the end of April: 'US military presence was opposed by some in the kingdom, and was among the reasons cited by Saudi-born Osama bin Laden for his al-Qa'ida attacks on America on September 11th 2001,' said the newspaper *USA Today*.

Al-Qa'ida's target range in Saudi Arabia widened to include all foreigners, especially those working in the oil industry. If there were to be a mass evacuation of key workers, they reasoned, Saudi oil production would be impaired, undermining the regime and the petrol-hungry US. Ayman al-Zawahiri had been urging *jihadis* to target oil production as a means of attacking the US since 2002.

Al-Muqrin, by now the leader of al-Qa'ida in the Arabian Peninsula and an experienced *mujahed* who had fought in Bosnia and Somalia, organized the next major attack on 8 November 2003 – a suicide bombing of the al-Muhayya housing compound in Riyadh. Though this had formerly housed US nationals (employees of Boeing) there were few Americans living there at the time. Again, the majority of the eighteen who were killed were Saudis or other Muslims. Followed by attacks targeting individual members of the security forces, this can be seen as a grave strategic error by al-Qa'ida, whose popularity took another nosedive, leading to problems with recruiting new members.

'It seems unlikely bin Laden would sanction attacks on Saudi nationals or Muslims at that time,' al-Faqih says. 'There were communication problems, obviously, since bin Laden and al-Zawahiri were on the run. Probably the al-Qa'ida operatives in Saudi Arabia had only the crudest sanction from the leadership – they sent them very rough requests for permission and bin Laden gave a very rough answer . . . there's no way, then, that he could know all the details or give them clear instructions as to what to do or how to select the best targets.'

Explicitly targeting the oil industry, four al-Qa'ida gunmen attacked the Yanbu Petrochemical company complex on 1 May 2004, killing two Americans, two Britons and one Australian. On 29 May 2004 there was a sustained and well-planned attack on various complexes and offices used by Shell, Lukoil and the Arab Petroleum Investment Company. Lasting twenty-five hours, the *jihadis* apparently made efforts to avoid killing Muslims when they opened fire. Nevertheless, of twenty-two dead, three were Saudi nationals.

Between May and September 2004 al-Qa'ida launched a new and deadly campaign of psychological warfare, targeting individuals.

There was a spate of street shootings and kidnappings in which eight Westerners died; the most gruesome was the beheading of an American Lockheed Martin employee, Paul Johnson, Jr. Again, the intention was to terrorize key foreign workers out of the country, thus undermining the economy.

Another shift in target occurred in December 2004, with the first al-Qaʻida attacks on 'hard targets' – first the US consulate in Jeddah on 6 December, when five non-US staff were killed, and 29 December when the Ministry of the Interior and Special Forces recruitment offices were bombed in simultaneous attacks.

Meanwhile the continued occupation of Iraq fanned the flames of Muslim resentment and anger. On 6 November 2004, twenty-six Saudi Islamic scholars signed an open letter calling on Muslims to fight the US in Iraq and consider it *jihad*. According to al-Faqih, official Saudi figures showed 3,000 nationals having left for Iraq since the insurgency began. Muhammad al-Masari alleges that 'the Saudi regime is happy that these *jihadis* are going to Iraq and are not staying to carry out operations inside the country'. He also suggests that, for this reason, border security is not as tight as the US would like it to be.[13]

It has often been claimed that the Saudi security services themselves harbour many al-Qaʻida sympathizers. According to Saad al-Faqih the official figures cited above attest to this: 'Five hundred of those who headed for Iraq were from the National Guard, and a further 500 from the army and security services,' he claims.

The late *emir* of al-Qaʻida in the Arabian Peninsula, Saleh al-Ufi (who was killed in August 2005) was a former policeman; the leader of the Jeddah attack on the US consulate, Awad al-Juhaini, was a former member of the religious police. Some commentators claim that the Jeddah and Khobar compound attacks would not have been possible without the collusion of the National Guard and other security forces, as they were both so heavily protected.

Assassinations in 2003 and 2004 show that al-Qaʻida was party to intelligence information about their victims. Robert Jackson, for example, was officially in the kingdom as a civil engineer, but in fact he was an undercover military 'advisor', a specialist in Apache helicopters. The gunmen who shot him down knew exactly where to find him, as they did a subsequent victim, Frank Gardner of the BBC, who was ambushed while filming with his cameraman.

In December 2004 the Saudi government enlisted the help of Jordanian anti-riot forces to suppress demonstrations in Riyadh and Jeddah, rewarding them with inflated salaries and plying the Jordanian government with gifts of millions of dollars and free supplies of oil. This shows how little the regime trusts its own security forces. Dr al-Masari claims that during the April 2005 attacks at al-Rass on al-Qa'ida strongholds, no National Guardsmen were used – suggesting that their loyalty could not be trusted in such operations.

Al-Masari also makes the astonishing claim that some Saudi officials are sympathetic to al-Qa'ida, and he is not alone. The same suggestion appeared, for instance, in the American academic journal *Foreign Affairs*.[14]

The invasion of Iraq, the subsequent insurgency and the emergence of Abu Mus'ab al-Zarqawi's al-Qa'ida in the Land of the Two Rivers have revived al-Qa'ida's fortunes in Saudi Arabia, according to many commentators. 'Al-Qa'ida would have suffered great difficulties because of its mistakes in Saudi Arabia,' according to al-Faqih. 'Its whole global campaign would have suffered if the US hadn't invaded Iraq. All that was needed was to get rid of Saddam and mobilize the people against the invader.'

Economic Jihad

Al-Qa'ida's operations in Saudi Arabia had serious repercussions for the world's financial institutions. The Western media began to speak of a 'terror premium' on oil with George Washington, a chief economist in the petroleum industry, assessing this at about $8 per barrel in November 2004 and adding that a successful attack on one of

Saudi Arabia's main oil export terminals would see prices shoot through the roof. He identified this as the single most serious risk to the global economy.

Saudi Arabia is by no means the only oil-rich country on the planet, however, and much has been written about the increasing importance of other oil-producing nations. Nevertheless, careful analysis shows that Saudi Arabia is, and remains what *The Economist* calls 'the indispensable nation of oil'.[15] In an article in May 2004, the magazine emphasized the fact that Saudi Arabia still has one quarter of the world's known oil reserves, but reminded readers that the country's role as a swing producer is even more crucial: 'Unlike other countries, the Saudis keep several barrels per day of idle capacity on hand for emergencies.' No other oil producer comes anywhere near Saudi levels in this respect.

The Saudi-US agreement that exchanges oil for protection is as relevant as ever. Only the details have changed: America no longer needs a military presence to assure itself of the continuing alliance with the House of Al Saud, which has isolated itself in the region through its willingness to participate in the US-led wars in Afghanistan and Iraq. The regime needs its superpower friend more than ever, and with oil prices reaching all-time highs the US needs to keep on the right side of the Saudis, who can control prices by adjusting their production levels. The curious sight of George W. Bush and King Abdullah holding hands at Bush's ranch in Texas in April 2005 dispels any doubt about the way they view their mutual future. In addition, these two now have a mutual enemy in al-Qa'ida.

If al-Qa'ida damages the Saudi oil industry (or, indeed, the supply of oil in general) it also hurts the US. Exploiting this economic interdependence has recently moved to the top of the al-Qa'ida agenda. Oil remains crucial not only to both economies but to the American global project as a whole. Eighty per cent of Riyadh's budget is generated by oil revenues, and the US not only relies on Saudi oil for its own consumption but, by controlling its sale and distribution, can fend off burgeoning competition from countries like Japan, India and China.

Since 2002 al-Qa'ida's leaders have been urging OPEC ministers to reduce oil production with the intention of pushing prices up and squeezing Western economies. Pipeline attacks in Iraq have been a frequent occurrence since the insurgency began, and oil prices have risen to unprecedented levels – nearly $70 a barrel in August 2005.

In a taped message broadcast on an Islamic website posted on 16 December 2004, bin Laden proclaimed that 'oil prices should be at least $100 per barrel'. Almost immediately, al-Qa'ida in the Arabian Peninsula issued a statement urging *jihadis* there to focus on oil targets. These announcements alone caused that month's crude oil to spike by 5 per cent on the NYMEX commodities exchange.

Some analysts doubted al-Qa'ida's capacity to attack Saudi Arabia's oil production facilities. They are heavily guarded by both Saudi and US security forces and are in the largely Shi'ite east of the country on the Persian Gulf, where al-Qa'ida has no infrastructure or support. However, on 24 February 2006 al-Qa'ida very nearly succeeded in blowing up the Abqaiq refinery, the largest oil processing plant in the world, when two car bombs were halted by security guards at the entrance and detonated prematurely, killing two guards and wounding eight. Economists concur that even an abortive attempt could disrupt Saudi oil production and cause spiralling prices damaging to Western economies. The US clearly has doubts about security and has secretly stored up to 700 million barrels in salt caverns in Texas and Louisiana. This could keep it going for three months, and could also be used to reverse any dramatic and unexpected oil price rises.[16]

While high oil prices benefit the Saudi economy and increase the Al Saud's ability to 'buy loyalty' as Saudi commentator Maadawi al-Rashid points out, if al-Qa'ida remains active in the kingdom it could be disastrous for the economy. 'Photos of beheaded corpses . . . and al-Qa'ida's hunting of foreign employees . . . are troubling and discomforting,' says al-Rashid, who spoke to many Western businessmen weighing up the pros and cons of investing in the kingdom. 'Investment and attracting foreign capital . . . depend totally on security.'[17]

This issue is of particular concern to the Saudi government now, as a strong trend emerges among Gulf investors to bring their money back home from Western stock markets and investments (fearing their assets might be frozen). The Gulf states are experiencing an economic boom manifested by active construction and an astronomical rise in the value of stocks in local markets. In Saudi Arabia the Tadawul All-Share Index rose by more than 70 per cent in 2005, and is now the biggest emerging stock market in the world.[18]

Western dependence on Saudi oil has resulted in unspoken complicity with human-rights abuses and corruption. However, Saudi Arabia's accession to the WTO might improve this situation. The reforms and changes demanded in order to fulfil the requirements of the WTO will present their own challenges. *Shariʻah* law is hardly going to be compatible with membership in this American-dominated club. The judicial system will have to be completely rewritten to incorporate secular concepts of justice and litigation. Many clerics and ordinary civilians currently languishing in jail are guilty only of attending peaceful demonstrations banned by the regime, though there have been slight improvements since the death of King Fahd in August 2005. His successor, King Abdullah, has already pardoned and released several political prisoners.

Endgame

The Saudi regime has made fitful attempts to bring bin Laden back into the fold, such as the 1996 offer to return his citizenship in exchange for a public declaration that the king was a true Muslim. The Al Saud also offered to double the $200 million they had frozen in his bank accounts if he would cooperate. Bin Laden refused. It would seem that there is no remaining scope for negotiation in the battle between al-Qa'ida (now described as a 'deviant group' by the government-controlled Saudi press) and the regime.

Saudi Arabia is a key country for many reasons: for bin Laden and for 1.3 billion Muslims it is the heart of the Islamic nation and faith; its oil resources are crucial to America's global project and the Al Saud imagine they can use their petrodollars to buy power and influence at home and abroad; geographically, it is placed at the centre of one of the world's most volatile and important regions.

Al-Qa'ida's strategy in Saudi Arabia changes as historical opportunities and advantages present themselves. Commentators concur that the ultimate local aim remains to bring about the downfall of the regime, and that this is inextricably linked to an overriding ambition to defeat America.

There are two main schools of thought in terms of the long-term al-Qa'ida aim in Saudi Arabia: if the House of Al Saud is targeted and brought down, that will undermine the American project in the area; alternatively, if the US itself is targeted, *jihadi* strategists believe that those who are against the Bush administration would become very much more militant bringing about damaging internal divisions and clashes, making it easier for al-Qa'ida and affiliated groups to remove the Al Saud from power.

In either case, most commentators say they expect a member or members of the Al Saud family to be targeted in the near future. Al-Qa'ida has a history of carrying out such attacks as a 'message', and in December 2004 bin Laden explicitly threatened to start 'armed operations against the rulers of Riyadh'.

Al-Qa'ida in the Arabian Peninsula experienced four successive changes of leadership in the space of just over a year. Al-Ayeri was killed in June 2003 in a shootout with Saudi security forces at a roadblock; he was succeeded by Khaled al-Hajj, who was ambushed and killed in Riyadh on 16 March 2004; al-Muqrin followed, until he was killed by police on 18 June 2004. His successor was Saleh al-Ufi, the ex-policeman, who was killed in August 2005. Successful operations by the Saudi security forces mean that few of the Afghan

Arab veterans are left, but reports suggest a new generation of *jihadis* has sprung up.

Nevertheless, there is unlikely to be a great deal of al-Qa'ida activity in the kingdom until the insurgency in Iraq is over because thousands of Saudi *jihadis* are engaged in battle there. According to al-Faqih, al-Qa'ida leaders in Iraq despatched a small group of *jihadis* back to Saudi Arabia in May 2005 to 'carry out some operations and remind them that they haven't gone away'. The attack on the Abqaiq oil refinery in February 2006 was just such a reminder.

When thousands of well-trained and battle-hardened *mujahedin* return from Iraq, ready to do the bidding of al-Qa'ida leaders, the Saudi regime may well have something to fear. For then, as al-Masari predicts, 'it will be settlement day.'

6

Al-Qaʻida in Iraq

When I met bin Laden in 1996 he explained his long-term strategy to me. He knew he would never be able to defeat his enemy, the giant military superpower America, on its own soil using conventional weapons. He had another plan, one that would take many years to reach fruition. We are witnessing part of that plan now, in the battlefields of Iraq.

Patience has always been one of the main weapons in the al-Qaʻida arsenal, and patience would be required if bin Laden was to do as he intended: 'We want to bring the Americans to fight us on Muslim land,' he said as we walked through the woods in the high mountains at Tora Bora. 'If we can fight them on our own territory we will beat them, because the battle will be on our terms in a land they neither know nor understand.'

The arrival of 150,000 US troops in Iraq in March 2003 created exactly the turning point in al-Qaʻida's history that bin Laden dreamed of.

Al-Qaʻida Nearly Destroyed

Five years after I visited bin Laden in his Afghan sanctuary, the Tora Bora area was pounded by massive cluster bombs as the US sought to avenge 11 September by destroying al-Qaʻida and the Taliban regime that harboured them. Twenty thousand Afghan civilians died in this and subsequent bombardments, which went on for eleven weeks from 10 October 2001 and devastated 128 Afghan cities and towns.

Just one Taliban leader, Security Minister Qari Ahmadullah, was killed in this demonstration of military might. Bin Laden and the inner core of the al-Qa'ida leadership had already left by the back door, into Pakistan, with the help – it is alleged – of that country's intelligence service, the ISI.

Though its leaders had avoided capture or death, this could have been the beginning of the end for al-Qa'ida. The US onslaught in Afghanistan had succeeded in destroying more than 80 per cent of its military capabilities and infrastructure. They lost their safe haven and their training camps there; they lost support among more moderate Muslims who felt tremendous sympathy for the victims of the 11 September attacks and, crucially, there was dissent within al-Qa'ida itself.

Several key figures in the organization had been against the 11 September attacks, including Abu Mus'ab al-Suri[1] and, most notably in the context of this chapter, Abu Mus'ab al-Zarqawi, who would later become infamous as the *emir* (leader) of al-Qa'ida in Iraq.

According to Omar Mahmood Othman abu Omar, better known as Abu Qatada, a radical cleric believed to be al-Qa'ida's spiritual leader in Europe, al-Zarqawi's disapproval of the 11 September operation was the main reason he had not pledged allegiance to bin Laden at this point, preferring to operate independently of al-Qa'ida.[2] Abu Qatada also said that some inner-circle al-Qa'ida members actually left the organization at this time as a result of what they considered to be a catastrophic decision. They predicted that the US would respond with unparalleled ferocity, destroying the Taliban's ideal Islamic state (as they perceived it). Most importantly, al-Qa'ida would lose the safe haven essential to its survival and expansion.

The US was quick to claim victory over al-Qa'ida. Nevertheless, despite its leadership being forced into hiding, the organization still had enough of a global presence and capacity to carry out several attacks in 2002, including the 11 April bombing of a synagogue in Djerba, Tunisia and the 12 October nightclub bombing on Bali. This should have made it clear to the US that its enemy was damaged but not yet defeated.

In a moment of great historical irony, just eighteen months after it had been sent reeling from Afghanistan, al-Qa'ida's flagging fortunes were revived by the US when it took the decision to invade Iraq on 19 March 2003. The US seriously misjudged the level of Muslim anger this move would provoke. Perhaps because Saddam was a secular leader, it was believed that the people would be glad to see a 'regime change'. It didn't help that, according to Palestinian Prime Minister Mahmoud Abbas (in June 2003), George W. Bush had told him that 'God' instructed the president to attack al-Qa'ida and Iraq. This alleged remark, widely reported, was outright blasphemy for many Muslims and evoked the Crusades.

Historical grievances, and the attendant sense of humiliation and the frustrated anger of the *umma* were inflamed in great measure by what many Muslims perceived as the arrogance of the US agenda. The US military seemed oblivious of the religious and cultural significance of oil-rich Iraq, which is not only a Muslim land but contains more Islamic holy places and shrines than anywhere else on earth; its capital, Baghdad, was the ancient seat of the caliphate[3] so dear to Salafi-*jihadi* hearts; Iraq is as important to Muslims as Palestine and Saudi Arabia.

Regime Change

Historically, Iraq – which comprises the three formerly Ottoman regions of Mosul, Baghdad and Basra – has been no stranger to regime change. In the twentieth century alone, it went from being a British mandate (1919) following World War One to a British-installed Hashemite monarchy upon independence (1932). The monarchy was overthrown in a popular uprising in 1958 with a military, leftist regime under Brigadier General Abdul Karim Qassim taking the reins. This government in turn was usurped by Colonel Abdul Salam Arif (1963), and the regime he established was put out of business by the Arab Socialist Ba'th ('Rebirth') Party in 1968. Saddam Hussein was a leading light in the Ba'th, which combined nationalism, militarism, Arab socialism and Pan-Arabism. He became President of Iraq in 1979.

It is beyond doubt that Saddam was a ruthless dictator. Kurds, dissidents, communists, army deserters and others were massacred during his rule. His method of dealing with political opponents was markedly brutal – in 1979, to take one example, having forced the resignation of his predecessor Ahmad Hassan Bakr, he compelled his fellow Ba'th leaders to personally execute sixty-eight civilian and military leaders (also members of the Ba'th) because he thought they might challenge his legitimacy.

Saddam Hussein's worst atrocities were committed during and shortly after the 1980–8 war with Iran, when up to 7,000 Kurds were killed by chemical bombs in Halabja in the spring of 1988. The US and the UK had been aware of Saddam's atrocities for decades, and taken no action to prevent them or hold him accountable. In 1988 the US doubled financial aid to Iraq. The UK was also eager to help, with the government's Export Credits Guarantees Department underwriting a £175 million (then approximately $309 million) loan to Saddam in 1988 and a further £340 million (then approximately $535 million) in 1989.

The first instance of American and British military intervention in Iraq, post-independence, goes back to July 1961, when British troops moved in to defend Kuwait against Iraqi troops massing on its border. Iraq claimed Kuwait based on the fact that as part of the Ottoman Empire it had been subject to Iraqi suzerainty. Kuwait was key to US-UK interests in the region; Gulf Oil (owned jointly by British and American interests) had been extracting oil from the Burgan oilfield there since 1946. In December 1961 the Iraqi prime minister, General Qassim, had his revenge for the country's frustrated military incursion when he deprived the Iraqi Petroleum

Company (in which American companies had a 25 per cent share and the British slightly more) of 99.5 per cent of its concessions in Iraq. Many suspect subsequent CIA involvement in the coup which overthrew Qassim in February 1963. His successor, President Abdul Salam Arif, recognized Kuwait's right to independence in October the same year. The Baʻthists seized power in 1968, and in June 1972 all Iraq's oil interests were nationalized.

A year after coming to power, Saddam attacked Iran. The Iran-Iraq war was a very long and bloody battle which became a war of attrition, ending with both countries' borders unchanged. In the course of this fruitless war Iraq had suffered 1 million casualties and was now $60 billion in debt. Though the US had supported Iraq militarily and financially throughout the war, no financial aid was offered to help rebuild it, and international financial institutions were warned off providing loans or rescheduling the nation's debts.

Saddam was now perceived as an emerging military threat in the region. He had gained a lot of military and strategic experience in the course of the war with Iran, and was pursuing nuclear ambitions. He had already accumulated an arsenal of weapons of mass destruction (WMD), which posed a direct threat to Israel and that nation's military supremacy in the Middle East. The US had come to perceive Saddam as a monster of its own creation.

Kuwait and the United Arab Emirates flooded the market with surplus oil, which severely hurt the already ailing Iraqi economy (which is almost totally dependent on oil revenue). Prices tumbled to $10 a barrel, and Kuwait suddenly called in the $30 billion loan it had given Iraq during the course of the war with Iran. Increasingly desperate to increase Iraq's oil revenues to pay off its debts, Saddam decided to annex Kuwait, and sent 100,000 troops to the border. The US intervened swiftly, and the first Gulf War began on 17 January 1991 with 'Operation Desert Storm', ending just six weeks later in an inevitable victory for the US and its allies.

The US had feared the Iraqi push would extend beyond Kuwait and threaten Saudi Arabia, its main oil producer and Arab ally in the

Middle East. Now it was beginning to turn its gaze to Iraq's own oil reserves – and with good reason.

Iraq has the second-largest potential oil reserves in the world after Saudi Arabia, in excess of 300 billion barrels. Along with Saudi Arabia, Iraq's oil is the cheapest to produce because it is found in enormous oilfields that can be tapped by relatively shallow wells. It has a high flow rate due to its sheer volume and because of high pressure on the oil reservoir from water and associated natural gas deposits. According to *Oil and Gas Journal*, Western oil companies estimate that they can produce a barrel of Iraqi oil for less than $1.50 and possibly as little as $1. By comparison, a barrel of oil costs $5 to produce in other relatively low-cost areas like Malaysia and Oman. Production costs in Mexico and Russia are potentially $6–8 per barrel (higher under current production arrangements by local companies). In Texas and other US and Canadian fields, deep wells and small reservoirs push production costs above $20 a barrel. When world market prices dip below $20 a barrel, the North American fields yield no profit at all, whereas Iraqi oil remains viable.[4]

For another take on just how desirable the Iraqi oil prize is, American economist Jeremy Rifkin has calculated how long current known oil reserves in various countries will last. The findings are very revealing: in the US they will last just 10 years; in Iran, 53 years; in Saudi Arabia, 55 years; in UAE, 75 years; in Kuwait, 116 years; and in Iraq, an astonishing 526 years.[5]

To the US, Saddam represented a threat to its Middle East agenda, and moreover had, during the course of the first Gulf War, launched missile attacks on Israel. It was no longer a matter of whether or not, but when and how they were going to get rid of him.

Throughout the 1990s the US sanctions programme resulted in thousands of Iraqi citizens dying every month from malnutrition and lack of medicine. When asked about the deaths of half a million Iraqi children due to sanctions, Secretary of State Madeleine Albright famously remarked that it was 'worth it'.[6] The sanctions era helped transform Iraq from a modern state with excellent public services into a poverty-stricken ruin.

Realizing that Saddam, apparently impervious to *coups d'état*, was not going to be dislodged by a popular uprising or localized revolution, the US played the WMD card. As we now know, there were no weapons – they had been destroyed or had degraded (they only have a life of two to four years) after the first Gulf War and during the intervening period. That did not prevent the US, with the UK's full participation, from invading in March 2003.

In August 2004 I spoke to a former high-ranking US military strategist. In an off-the-record conversation he told me about the 'dilemma' the US administration had faced before invading Iraq. It had been a straight choice between allowing UN inspectors to finish their job or an all-out invasion. If the inspectors found no evidence of WMD, the US would have to lift the sanctions, and Saddam would be reinvented as a great hero in the Arab world. There were two schools of thought in the Pentagon as to how best to get rid of Saddam, he told me – one advocated a 'hit-and-run' approach in which troops would swiftly occupy Baghdad and assassinate Saddam and his entourage before withdrawing immediately, leaving the Iraqis to sort out their problems in their own way. The other recommended a full-scale occupation, dismantling the state and its institutions, which would then be rebuilt according to the 'democratic model'.

In February and the first half of March 2003, the US and Britain lobbied UN Security Council members relentlessly in an effort to legitimize their intended invasion of Iraq. However, only Spain and Bulgaria committed to voting in favour of military action. As nine votes and no vetoes among the fifteen members were required to get a resolution, the US simply decided not to bother with a vote at all but to go ahead and invade.

On 19 March the US launched air strikes on buildings where it believed Saddam Hussein and other leaders would be, killing scores of civilians instead. On 20 March the ground invasion began, with troops entering the country from Kuwait. The 'Shock and Awe' campaign, a relentless barrage of bombing and advancing troops, met with limited, though courageous, resistance. By 9 April Baghdad had fallen, and on 1 May the 'end of major hostilities' was announced by George W. Bush.

Resistance

The real war began after 1 May 2003. All potential insurgents, from the Ba'thists to al-Qa'ida and the Kurdish *jihadi* groups in the northern mountains, had realized there was little point in engaging in conventional warfare, given the US's immense military superiority. According to sources, most of them decided to keep a low profile and simply bide their time.

Resigned to the inevitable US invasion, Saddam had begun making contingency plans months before it began. Sources close to the Ba'th regime told me that Saddam used to send messengers to farmers in Sunni areas and buy small plots of land from them. In the middle of the night, groups of soldiers would bury arms and money caches for later use by the resistance. Even while in hiding, Saddam continued to make provision for the escalating insurgency until he was captured on 13 December 2003.

On 28 April 2003 my newspaper received a faxed letter from Saddam, then still in hiding, indicating that he knew the real war would be one of insurgency and would begin when the US believed the war was over. He urged the ordinary Iraqi people to rise up against the US: 'Bush will never be victorious as long as there is resistance in your hearts and minds,' he wrote.

As if realizing that the resistance in Iraq would be inextricably linked with a Muslim sense of identity, the *umma* and *jihad*, his tone in this and subsequent letters is increasingly Islamic, peppered with quotations from the Qur'an. Considering he had long been secular, this struck me as very significant at the time. We received several more letters, the last one at the beginning of June 2003. After that he communicated with his people via audiotapes which were sent to al-Jazeera, just as bin Laden was doing at that time.

By not squandering their energy or resources and choosing the right moment to start their fight, the various insurgent groups were immediately effective when the battle began. The US found itself facing a stubborn and indomitable resistance composed of several groups from very different backgrounds.

In order to make sense of the postwar situation in Iraq we need to briefly consider the groups that were active in Iraq prior to the American occupation.

Background to the Resistance

Before the US invasion there were several Sunni organizations opposed to Saddam's secular regime in Kurdistan, in the north of the country near the borders with Iran and Turkey.

The Islamic Movement Tanzim al-Harakah al-Islamiyah, founded in 1988, was a *jihadist* organization, and it is significant in that Mullah Krikar, who would later head Ansar al-Islam, was in the core group. Much has been made of a possible organizational or financial connection between Ansar al-Islam and al-Qaʿida in the course of US intelligence efforts to link Saddam and bin Laden, implicate Saddam Hussein in the 11 September 2001 attacks and thus legitimize their invasion of Iraq.

I met Mullah Krikar in Oslo in April 2005, and he vigorously denied that al-Qaʿida had helped Ansar al-Islam in any way. He did, however, concede that he had approached bin Laden for financial help in 1988 when he and two other members of the Islamic Movement went to Peshawar to raise funds for their battle against the Baʿth regime. Initially the men had met with Abdullah Azzam, who very much supported the Kurdish Salafi-*jihadi* groups as he considered Saddam a *kafir*. Azzam introduced them to a Saudi prince who said he would finance them if they would export their fight to target the Iranians, whom he considered much more dangerous. At the time Saddam was at war with Iran, financed and supported by Saudi Arabia, among others.

After the meeting, Mullah Krikar told me, someone had pointed out a tall, thin man who had remained silent throughout the discussions even though he was in the prince's immediate entourage. 'That is Osama bin Laden,' he was told. 'The Sheikh of the Arabs in Afghanistan. You should ask him about money.' Azzam duly arranged another meeting, but this too ended in failure. 'Osama bin Laden told me that all the money he had was dedicated to financing the Arab *mujahedin* in Afghanistan,' Mullah Krikar recalled. 'He said he had no authority to give it to anyone else and that was the last time I met him.' It must be added that many sources dispute that this was the last meeting between Mullah Krikar and bin Laden.

Ansar al-Islam emerged in December 2001 out of several other groups. Its stronghold was near the border with Iran, and until March 2003 it imposed a Salafi lifestyle on around 1,500 people living in the ten villages under its control. Shops closed at prayer time, no alcohol was allowed and the group urged its followers to prepare themselves for *jihad*. Barham Rahuf, a teacher in Sargat, in the region, described the experience: 'They refused to allow women to leave their homes without a veil. They banned all satellite dishes, parties where men and women mixed and music. They told people these were the rules and that we must obey them.'

Many Afghan Arabs fleeing the US bombardment in Afghanistan in October and November 2001 found refuge with Ansar al-Islam, which is another reason people have erroneously inferred organizational (as opposed to personal) connections between the group and al-Qa'ida. Ideologically, the two groups are close: like al-Qa'ida, Ansar al-Islam is Salafi, Sunni and advocates *jihad*. It is influenced by the ideology of Sayyid Qutb and groups such as Egyptian Islamic Jihad. Led by an *emir* and two deputies, and with various committees for military planning, information, security, *shari'ah* guidance and a *shari'ah* court, it is also structurally similar to al-Qa'ida.

There were also several Shiʻite resistance groups, opposed to the preponderance of minority Sunni Muslims in the Baʻth government. All of these parties, except the radical cleric Moqtada al-Sadr's many followers, cooperated with the American invasion sooner or later. The main Shiʻite groups are al-Daʻwa ('The Call') – whose spokesman Ibrahim Jafari was briefly Prime Minister of Iraq – and the Supreme Council for Islamic Revolution in Iraq (SCIRI), whose ferocious Badr Brigades militia is now fighting the Sunni insurgents alongside US and coalition forces.

Among the Kurdish secular organizations the Patriotic Union of Kurdistan, led by Jalal Talabani, and the Kurdistan Democratic Party, led by Masud Barzani, dominated. These two ex-guerrilla leaders are now, respectively, the president of Iraq and the president of the Kurdish Assembly. Kurdish militia fighters, the *pershmerga*, are also cooperating with US and coalition troops trying to quash the insurgency.

Mullah Krikar told me that when Jalal Talabani was invited for talks with the Bush administration prior to the US invasion, he agreed to help the American forces on the condition that they would destroy Ansar al-Islam. He said Talabani told the US that al-Qaʻida was running training camps in the areas under Ansar al-Islam's control, that they had the capability to manufacture chemical weapons and were collaborating with Saddam Hussein. Despite the fact that none of this was true, the US began an eight-day bombardment of the Ansar al-Islam enclave on 21 March, killing hundreds and forcing the rest to flee into neighbouring countries.

Rather than seeking to link Saddam with Ansar al-Islam and al-Qaʻida, the US could have highlighted the very real relationship between Saddam and the Iranian anti-clerical group, the Mujahedin-e Khalq (MK), which had been on the US State Department's list of terrorist organizations since 1997. With its headquarters in Baghdad since 1986, the MK and its National Liberation Army had been supported and trained by the Iraqi military and had carried out several terrorist attacks against the Iranian regime. Even though the MK heralded the attacks of 11 September as 'God's revenge on America'[7] its political wing, the National Resistance Council of Iran, maintained offices in Washington until 2003.

Al-Qa'ida in Prewar Iraq

Most commentators agree that al-Qa'ida was present in Iraq before the US invasion. The question is for how long and to what extent. Sources concur that Abu-Mus'ab al-Zarqawi was operating independently of bin Laden and al-Qa'ida at that time. He was based in the north, in the Ansar al-Islam enclave, where he had several contacts among the Jordanian fighters who had fled there following the bombardment in Afghanistan.

According to Muhammad al-Masari, Saddam had established contact with the Afghan Arabs as early as 2001, believing he would be targeted by the US once the Taliban was routed. In this version, which is disputed by other commentators, preparatory talks resulted in Saddam funding al-Qa'ida operatives to move into Iraq six months prior to the first bombardments, with the proviso that they would only attack American and coalition targets while doing nothing to undermine the Ba'th regime.

According to al-Masari, Saddam realized that Islam was emerging as the new unifying force among Muslim nations; Arab nationalism, he inferred, had had its day. He saw quite clearly that Islam would be key to the formation of a cohesive resistance in the event of invasion. Iraqi army commanders were ordered to become practising Muslims and to adopt the language and spirit of the *jihadis*. Al-Qa'ida operatives were put in touch with these commanders on arrival and later this network of ex-officers would facilitate the distribution of arms and money from Saddam's caches to al-Qa'ida and various other insurgent groups. Saad al-Faqih concurs that al-Qa'ida operatives began arriving in Iraq a few months prior to the invasion, but not at Saddam Hussein's instigation and possibly without his knowledge. Al-Faqih says that a group numbering about 300 was sent by the al-Qaʿida leadership to establish itself in the Sunni Triangle between Baghdad and Mosul. He agrees that they were instructed to make contacts with Iraqi army personnel 'with Islamic tendencies'.

In the run-up to the war, thousands of Arabs arrived from various different countries to support Iraq, and al-Qaʿida agents went unnoticed by US intelligence. Like the rest of the groups which would form the insurgency, they were prepared to lie low and bide their time.

Abu Musʿab al-Zarqawi

Al-Zarqawi was killed by US forces in early June 2006. His death was announced on 7 June, the day the new Prime Minister, Nouri al-Malaki, announced the completion of his cabinet. I am not convinced by this 'coincidence', and believe al-Zarqawi may in fact have been killed some time earlier. Al-Zarqawi shot into the limelight from a position of relative obscurity. He had not been a key figure in al-Qaʿida in Afghanistan, preferring to establish his own group, Al-Tawhid wal-Jihad, with an independent training camp at Herat. When he left Afghanistan for Iraq via Iran, he seemed to have been acting on his own initiative – 'in search,' as one commentator puts it, 'of a mission'.[8]

It is worth looking at the origins and background of the man who some say has become as important a figure as bin Laden in al-Qaʿida's history. Even though my newspaper has published a profile of al-Zarqawi, many details about this man remain hazy with nearly every source suggesting something different – even the question of how many limbs he had is open to debate, with some reporting that he had lost a leg and others adamant that he retained the full set. Where this is important I will offer the alternatives.

Al-Zarqawi was born 20 October 1966. He had several aliases, but his real name was Ahmad Fadil al-Khalayilah. He was born in a ghetto in the Jordanian city of Zarqaa, fifteen miles northeast of

Amman. Hence his *nom de guerre* – 'al-Zarqawi' simply means 'the one from Zarqaa'. He belonged to the Abu al-Hassan or Banu-Hassan tribe, a minor Bedouin tribe from the desert.

His tribal origins are relevant in terms of his character and personality. The Bedouin people are known for their pragmatic spirit of cooperation and generosity, which they evolved in order to survive their harsh desert habitat. They are also famous for their courage and fighting spirit. Iraqi sources aver that the Bedouin are immensely unforgiving, however, brought up from an early age to exact revenge for harm done by an enemy no matter how long ago. If the English say 'revenge is a dish best eaten cold', the Bedouin say a man is hasty if he waits forty years to take revenge. Like his *emir* bin Laden, al-Zarqawi possessed that great asset, patience.

Al-Zarqawi's father was either a retired army officer or a practitioner of traditional medicine depending on the source. He died in 1984, leaving the family with a small pension on which to survive. Al-Zarqawi is said to have seven sisters and two brothers. Like bin Laden, his father died when he was still very young and he is extremely fond of his mother.

Al-Zarqawi left school at seventeen to help the family finances but, it seems, swiftly degenerated following his father's death, becoming something of a street thug. Known for his heavy drinking and nicknamed 'the Green Man' because of his tattoos, it seems he was at once feared and revered on the street, displaying ferocious courage when defending himself or friends, but always with the tendency to extreme violence that would mark him out, even in the ranks of al-Qaʻida. He became a petty criminal and spent time in jail; one sentence was for 'wounding with a knife'. He was also arrested for shoplifting and drug dealing, and was once accused of rape.

The turnaround in his character seems to have happened towards the end of the 1980s, when he suddenly developed an interest in radical Islam. His life of petty crime often took him to the nearby Palestinian refugee camp, al-Ruseifa, which housed many men with overtly *jihadi* sympathies. Observers say that at least 300 young men from the area round al-Zarqaa and al-Ruseifa went to fight in Afghanistan; the majority of Jordanian fighters in the current Iraqi insurgency also hail from there.

Al-Zarqawi began frequenting the bin Abbas Mosque, where most of the worshippers were associated with radical Islamic groups and extolled the virtues of *jihad*, urging the young men to go and fight in Afghanistan. The Arab media was also trumpeting the heroic *mujahedin* who enjoyed the wholehearted support of most Arab regimes, including Jordan. Donations were openly collected in mosques and public places to finance new recruits. Nevertheless, al-Zarqawi's family was surprised when, having recently married his cousin, he suddenly set off for Afghanistan in 1989, roused to action by Abdul Rasul Sayyaf (leader of the Islamic Union for the Liberation of Afghanistan), who had delivered a stirring sermon at the mosque.

Arriving just too late to participate in any actual fighting against the Soviet army, al-Zarqawi received military training in the camps and participated in the subsequent struggle to overthrow the government of the pro-Soviet Najibullah. According to sources he fought in the battle to liberate Khost in 1991 as well as on the fiercest battlefronts alongside the two notorious Afghan warlords Jalaluddin Haqqani and Gulbuddin Hekmatyar. He witnessed the fall of Kabul to the *mujahedin* in 1992 and the subsequent demise of Najibullah before returning to Jordan.

While in Afghanistan al-Zarqawi met two men who would prove key to the formation of his ideology: Abdullah Azzam and Abu Muhammad al-Maqdisi. Azzam was running the Maktab Khadamat al-Mujaheddin – a clearing-house for *mujahedin* on their way to Afghanistan – in Peshawar. He had proved a powerful influence on bin Laden, who often assisted him in his work. Al-Zarqawi was also deeply impressed by Azzam; he began to attend his lectures, read his work and often repeated his words.

Al-Maqdisi (real name: Issam Muhammad Taher al-Burqawi) is

a Salafi scholar of great repute, currently serving a long prison sentence in Jordan as a result of his political activities. A Palestinian who acquired Jordanian citizenship, he was accompanied in Afghanistan by another Palestinian, Abu Qatada, who had been living in Jordan and knew al-Zarqawi well. Abu Qatada introduced the two men.

Al-Zarqawi and al-Maqdisi established Bayat al-Imam ('The Imam's Fealty or Pledge of Allegiance') while still in Afghanistan, an organization designed to coordinate and organize Jordanian veterans when the *jihad* in Afghanistan was over. This foresight and an emphasis on planning ahead would be key to al-Zarqawi's deadly efficiency in the future.

On leaving Afghanistan in 1992, al-Maqdisi found himself unable to return to his home in Kuwait, where the government had decided to expel its 250,000 Palestinian refugees. He was one of the 160,000 so-called 'returnees from Kuwait' – many of them with a Salafi-*jihadi* outlook – who gravitated to al-Zarqaa. Here they found like-minded companions, and a flourishing *jihadi* trend took root.

Al-Maqdisi became the *emir* of a new group called al-Tawhid ('Monotheism') and al-Zarqawi swiftly took an active role in this organization. With al-Maqdisi as his spiritual mentor, he set about mobilizing other young men and acquiring arms, initially for training but with the ultimate aim of *jihad* – possibly in Palestine.

In July 1994 Jordanian security forces found several caches of explosives and weapons, apparently part of an organized plot to overthrow the regime. Both al-Maqdisi and al-Zarqawi were found in possession of arms and were sentenced to fifteen years each for conspiracy, to be served in the Suwaqah prison, eighty-five km south of Amman in the heart of the desert.

The prison authorities placed all the Islamists together in one large cell, creating an emirate behind bars. Many commentators say that this, rather than the Afghan war, was the crucial period of al-Zarqawi's formation as an al-Qa'ida leader. Here he engaged in lengthy theological and ideological discussions led by al-Maqdisi and embarked on learning the entire Qurʾan by heart, creating a tent for his own private study and contemplation by hanging blankets over his bunk.

An inherent part of any Islamic group is the establishment of an *emir* or leader. Initially this role naturally fell to al-Maqdisi, but within two years the scholar found himself replaced by al-Zarqawi. Fellow inmates had chosen the younger man over the more gentle-mannered al-Maqdisi; they admired al-Zarqawi's confrontational approach to authority, his physical strength and obvious toughness.

Yusef Rababaʾa was in prison with the men for three years, and he describes the strict regime al-Zarqawi established among the Islamists, banning his men from reading anything other than the Qurʾan and meting out violent punishments to anyone who dared disobey him. 'There were no grey areas,' Rababaʾa recalled.[9] 'Either you were with al-Zarqawi and al-Maqdisi or you were an enemy.'

Fuʾad Husayn[10] was also briefly detained in the Suwaqah prison in summer 1996. He told me that al-Zarqawi was a cool, self-contained person who would only speak when addressed. Turning the rules to his own advantage he dealt with the authorities with studied rudeness and would not allow them to address any member of his group except via himself as intermediary.

It seems that al-Zarqawi was effecting a deliberate and well-planned self-transformation. Self-discipline became crucial, and he worked out for long periods every day, using buckets of rocks as weights to build up his physical strength. Mornings were spent paying visits to inmates detained on civil or criminal charges. His motive was a canny mixture of offering Islamic direction and creating a pool of potential *jihadis* with a tough criminal edge. It seems he was successful, and gathered a following of hundreds of the most hardened criminals in Jordan. Most became ultra-religious, sources say, and many were subsequently killed in battles in Afghanistan or Iraq.

Al-Zarqawi became so widely respected in the prison that when the authorities put him in solitary confinement in 1996 a riot ensued. Inmates sabotaged security cameras, and dismantled iron beds to make vicious weapons. The authorities backed down at the last moment and the next day al-Zarqawi returned, calm and unperturbed, resuming the mantle of *emir* which al-Maqdisi had borne in his short absence. (The latter was apparently happy to return to his research and writing.)

Many sources testify to al-Zarqawi's physical and mental resilience. He had been tortured to the extent that he had lost all his toenails and had endured eight and a half months of solitary confinement on a previous occasion. He did not appear to need the company of others unless it was to further his goals and intentions, which by now had become solely to promote and organize *jihad*.

His remoteness had earned him the nickname *al-Gharib* ('The Stranger') and he embraced this identity wholeheartedly. It was the name by which he preferred to be called, and he signed all his letters and cards to his family in this way.

In 1999 Jordan's new king, Abdullah II, granted a general amnesty, and al-Zarqawi was released. The security services had decided on a policy of harassing known Islamic militants, and al-Zarqawi could neither find work nor carry out any business. His mother had been diagnosed with leukaemia, and when doctors advised that she would be better off in the mountains he decided to return to Afghanistan. According to some accounts, al-Zarqawi plotted to bomb a Westerners' hotel in Amman before being foiled and forced to flee Jordan. In any event, he resurfaced in Afghanistan in 2000, having been briefly detained in Peshawar on unspecified charges.

In Afghanistan he visited al-Qa'ida training camps but did not pledge his *bayat* to bin Laden at this time. Instead he decided to go it alone. With the blessing and cooperation of the Taliban regime he set up his own camp in Herat in the west of Afghanistan, geographically as far removed from the al-Qa'ida operations in Jalalabad (far east) and Kandahar (southeast) as possible. Al-Zarqawi's choice of Herat seems to have been designed to facilitate the smuggling of recruits from Europe and various Arab countries into Afghanistan via Iran.

The camp in Herat accommodated up to 100 Syrians, Palestinians and Jordanians, many of whom had been living in Europe. It was then that al-Zarqawi established the organization that would become synonymous with the first chilling beheadings and suicide attacks in Iraq, Al-Tawhid wal-Jihad ('Monotheism and *Jihad*'). The core leadership was mostly from al-Zarqaa, including Abdul Hadi Daghlas, a Palestinian who was later killed in Iraq, Abu al-Qassim and Sheikh Yassin, the father of al-Zarqawi's second wife. How the camp was financed has been the cause of much speculation; some commentators claim al-Qa'ida funding and connections were used[11] while others assert that al-Zarqawi scorned donations from Saudi sources and was supported by an unnamed Afghan warlord.[12]

As mentioned previously, al-Zarqawi was dismayed by bin Laden's decision to go ahead with the attacks of 11 September 2001; he knew the security they enjoyed in Afghanistan would be lost forever. For al-Zarqawi the training camps and supportive Taliban regime were key ingredients to the evolution of a globalized *jihad*. Soon after the attacks on the World Trade Center and the Pentagon, apparently before the US retaliatory invasion of Afghanistan in October 2001 began, al-Zarqawi and his men fled to Iran via Pakistan. This point of departure could suggest a last-ditch meeting with bin Laden who was at that time still in eastern Afghanistan.

Al-Zarqawi was expelled from Iran in April or May 2002 after eleven members of Al-Tawhid wal-Jihad were arrested in Germany.[13] Crossing into Iraqi Kurdistan, al-Zarqawi arrived at the stronghold of Ansar al-Islam. Some Jordanian ex-members of Al-Tawhid had been with Ansar al-Islam since the Jordanian amnesty of 1999; still others had fled to Iraq after the US bombardment of Afghanistan in 2001. These contacts smoothed the way for al-Zarqawi to gain the organization's support and trust as he established his own camp in the enclave.

Believing an American invasion of Iraq was inevitable, al-Zarqawi began establishing local support networks in Baghdad and the Sunni Triangle. Interestingly, this was the very same tactic al-Qa'ida was employing, suggesting either that some level of cooperation was already in place or that al-Zarqawi's strategic intuition was naturally close to that of the al-Qa'ida leadership. Al-Zarqawi also investigated the best routes for recruits to enter once battle began – deciding on Syria as the most 'porous' border.

In March 2003 – it is not clear whether this was before or after the US invasion began – al-Zarqawi met Muhammad Ibrahim Makkawi, al-Qa'ida's military strategist. At this meeting al-Zarqawi agreed to facilitate the entry of al-Qa'ida operatives into Iraq.

Al-Tawhid wal-Jihad rapidly gained importance as it provided coordination and logistical support to newly arrived Arab recruits, including al-Qa'ida operatives, who had to rely on al-Zarqawi's contacts and local knowledge. His well-established intelligence-gathering capacities also facilitated coordinated attacks, which were instantly more effective than random independent operations.

Al-Zarqawi had effectively become the *emir* of the foreign *jihadis* in Iraq as early as autumn of 2003, though he would not pledge his allegiance to bin Laden or join al-Qa'ida for another year.

Stirring up the Hornet's Nest

The conventional war in Iraq lasted less than six weeks. There was little resistance to the enormous might of the American military 'Shock and Awe' campaign as it pounded Baghdad, Kirkuk, Mosul and Basra with massive cluster bombs and even napalm, banned by a UN convention in 1980.[14] The whole enterprise was broadcast live on TV to American viewers with the grim reality of death almost entirely edited out. A modest estimate puts Iraqi civilian fatalities during this period at 7,000. Forty-five thousand Iraqi soldiers were killed or injured, and 141 US military personnel died.

The US and Britain produced a blueprint for postwar Iraq. In this document, which was adopted by the UN in Resolution 1483 on 22 May 2003, the allies not only identified themselves as 'occupying powers' but awarded themselves total control of Iraq's oil revenues on the basis that it would be needed to rebuild Iraq's infrastructure. The US was aware that there would be a lot of resistance to oil privatization, which would see Iraqi oil handed over to multinational corporations. But quite apart from the enormous financial incentive, there is a crucial political goal. If the US can implement privatization of the Iraqi oil industry this will undermine the enormous power that the OPEC cartel currently wields on the global energy market – and perhaps OPEC countries might follow suit, with an oil privatization bonanza in the Middle East.

General Jay Garner was the Bush administration's proconsul in Iraq as the war ended. Criticized for mismanagement, which included prioritizing elections and the establishment of independent Iraqi self-rule, he was replaced by the bellicose Paul Bremer, who arrived in Baghdad in May 2003. His attitude was concisely expressed in a BBC interview in June: 'We dominate the scene and we will continue to impose our will on this country.'[15] A year later, Bremer was still in post as head of the 'interim' US-led administration and bin Laden famously offered '10,000 grams of gold to whoever kills the occupier Bremer'.

During his period in office, Bremer issued orders for the privatization of Iraqi state-owned industries including oil, and these were written into Iraq's transitional laws. By the end of 2006 the Iraqi Oil Minister (currently Ahmad Chalabi) will have passed a new oil law through parliament enabling the government to sign contracts with US- and UK-based multinational oil companies. Fiscal pressure is also being exerted on the fledgling government, which inherited Saddam's massive foreign debt, much of it accumulated through the purchase of armaments from the US. (The debt has not been written off, perhaps the better to serve as a useful bargaining tool, adding to the pressure to implement the privatization orders and sign agreements with multinational oil companies at bargain prices.) Fearing a challenge to oil privatization from another quarter – the newly revived Iraqi oil workers' union – a law prohibiting public-sector unions which was passed under Saddam's dictatorial regime is still in force, at the instigation, commentators claim, of the US.[16]

Some Shi'ite and both main Kurdish groups allied themselves from the outset with the occupying forces, seeing this as their historic moment to seize power. The interim Iraqi Council established by Bremer in July 2003 included Jalal Talabani and Masud Barzani, as well as Grand Ayatollah Abdul Aziz al-Hakim, the leader of the SCIRI, who would be assassinated in August. At the press conference introducing this interim council, the then Deputy Prime Minister Ahmad Chalabi thanked the US 'on behalf of the Iraqi people . . . for helping us liberate ourselves from the scourge of Saddam'.

Al-Hakim's rivals among Shi'i leaders, Grand Ayatollah Ali al-Sistani and Muqtada al-Sadr, refused to collaborate with the occupation authorities, although al-Sistani had issued a *fatwa* on 3 April 2003 ordering Iraqis not to impede the progress of coalition troops.

Even while the war was in progress, the flames of the resistance that would follow it were being fanned. On 8 April, bin Laden issued a tape urging people to take up arms and join a *jihad* against the Muslim governments which supported the US invasion – namely Pakistan, Afghanistan, Bahrain, Kuwait and Saudi Arabia. He also addressed those already carrying out guerrilla operations inside Iraq to start a campaign of suicide bombing: 'Do not be afraid of their tanks and armoured personnel carriers,' he said, 'these are artificial things. If you start suicide attacks you will see the fear of the Americans all over the world.'

On 11 April the entire Iraqi army's Fifth Corps surrendered as US troops entered Mosul. The old regime began to fall, and by 2 May 2003 seventeen of its fifty-five 'most wanted' had been arrested. (These 'most wanted' were famously represented as a pack of playing cards by the US, which many Iraqis felt insultingly trivialized a war that had claimed thousands of lives.)

Humiliation is a dangerous game. Iraqis are very proud people and, though the majority did not support Saddam, they have a great love for their country. They are generally well-educated (in the 1980s Iraq achieved a 90 per cent literacy rate), with a large professional class. As one Iraqi currently living in London observed: 'The sense that our people, our erstwhile leaders, our country, our culture and our history were being spat on by US soldiers, themselves pitifully lacking in history, education, culture and respect, was too much to bear.'

On 18 April tens of thousands of ordinary Iraqis, Shiʿi and Sunni alike, took to the streets to demonstrate against coalition troops being billeted in a school. When Iraqi citizens staged another anti-American demonstration near Baghdad just ten days later, US troops opened fire on them and killed at least thirteen, wounding seventy-five.[17] Two days later a demonstration protesting these shootings was held in Falluja, and more shooting followed, this time killing at least two more Iraqi civilians.

On 1 May, George W. Bush announced the end of 'major combat' just as the first act of real insurgency occurred in retaliation for the shootings of demonstrators in Falluja. A group of civilian men lobbed hand grenades into the US army base there, wounding seven soldiers.

By Monday 26 May the insurgency had begun in earnest, with a string of attacks against US forces in Baghdad and Falluja during the week that followed. The first US deaths at the hands of non-military combatants occurred when two soldiers were killed and four injured in gun and RPG attacks in Baghdad. As he would continue to do for many months, Bremer repeatedly insisted that the insurgency was being conducted by the remnants of Saddam's regime and would soon fizzle out. Then photographs of the humiliation and torture of Iraqi prisoners appeared on 30 May showing, among other things, one prisoner dangling terrified from a forklift and another lying with his head in his own excrement. These did little to calm the unrest that was spreading across the country.

Evidence of Israeli-style tactics used in the Occupied Territories also emerged. Robert Fisk noted that US soldiers adopted these in raids on civilian homes, inflicting brutal collective punishments following insurgency operations: in one instance a rural village had its date palm groves and citrus orchards torn out of the ground by bulldozers while soldiers blasted music through loudspeakers.[18] On 9 December 2003 the *Guardian* reported that Israeli military 'consultants' had briefed US commanders in Iraq on their experience in urban guerrilla warfare. This advice was put into practice during the siege of Falluja, which began 7 November 2004.

The Map of Post-invasion Iraq

By 2 July 2003 the resistance was already beginning to organize. Regular gunfire and RPG attacks had killed at least thirty US soldiers since 1 May. A new phase of deadlier, symbolic attacks was heralded on 7 August by a massive car bomb using military explosives outside the Jordanian embassy in Baghdad, which killed nineteen people.

The Bush administration issued its '100 days in Iraq' report on 11 August 2003 and concluded that the 'low-intensity conflict' with insurgents – whom they still identified as Ba'thist stragglers – was all but over. 'Most of Iraq is calm,' it commented. 'Only in isolated areas are there still attacks.' Eight days later a suicide bomber drove a truck laden with 10,600 lbs of military explosives into the UN's headquarters, demolishing the building and killing twenty-three people including the UN's special representative to Iraq, Sergio Vieira de Mello. (The UN was considered a justifiable target, presumably because of the thirteen years of sanctions it had endorsed, which damaged Iraq badly; moreover, al-Zawahiri had identified it as a legitimate target in his book *Knights Under the Prophet's Banner*.) The attack was almost certainly the work of al-Zarqawi, and whether or not it was intended as a message to international organizations to leave Iraq, the International Monetary Fund and the World Bank hurriedly removed their staff, and India, Pakistan and Bangladesh – all of whom had offered troops for the peacekeeping forces – now refused to help. By contrast, the insurgency was becoming increasingly multinational.

Sabotage became rife as the Bush administration issued lucrative reconstruction contracts to US multinationals and conglomerates. Water mains were blown up and oil pipelines bombed, disrupting production which now plummeted to 700,000 barrels a day – less than a third of prewar levels. As the US was counting on Iraq's oil revenues to pay for reconstruction, this was a devastating blow.

On 18 October bin Laden posted a videotaped message on Internet sites urging Iraqis to 'wage a holy war against the American Crusaders in Iraq'; additional messages from unnamed militants included one in clear English: 'We want all Christians and Jews to go out from our Islamic countries and release our brothers from jail and stop killing Muslims or we will kill you.' The message adds: 'We promise we will not let you live safely, and you will see nothing from us but bombs, fire, destroying homes and cutting heads.' It was a chilling preview of what was to come.

At the time of writing, three years down the line, it is clear that there are three main groups within the insurgency:

The Islamist groups
On 15 January 2006, several different Sunni Islamist groups announced the formation of the umbrella Mujahedin Shura Council in Iraq. These included Jaish al-Taiifa al-Mansoura, Monotheism Supporters Brigades, Saray al-Jihad, the al-Ghuraba Brigades, the al-Ahwal Brigades and al-Qa'ida in the Land of the Two Rivers, at that time led by Abu Mus'ab al-Zarqawi, who initially also assumed leadership of the Council. The Council replaced the previous umbrella grouping, Jaish Ansar al-Sunnah (JAS), which had been created five months after the occupation. Al-Zarqawi's former group, Al-Tawhid

wal-Jihad, was not formally part of JAS, although the aims of most Islamist insurgent groups were, and remain, broadly similar – to establish an Islamist state in Iraq having expelled the occupying forces.

In April 2006, al-Zarqawi was effectively demoted when Osama bin Laden urged him to restrict himself to military activities. His presumption that he could speak for the Iraq people and resistance was alienating indigenous fighters and had infuriated fellow insurgents and several Imams. Nevertheless, it is clear that al-Zarqawi's strategy in Iraq has formed the basis of the insurgency from the outset. His stategy seems to have had four main strands:

1. To isolate America from potential allies and supporters; the targeting of the UN is a prime example. Al-Qa'ida took this cue with subsequent bombings abroad in Madrid, following which Spanish troops withdrew from Iraq, and in London.

2. To prevent Iraqis from cooperating with the occupiers. Repeated suicide bombings at army recruitment centres and police stations have proved very effective. Al-Zarqawi is also behind assassinations and attempted assassinations of politicians who cooperate with American-initiated plans for the new administration.

3. To commit atrocities that have a dual impact, waging psychological warfare on one hand while obstructing the efforts of those involved in the reconstruction of Iraq. Al-Zarqawi leads the way in kidnapping and gruesome murders, including the beheading of American businessman Nicholas Berg which, it is alleged, he carried out himself.

4. Fomenting secular conflict by targeting Shi'is. Initially this seemed to be designed to warn Shi'is against further cooperation with the US, but now appears to have far more lethal intentions. I believe that al-Zarqawi's aim is to drag the Shi'is into a civil war. His choice of provocative targets bears this out: he was almost certainly behind the massacre of 185 Shi'i

pilgrims who were killed by a total of four suicide bombers and five bombs in Karbala and Baghdad during Ashura[19] on 2 March 2004, and a string of other attacks on Shi'i civilians. He also claimed responsibility for the August 2003 assassination of Shi'i leader Ayatollah Muhammad Baqr al-Hakim, and there have been several attempts on the life of his successor, the current SCIRI leader Abdul Aziz al-Hakim.

Al-Zarqawi's language with regard to the Shi'is was extremely vitriolic. In a letter to bin Laden dated 15 June 2004, he describes them as 'the lurking serpent', claiming that 'they can inflict more damage on the *umma* than the Americans'. He elaborates: 'These are people who have added to their heresy and atheism [sic] with political cunning and a burning zeal to seize upon the crisis of governance and the balance of power in the state . . . whose new lines they are trying to establish through their political organizations in collaboration with their secret allies, the Americans . . . they have been a sect of treachery and betrayal through all history and all ages.' Al-Zarqawi's letter baldly states that if bin Laden and al-Zawahiri will not endorse an anti-Shi'i campaign, he will not join al-Qa'ida.

Al-Zarqawi had been in negotiations with the al-Qa'ida leadership for nearly a year when they finally announced their alliance on 28 December 2004. Already established as a formidable leader of his own group in Iraq, al-Zarqawi had obviously waited to negotiate from a position of strength. Fiercely independent and not known for humility, these were the only circumstances under which he would talk. Perhaps he would have preferred to usurp bin Laden as leader of al-Qa'ida as he had usurped al-Maqdisi as *emir* in prison, but he had the strategic sense to realize this was not going to be possible and therefore decided to submit. He needed the legitimacy and status that bin Laden's blessing and the al-Qa'ida name would bring him.

In October 2004 al-Zarqawi had announced he was changing the name of his Al-Tawhid wal-Jihad group to al-Qa'ida in the Land of

the Two Rivers. In December bin Laden gave al-Zarqawi his blessing as the *emir* of this latest franchise in an increasingly global
network. In June 2005 Abu Qatada told me that since bin Laden
was in hiding, al-Zarqawi had not been able to pledge his *bayat* in
person to the al-Qaʿida leader, and that he had given it via Abu
Qatada instead.

Commentators are divided as to who gave in to whom concerning al-Zarqawi's June ultimatum, but as attacks against Shiʿite targets
have escalated since the allegiance was made it would seem al-
Zarqawi had his way. My information, from sources close to
al-Qaʿida, is that bin Laden and al-Zawahiri did endorse the fight
against the Shiʿis, and it was at this point that al-Zarqawi pledged his
bayat to bin Laden.

Al-Zarqawi's agenda was to prove even more radical than that of
the al-Qaʿida leadership; in May 2005, firmly under the al-Qaʿida
banner, al-Zarqawi declared that 'collateral killing (of Muslims) is
justified under *dharura* [overriding necessity]'. He can also be 'cred-
ited' with bringing a new level of psychological terror to al-Qaʿida
operations with his ferocious reputation and bloody deeds.

At the time of the new alliance, al-Qaʿida's fortunes were lagging.
The attacks on Afghanistan and increased security measures the
world over had seen its numbers dwindle; its 2003 attacks on indigenous security forces and civilians in Saudi Arabia had adversely
affected its popularity in the kingdom. A new presence in Iraq,
especially with such a high-profile, magnetic (if terrifying) leader as
al-Zarqawi, promised a new lease on life. They were not to be disappointed.

In its turn, the blessing of bin Laden gave al-Zarqawi a new legitimacy and status, ensuring that thousands of new recruits from all
over the world (and not just from Arab countries) headed for Iraq
urged on by the rhetoric of both bin Laden and al-Zarqawi, who
have issued many communiqués exhorting young *mujahedin* to join
the battle. Al-Qaʿida in Iraq still trains and organizes the majority of
foreign fighters arriving in the country.

Two new studies, one by the Saudi government and one by an Israeli think tank, analysing the backgrounds and motivations of hundreds of young men entering Iraq to fight the US, discovered that the majority of foreign fighters were not *jihadis* before the Iraq war, but were 'radicalized by the war itself'. This explains the apparently bottomless pit of raw recruits presenting themselves for 'martyrdom' in Iraq every day.

Sources say that 'sanctions generation' Iraqis have started to join the ranks of al-Qa'ida in Iraq. This creates the unprecedented phenomenon of Iraqi suicide bombers. Evidence for this is found in the leaflets dropped after suicide missions in which the 'martyrs' are named. An increasing number have an Iraqi *nom de guerre*, usually based on the towns they come from, in keeping with the habit of al-Zarqawi's group. As noted, the sanctions era engendered a mood of anger and despair amongst Iraqi youths, who are now drawn by the promise of a better life after death. Their greater exposure to Islam than previous generations may help explain why younger Iraqis seem to be more susceptible to *jihadi* talk.

The situation to date, then, is that there are two strands of the Sunni Islamist insurgency in Iraq: the Jaish Ansar al-Sunnah coalition and al-Qa'ida in the Land of the Two Rivers.

The secular groups

According to our sources there is a very substantial secular contingent within the resistance movement consisting of up to 50,000 Ba'thists, ex-Iraqi army personnel, ex-members of Saddam's security forces and radicalized citizens.

Initially formed into brigades with names like Jaish al-Mujahedin, the Brigade of Omar, and General Command of the Iraqi Armed Resistance, they have come together under an umbrella organization called the National Council of Resistance (NCR). Led by former generals from Saddam's army, they are well-disciplined, well-armed and well-trained. Since every young Iraqi male had to do military service in the Saddam era, all the indigenous insurgents are capable fighters, versed in the use of small arms and explosives. The NCR recruits from among increasingly disaffected Iraqi youth and ordinary citizens angered by US brutality and the escalation in civilian deaths. The cultural imperative to avenge the deaths of women and children also galvanized many Iraqi men into action.

The NCR is a very professional organization, conducting formal assessments of volunteers' suitability for joining its ranks and establishing training camps along the Syrian border. NCR insurgents use classic guerrilla warfare tactics and eschew suicide bombings. Records show that there are 24 million guns in the possession of Iraqi civilians. NCR leaders also know the whereabouts of secret caches containing money and weapons, and is in control of most of Iraq's roads, making sure that none are safe for coalition troops. Its knowledge of the terrain and of the small details of daily life in Baghdad and other cities also facilitates frequent kidnappings and assassinations.

The extent of cooperation between the secular insurgents and al-Qa'ida is not entirely clear. However, in November 2004, a joint statement, authored by the Ba'th Party and signed by several groups including al-Zarqawi's, appeared on several *jihadi* websites. 'We are committed to intensifying armed attacks against coalition forces and their spies and agents,' it read. However, the Islamists added this qualification: 'We are not signing this statement because we support the Ba'th Party or Saddam, but because it expresses the demands of the resistance groups in Iraq.' Some degree of operational collaboration seems likely; in Mosul, Samarra and Falluja, Islamist and Ba'thist fighters reported to the local committee of Sunni Islamic leaders.[20] During the uprising in Mosul (10–11 November) *jihadis*, the JAS and the NCR united to battle US troops, the National Guards and Kurdish *pershmerga* militia.

Rebel leaders repeatedly call on Iraqi soldiers, security service personnel and policemen to desert rather than collaborate with the occupation forces. These calls are often successful: during the siege of Falluja an entire Iraqi battalion deserted, one of four which had been integrated with US troops. During the Mosul uprising four-fifths of the 4,000-strong police force either fled or joined the insurgents.[21]

The Iraqi security forces have been infiltrated by insurgents. Some sources say that police forces in Sunni towns often contain more spies than genuine officers; as a result, the insurgents have been picking off policemen at an average rate of 100 per week. Insurgents have often mounted attacks wearing police uniforms, which can only be provided by serving officers, and the assassinations of the governors of both Falluja and Mosul are widely believed to have been carried out with the collaboration of the security services.

The Shi'ite resistance groups

The only indigenous Shi'ite group which remained implacably opposed to the occupation was the Sadrists (followers of the radical cleric Moqtada al-Sadr), whose military wing is called the Mahdi Army. It is worth noting, however, that Lebanese Hizbullah has been active in Southern Iraq.[22] The Mahdi Army was created by al-Sadr in June 2003, in direct response to the American invasion. The cleric's father, Grand Ayatollah Muhammad Baqir al-Sadr, was assassinated in 1999 when he angered the Ba'th regime with his outspoken criticism of its policies. Many of his supporters trans-ferred their loyalty to his son.

Prior to the invasion, Moqtada al-Sadr had been keeping a low profile, fearing a fate like his father's. Resurfacing after the fall of Saddam, he issued a call to arms, and many thousands of his fol-lowers joined the Mahdi Army. Al-Sadr has a considerable power base, and funding through a network of Shi'ite charitable institu-tions founded by his father. The Mahdi Army is amply armed with light weapons, Kalashnikovs and RPGs.

Though outspokenly opposed to the US invasion from the outset, al-Sadr initially urged peaceful protest and non-violence. However, when the US occupation authorities banned his news-paper *al-Hawza*, on 4 April 2004 he led the first major armed uprising in the postwar period, ordering his followers to 'terrorize' the enemy and threatening to begin using suicide bombers. The uprising lasted until 6 June when a truce was established.[23]

World attention again focused on the Mahdi Army in August 2004, when the US tried to arrest al-Sadr in Najaf, the Shi'is' holiest city. A major battle ensued between 2,000 US Marines, 1,800 Iraqi security forces despatched by Interim Prime Minister Ayad Allawi[24] and 2,000 members of the Mahdi Army. The siege of the mosque where al-Sadr and thousands of followers took refuge, and the subsequent devastation of the city, lost the US key allies among moderate Iraqis.

Supporters of Moqtada al-Sadr fought alongside the Ba'thist and *jihadi* groups during the battle of Falluja in a short-lived alliance of Sunnis and Shi'is, who now found themselves brothers-in-arms. The situation in Falluja also brought 200,000 Sunnis and Shi'is together for joint prayers on Friday, 9 April, at the Umm al-Qura mosque in Baghdad. Al-Sadr was moved to address his 'enemy Bush', telling him: 'You are now fighting an entire nation.' This display of secular unity has not endured, however. Recently al-Sadr has moved closer to the Shi'i leaders of the new regime, and his militia is embroiled in bloody sectarian conflict with Sunni groups.

Another Failed State

In October 2006 President George W. Bush admitted that the situation in Iraq was comparable to the 1968 Tet offensive in Vietnam, the endgame in a war that was ultimately unwinnable. Iraq is on the brink of all-out civil war, with more than 665,000 civilians dead and more than two million displaced by ethnic cleansing or voluntary exile. As the Afghan experience has shown, the US may be able to impose a government on an occupied nation, but it cannot uphold it. Eighty-one per cent of Iraqis view the US troops as occupiers rather than 'liberators' and a mere 13 per cent say the invasion was morally justified.[25] Very few people in postwar Iraq believe that their lives have been improved. Unemployment is currently running at around 50 per cent,[26] and most areas are still without regular water and electricity. As schools and hospitals require electricity to function, even the most basic public services are virtually nonexistent. Water plants reconstructed by the Bechtel corporation break down constantly and are regularly attacked by insurgents, leaving most Iraqis without clean water to drink. Ordinary people have become too frightened to walk the streets of their native towns and cities for fear of being caught up in battles between rival militias or insurgents and troops. Demonstrations and riots are becoming increasingly widespread as people protest the new government's inability to provide services.

The advent of 'democracy' in Iraq, it can be argued, is a fiction, with Shiʻi and Kurdish ministers representing their own interests and the Sunnis, for the most part, boycotting the whole process. Surely a system cannot be called democratic when it does not represent the whole of society, and its differing interests and needs. Furthermore, elections do not fill a man's car with petrol, and ballot boxes do not feed children.

The political future of Iraq is further complicated by the implacable ideological stance of al-Qaʻida and the Salafi groups, which hold democracy to be 'heresy' and demand the establishment of a Salafi Islamic state.

A week before elections were to take place on 30 January 2005, al-Zarqawi posted a speech on Islamist websites denouncing democracy and urging the Iraqi people not to participate. His argument, which reflects the view of many Islamists, was that in a democracy, legislative authority is performed by representatives who act as proxies for the people; in this way man must be obeyed, not Allah – 'the very essence of heresy, polytheism and error'. Democracy, the argument goes, allows freedom of religion, including the conversion to another religion but according to Islam, 'if a Muslim apostatizes from Islam to heresy, he should be killed'. Other aspects of democracy al-Zarqawi claimed in his speech are unpalatable include freedom of expression which, he suggested, would allow the use of language that might hurt or offend the Divine Being and the fact that a secular state confines the presence and influence of Allah to places of worship. He found the idea of majority rule 'totally wrong and void because truth according to Islam is that which is in accordance with the Qur'an and the Sunnah, whether its supporters are few or many'.

Democracy in Iraq is characterized by corruption, treachery and greed. Business opportunities abound: a 'Rebuild Iraq 2006' conference was held in Amman, Jordan, for companies who wish to exploit the opportunities created by the war. 'Emerging Iraq is in desperate need of a full range of infrastructure products, services and systems,' the prospectus announces eagerly. 'Be a player in the region's most promising market,' it urges. 'No country in the region has more business-generating potential [. . .] the US government has set aside $18.6 billion for the rehabilitation of Iraq.'[27]

Iraqis who work with American big business can benefit in a number of ways. They can win subcontracts producing inflated returns or, for those in administrative positions, receive large bribes in exchange for awarding lucrative contracts.

The 'new Iraq' gets nearly $100 billion in foreign aid. The corruption watchdog Transparency International says the situation could produce 'the biggest corruption scandal in history'. It is widely acknowledged that bribery is an integral part of the new economic system. Ministers and officials, it is alleged, routinely expect 5 or 6 per cent of the contract price in exchange for accepting a bid. Australian journalist Paul McGeough reports on one tender made at the Ministry of Electricity: 'The work was worth about $15 million,' an Iraqi businessman told him in Baghdad, 'but the minister's staff wanted a rake-off of about $40 million. They advised the bidder to inflate the price to $70 million so that they could have their cut and the bidder would make a good profit too.'[28] These 'entrepreneurs' clearly care little for the fact that the parlous state of the Iraqi electric grid is currently crippling the entire nation.

Ahmad Chalabi, former deputy prime minister and currently Oil Minister, was once sentenced to twenty-two years in jail for his role in a $200 million banking scandal in Jordan. He regards the charges as politically motivated. He later resurfaced in London, where he chaired the Iraqi National Congress, a 'government-in-exile' funded by the US to the tune of $97 million. The US allegedly paid Chalabi $1 million for 'information' regarding Saddam's arsenal of WMD, which proved fictitious but temporarily provided George W. Bush with a reason to invade.[29] Despite a rift in 2004 when it was 'discovered' that the WMD information was incorrect, Chalabi retains close ties to Washington.

Politically, economically and morally, the new government of Iraq is a failure. In terms of security, it is an unmitigated disaster. Sunni and Shi'i militias rule the streets amid spiralling sectarian violence. Fighters are becoming more audacious and brutal by the day. The level of military and strategic skill employed by the insurgents has developed to such an extent that even battle-hardened US army officers cannot help but be impressed, as one told *The New York Times* during the siege of Falluja: 'They cover the infantry advances with mortar supporting fire. That's a very, very difficult small-unit tactic.'

This increased level of skill is matched by mounting savagery and indiscriminate killing of civilians along with more 'legitimate' targets. Indeed, the level of violence is proving too much even for some hardliners: in August 2005 Abu Nasir al-Tartusi, the Syrian Salafi-*jihadi* theorist, reminded al-Qa'ida of the Prophet's saying: 'Whoever hurts a Muslim has no *jihad* reward'; in July 2005, Sheikh Abu Muhammad al-Maqdisi – still in jail in Jordan – spoke out against his erstwhile protégé al-Zarqawi, questioning his attacks on civilians, especially women and children, and his targeting of Shi'is. Al-Zarqawi responded with an Internet posting asserting that 'al-Maqdisi is being lured into the path of Satan to drive a wedge into the ranks of the *mujahedin*'.

As of September 2006, the US admits to 2,084 military deaths, with 44,779 injured. A recent report published in the *Lancet* in October 2006 puts the number of Iraqi civilian casualties at 665,000.

Full-scale attacks on insurgency bases such as 'Operation Quick Strike' in al-Anbar province in August 2005, the bombardment of Ansar al-Islam in the north at the outset of the invasion or the devastation of Falluja, have had only a temporary and limited effect. The insurgents have a remarkable ability to slip through the security net and regroup elsewhere. To put it simply, the US does not have control in much of Iraq.

The insurgents are not only winning this bloody war, but winning it spectacularly. No matter how many insurgents coalition forces kill, they are always faced with a new wave of young men longing to be 'martyred' and take as many of their enemy with them as they possibly can. Military theorists calculate that for an armed invading force to win a guerrilla war, its casualties should be one to ten of its enemy's. That would require 20,000 casualties among the insurgents; while figures are hard to come by, it is highly unlikely that insurgency fatalities approach even half that. The popularity of the insurgency among ordinary Iraqi citizens is another sign of US failure. Sales of pro-resistance music tapes and CDs continue to soar. The most popular singer is Sabah al-Janabi, with lyrics like 'America has come and occupied Baghdad/The Army and people have weapons and ammunition/Let's join the fight and call out the name of Allah'.[30]

The US faces the very real danger of the *jihadi* tendency spreading to surrounding countries, many of which are already supporting the Iraqi insurgency with fighters and supplies. In northern Iraq, Turkish *jihadis* found common ground with Kurdish groups and the presence of Turkish fighters has been noted in Sulaymaniyah, Kirkuk and Mosul. There are tribal connections throughout the region, especially between Iraq, the Gulf and Syria. Most of these tribes are Sunni, and such interconnectedness and family relations make it easy for the many young *mujahedin* from these tribes – whether members of al-Qa'ida or those who share its ideology – to move in Iraq.

An atmosphere of fear and dread, instability and paranoia reigns. Reports of war-related mental illness among US troops cite figures from 17,000 to 100,000 and there were thirty suicides among American soldiers by the end of 2004.[31] According to Said Aburish, the Palestinian writer and Middle East expert, there have been persistent anecdotal reports of American soldiers defecting to Turkey.

Perhaps the biggest and most serious aspect of the American failure in Iraq was highlighted in an 18 July 2005 paper published by Chatham House (formerly the Royal Institute of International Affairs). International security experts noted that the situation in Iraq had provided 'a boost to the al-Qa'ida network's propaganda, recruitment and fundraising, caused a major split in the coalition, and provided an ideal targeting and training area for al-Qa'ida-linked terrorists'.

The Future

For the US, the second Gulf War has become a war of attrition that has so far cost $337 billion and is expected to top $700 billion in a few years if it continues. With the federal budget deficit approaching $500 billion, the American economy is in trouble. 'Osama (bin Laden) doesn't have to win, he will just bleed us to death,' said Michael Scheuer, a former CIA counterterrorism official;[32] this in addition to the mounting death toll of US military personnel.

Recently there has been talk of a phased US withdrawal, and former CIA chief John Deutch wrote an outspoken piece in *The New York Times* advocating just that. 'Those who say we should stay the course [. . .] must consider the possibility that we will fail in our objectives in Iraq and suffer an even worse loss of credibility down the road,' he wrote. 'The underlying destabilizing effect of the insurgency is undiminished,' he added, recommending that Iraq be allowed to 'evolve peacefully and without external intervention'.

In May 2005 the *Washington Post* reported Pentagon plans for four large airbases: Tallil in the south, al-Asad in the west, Balad in the centre and either Irbil or Qayyarah in the north. These four fortified strategic hubs will each support a brigade combat team, along with aviation and other support personnel, the newspaper said. In January 2005 it was reported that the Pentagon was building a permanent military communications system in Iraq.[33] All of this casts significant doubt on the prospect of any complete withdrawal of US troops in the near future.

If the US were to withdraw its troops and the Iraqis began to sort out their own administrative processes, the *jihadi* groups would be deprived of their pretext for the killing and maiming that has become their hallmark. A united Iraq would leave them as they were left in Bosnia, with no role to play in an emerging nation-state.

In this case, it is likely that many *jihadis*, well-trained and experienced from Iraq, would return home to start wars against their own governments. This happened after the Afghan war, which re-ignited conflicts and threatened to destabilize corrupt and dictatorial regimes in Algeria, Egypt and Saudi Arabia. *Mujahedin* returning from Iraq would enjoy enormous public support at home, as many Arabs consider the fight against US troops in Iraq to be entirely legitimate.

Saudi Arabia in particular has a lot to fear from its native *jihadi* sons' return from Iraq. The terrorist threat in Saudi Arabia had already caused crude prices to spike and regular sabotage of oil pipelines and tankers by insurgents in Iraq has sent prices soaring to record levels. 'Our dependence on foreign oil is like a foreign tax on the American dream,' said George W. Bush in May 2005, declaring that the US urgently needs to find alternative energy sources.[34]

As long as the occupation continues, globally organized resistance will mushroom. Military intervention by the US and its allies in Iraq and Afghanistan has had global repercussions of an unprecedented force. The Madrid and London bombings were in direct response to the Spanish and UK governments' military support for the US occupation of Iraq. These attacks were threatened and then carried out. There is a ruthless efficiency about al-Qaʻida's *modus operandi* that is entirely new in 'terror groups'.

The phenomenon witnessed in London, of homegrown *jihadi* youths prepared to kill, is a new horror for the West to digest. Continued support for the US occupation by any government will only increase the level of frustration, alienation and hatred that produces such extremes of violence.

The US has created the perfect training ground in Iraq for al-Qaʻida and any other *jihadi* group or individual seeking action. In Iraq there are arms, money, comrades and trainers. There the Arab *mujahedin* do not face a language barrier as they did in Afghanistan, where people speak Pashtu, and there are fewer cultural differences. Just as the Taliban proved sympathetic hosts to al-Qaʻida, Iraqi civilians provide the insurgents with safe houses, money and military hardware. Without this protection they would not be able to evade security forces or survive.

Furthermore, they have provided al-Qaʻida and other *jihadi* groups with new allies in their fight against a common enemy. The new and deadly combination of Islamists and Arab nationalists that we are currently witnessing in Iraq could have very serious implications for the whole region.

The current situation in Iraq was inevitable – a descent into a bloody, sectarian war with the Sunnis fighting the majority Shiʻis. Sources close to al-Qaʻida have told me that this is what al-Qaʻida strategists are aiming for. Not only does al-Qaʻida consider the Shiʻis to be heretics, but they hold them accountable for collaborating with the occupying forces. For the time being, an uneasy truce exists between the Sunni *jihadis* and al-Sadr's Mahdi Army. Al-Sadr's men are mainly Arabs with no links to Iran, whereas Grand Ayatollah al-Sistani's and Abdul Aziz al-Hakim's groups are composed of mostly Farsi Shiʻis and are Iranian-backed. On 25 August 2005 the Mahdi Army and Hakim's Badr Brigades clashed violently, leaving one man dead and thirteen wounded. Al-Zarqawi may well have had a strategy aimed at fostering divisions amongst the Shi'is based on ethnic lines in order to more easily overpower them at a later stage.

Sunnis are in the minority in Iraq, and al-Qa'ida believes that a sectarian war would expand their *jihad* in the region by bringing *mujahedin* from neighbouring countries to help them. Sunnis are in the majority in Turkey, Saudi Arabia, Syria and Jordan. I believe that al-Qa'ida would also very much welcome a US military intervention in Syria: extending the *jihad* there would bring the *mujahedin* closer to their other arch-enemy, Israel.

Ironically it is Iran, the long-term strategic enemy of the US, that has benefited most from US foreign policy and its military adventures in Iraq and Afghanistan. In the latter, the US put an end to the rule of Shi'ite Iran's theological enemy, the (Sunni) Taliban. In Iraq they disposed of Iran's secular enemy, Saddam Hussein. Furthermore, the Iranians took advantage of the US military engagement in Iraq to develop their own military and nuclear capabilities while nobody was looking, suddenly emerging as regional superpower. Iran achieved these two major victories without shooting a single bullet or losing a single soldier.

The US has effectively presented Iraq on a golden plate to Iran. Iraqi President Talabani was a trusted ally of Iran during the Iran-Iraq war; the prime minister and many ministers in the new Iraqi government were trained and financed by the Iranian Revolutionary Guard and SCIRI leader al-Hakim, whose Badr Brigades were based in Iran prior to the US invasion. Grand Ayatollah al-Sistani, the driving force behind the US political process in Iraq, was born in Iran. All of this is extremely problematic for the US – this powerful Iranian influence inside Iraq and, indeed, the very government the US is endorsing must be taken into account if they or Israel decide to neutralize Iran's nuclear programmes through military means.

Whatever the future holds, one thing is certain: the invasion of Iraq has ensured that a greatly strengthened, encouraged and invigorated al-Qa'ida has acquired the safe haven and training ground it so desperately needed, and activated tens of thousand of *jihadis* and potential *jihadis* all over the world who can produce just the kind of ruthless, devastating violence we have witnessed and condemned in New York, Madrid, London and elsewhere.

Postscript

It is now more than three years since President Bush declared the end of hostilities and Iraq now finds itself on the brink of a civil war. The bloody sectarian conflict between Sunnis and Shiʿis that has developed since the bombing of the Golden Mosque in Samarra in February 2006 was fomented, as part of a deliberate strategy, by the late Abu-Musʾab al-Zarqawi and has become even more deadly since his death. Furthermore, it has the potential to spread throughout the region if other countries such as Iran, Saudi Arabia, Egypt, Syria and Jordan become involved.

The concerted efforts of the US and British leadership, together with their allies inside Iraq, had not managed to get the much trumpeted National Unity Government started as a real, fully functioning political engine six months after the parliamentary elections of December 2005. Many Sunni groups still steadfastly refuse to be part of the US-led political process in Iraq and the last cabinet posts were only belatedly filled in June 2006, due to infighting and squabbling among the Shiʿi coalition ranks.

Ibrahim al-Jafaari was finally induced to make room for his successor Prime Minister Nouri al-Malaki in April 2006 but this represents little real change since both men are members of Shiʿite fundamentalist group al-Daʿwa, and both spent most of their adult lives in Iran. The close relationship between key National Unity Government figures and Iran presents the US with a new and unanticipated dilemma in the light of the recent nuclear crisis in Iran. Where the US might once have hoped to use a subdued Iraq as a springboard for an attack on Iran, they now find their 140,000 troops in the position of hostages to the Iranians on the one hand

and the Iranian-backed militia (in a new twist these now include Moqtada al-Sadr's Mahdi Army) inside Iraq on the other. The Iranians are effectively waging a war of attrition on the allies inside Iraq – Basra has become a volatile region for the first time and British troops have been killed by Shi'i militia using Iranian-manufactured bombs. Having spent billions of dollars on the National Guard and security forces, the US and Britain are now discovering that they have been training and arming members of the very Shi'i militia whose guns and bombs are killing allied soldiers. The invasion of Iraq is evolving into a situation that is actually counter-productive to US strategy for the region.

Whilst the Shi'i militia are united in the fight against the allied forces, they are also engaged in fighting each other for control of the new and highly lucrative business of oil smuggling – the fact that Iraq remains the only country in the world whose oil fields are not metered facilitates the theft of countless barrels. The country is in total chaos.

Although the death of al-Zarqawi in early June 2006 represented a victory for the security services in Iraq, many sources have since informed me that the al-Qa'ida leadership was relieved by his abrupt removal from the arena since he had become something of a loose cannon. Ayman al-Zawahiri and Osama bin Laden were reported to have been extremely unhappy with the attack, instigated by al-Zarqawi, on Western-owned hotels in Jordan on 9 November 2005. In the attack on the Radisson Hotel, the majority of the casualties were Jordanian nationals celebrating a wedding. These atrocities decimated al-Qa'ida's reputation and appeal in that country.

The video of himself that al-Zarqawi released on 25 April 2006 displayed none of the precautionary measures observed by other al-Qa'ida leaders mindful of their own security, which suggests he was operating independently and was not being advised appropriately – perhaps this is telling. Al-Zarqawi was shown, like an Arab Rambo, fiddling with machine guns in a desert location that US intelligence, with all their technological sophistication, can have had little difficulty in identifying geographically. Less than six weeks later he was killed in a US raid on his hideout.

The death of al-Zarqawi has not dampened the resistance – in fact Iraq is embroiled deeper in violence than ever. I fully expect to see the al-Qaʿida presence in Iraq become more numerous and even more active now that al-Zarqawi has gone. His presumption that he spoke on behalf of the Iraqi people alienated a lot of potential indigenous recruits, a problem for the organization that has not been overcome by the appointment of Abu Hamza al-Muhajir, an Egyptian who, like al-Zawahiri, was a member of Egyptian Islamic Jihad before joining al-Qaʿida. Along with many other commentators, I had expected Abdullah bin Rashid al-Baghdadi, an Iraqi national, to be installed as new regional leader.

7

Al-Qaʻida in Europe

> In what creed are your dead considered innocent but
> ours worthless? By what logic does your blood count as
> real and ours as no more than water? Reciprocal treat-
> ment is part of justice, and the one who initiates
> hostilities is the unjust one.
>
> Osama bin Laden, 'to the Peoples of Europe', 15 April
> 2004

The Madrid bombings of 11 March 2004, the London bombings of
7 July 2005, the assassination of Dutch filmmaker Theo Van Gogh,
the violent protests against the Danish cartoons depicting the
Prophet Muhammad and a host of other actions by Islamic militants
on European soil have brought it home that *jihad* is no longer a
battle being fought in remote corners of the world. From watching
on the sidelines, Europe now finds itself a prime target and second
battlefield for al-Qaʻida's war with the US and its allies.

Just as the wars in Afghanistan and Bosnia produced two waves of
returning battle-hardened *mujahedin*, many of whom found refuge
in Europe, the war in Iraq is generating a third wave of *jihadis* dedicated to spreading their theological message and military ambitions
in the West. The difference is that while the Afghan Arabs seeking
asylum in the early 1990s did not perceive the US and Europe as
their legitimate enemy, those returning from Iraq most certainly do.
Furthermore there has been a two-way flow – encouraged, and

sometimes overseen, by al-Qa'ida central leadership – of *mujahedin* from Europe to Iraq and back again.

In some European countries – Italy in particular – the presence of '*jihadi* tourists' is notably on the increase. These are (usually North African) Muslims who arrive in European cities with the intention not to apply for residency, but rather to recruit and establish cells either for their own local conflicts or, potentially, for attacks within Europe.

The war in Iraq has produced another new phenomenon – home-grown *jihadis* ready to attack their erstwhile hosts. These are second- and third-generation Muslim immigrants, disaffected and humiliated by the second-rate social status accepted by their parents' more passive generation, and whose anger is further fuelled by incessant media and online reports of outrages perpetrated against fellow Muslims as well as their own experiences of racism and Islamophobia. The increasing scrutiny and suspicion under which Europe's 32 million Muslims now find themselves will have serious repercussions, feeding and expanding the appeal of militant Islam.

Furthermore, Europe has become the arena for a new form of *jihad* identified by Osama bin Laden in his audiotaped communiqué of 23 April 2006: the cultural-moral battle. This is most clearly manifest in the riots following the publication of cartoons mocking the Prophet Muhammad in Denmark, the murder of 'blasphemous' filmmaker Theo Van Gogh and the controversy over the wearing of headscarves in France.[1]

The al-Qa'ida presence in Europe is diverse and elusive, often surfacing through other Islamist groups with a shared agenda or through self-initiated cells gaining motivation, expertise and contacts via the Internet. The days of the older, experienced, ex-*mujahedin* recruiter forming and leading networked cells are long gone. This state of affairs makes it particularly difficult for intelligence services to track the whereabouts and activities of new *jihadi* cells and creates ideal circumstances in which al-Qa'ida can thrive.

Islam in Europe – a Historical Connection

Islam has played a significant part in European history since the eighth century – first in Spain and then in the Balkans.

Spain

Muslim forces, drawn from throughout the Arab world, invaded from North Africa in 711 and conquered much of the Iberian peninsula, establishing the Andalusian Umayyad dynasty from 756 to 1031, which took Cordoba as its capital. The period under the Caliphate established by Abd-as Rahman III in 929 and lasting until civil war extinguished it in 1013 is widely considered the 'Golden Age' of Andalusia, although the Christians did not finally unseat the Islamic invaders until 1492.

Muslim Spain was a beacon of civilization to the rest of Europe. Cordoba, the seat of the Caliphate, had paved and lit streets and boasted bookshops and more than seventy libraries 400 years before the rest of Europe even learned how to make paper. Students flocked from the Arab and European world to study there.

Islamic Andalusia's advances in the fields of medicine, astronomy, mathematics, algebra (an Arabic word), law, history, medicine, pharmacology and so on produced a legacy which benefited Europe for centuries afterwards. The orange and lemon groves that characterize Andalusia today were imported from the Middle East, as were the irrigation techniques that enabled them to flourish.

The Balkans

The Ottoman Empire spanned seven centuries from 1299 until 1922. From 1517 onwards, the Ottoman Sultan was also the Caliph of Islam and the Ottoman Empire was synonymous with the Caliphate, or Islamic State, that al-Qa'ida ideologues wish to see re-established.

Rapid expansion from 1453 brought much of southeastern and central Europe under Ottoman control until the decisive battle of

Vienna in 1683, which was lost to the combined forces of the Polish and Habsburg armies. The Ottoman Empire remained a major global force until the Sykes-Picot agreement of 1916 paved the way for the French and British to carve it up in the aftermath of World War One.

Ottoman influence within Europe was most enduring in the Balkans, only losing its foothold in 1912 when Serbia, Montenegro, Greece and Bulgaria united to expel the crumbling empire's forces.

Today, Muslims represent 70 per cent of the population of Albania, 40 per cent in Bosnia-Herzogovina and 30 per cent in Macedonia.

This historical background helps explain the significance of Spain and the Balkans in al-Qa'ida's global vision. Once part of *dar al-Islam*, a country is considered Muslim territory forever.

Post-Afghanistan: the First Jihadi *Migration to Europe*

Many of an estimated 15–20,000 Afghan veterans were unable to return to their homelands in 1992 (when Najibullah was finally ousted) because they would face execution or imprisonment as terrorists. For these men there were three main possibilities: to continue *jihad* in conflict zones like Bosnia or Chechnya; to join Osama bin Laden, securely based in Sudan from 1992–1996; or to seek asylum in the West.

Bin Laden was very much opposed to Islamists asking for political asylum in the West at this time – he told me that he himself would 'rather die than live in a European state', and he shared al-Zawahiri's fear that the children of *mujahedin* would become 'Europeanized' and even issued a *fatwa* against settling in an 'infidel' country.[2] This problem was only overcome when the *mufti* of *al-jihad*, Dr Said Imam (Abdul Khadr bin Abdel Aziz), issued individual *fatwas* allowing people to 'go to Europe and live with the atheists on a temporary basis until a Muslim country applying true *shari'ah* is established for you to move to.' He did not consider Sudan to be such a country.

Thousands of Afghan Arabs dispersed throughout Western European countries during the early 1990s, benefiting from the liberal immigration and asylum policies adopted by many European states following World War Two and the de-colonization process. The most welcoming and the most liberal of the chosen destinations was London, making the British capital a magnet for *jihadis* and radical Islamists of all types, who were able to go about their business undisturbed.

Al-Zawahiri had already established contacts in Europe, consolidated during several trips he undertook in the late 1980s when he brought injured *mujahedin* from Afghanistan for treatment, mainly in Austria and Germany. During these visits al-Zawahiri would give talks in European mosques. Other emerging al-Qa'ida leaders, including bin Laden himself, also travelled in Europe during the 1980s garnering support for the *jihadi* effort.

These European contacts had proved their worth during the Afghan *jihad* by sending goods and equipment to the *mujahedin*. I do not believe that the al-Qa'ida leadership had any ambitions in Europe beyond this at that time, nor that there was a strategy to create a 'network' of *jihad* cells throughout Europe as has sometimes been suggested. It seems to me that this evolved almost organically out of a spontaneous dispersal of Afghan Arabs throughout the 1990s and the evolution of other Islamist movements, for example the Algerian Salafist Group for Preaching and Combat (GSPC) and the Moroccan Islamic Combatant Group (GICM), which became active in Europe and subsequently formed links with al-Qa'ida.

Bosnia: Jihadi *East-West Staging Post – the Second Wave*

There was a very strong Islamic fundamentalist presence in Bosnia, which Europe will be paying for in many decades to come, because had there not been those bases in Bosnia, terrorist activity in Europe would not have been possible.

Slobodan Milosevic speaking at his trial, The Hague, 3 February 2006

At the same time as the *mujahedin* were leaving Afghanistan, a new call to *jihad* was raised from Bosnia, presenting another option for the Afghan Arabs as well as an opportunity for willing new recruits from Europe to cut their teeth in battle.

The civil war in Bosnia from 1992–1995 claimed between 250,000 and 300,000 lives and was the bloodiest genocidal conflict in Europe since World War Two. The majority of those killed or displaced were Bosnian Muslims. Around 5,000 *mujahedin* flocked to help.[3]

Compared with Afghanistan, Bosnia was an easy place for European *jihadis* to enter. Geographically located between the Middle East and Europe, it was also an ideal platform for a westward expansion of al-Qaʿida ideology and connections. In Bosnia, battle-hardened Afghan Arabs mixed and fought with raw recruits from Western Europe. This was to be a key factor in the global expansion of *jihad*, in particular within Europe. For here, *mujahedin* with European passports made connections not only with each other but also with al-Qaʿida central leadership. Dr Ayman al-Zawahiri was in charge of al-Qaʿida's operations in Bosnia in 1993 and it seems bin Laden himself visited *mujahedin* camps in Bosnia three times between 1994[4] and 1996, having been issued with a Bosnian passport in Vienna in 1993.[5]

When the war was over a significant number of *mujahedin* exploited a loophole in the Dayton agreement that allowed them to stay in Bosnia if they married indigenous women and several small Salafist enclaves were established in villages such as Bocinja Donja, which became home to more than 100 veterans. This was not much to the liking of the 'Westernized' Bosnian Muslim population, and in that it failed to create enduring links with indigenous Muslims (unlike the experience in Afghanistan), al-Qaʿida's Bosnian experiment was largely a failure.

The majority of the *mujahedin* left Bosnia to seek refuge elsewhere. European countries as well as Canada welcomed the veterans of the conflict in Bosnia as they had the Afghan Arabs, with the exception of France, which had experienced Algerian terrorist attacks through the 1990s and refused asylum to any of the Afghan or Bosnian *mujahedin*.

Bosnia veterans who established themselves in the West quickly made their presence felt and were implicated in several actual and thwarted plots. At least two of the nineteen 9/11 suicide hijackers – Nawaf al-Hamzi and Khalid al-Mihdar – fought in Bosnia in 1995 as did Abdul Aziz al-Muqrin, who would later lead al-Qaʿida in the Arabian Peninsula (Saudi Arabia).

The Muslim Diaspora in Europe

Thirty-two million Muslims now live in Europe. The majority migrated in the aftermath of the World War Two, attracted by the promise of well-paid employment shoring up Europe's 'economic miracle'. Two generations down the line, many European countries now find these workers surplus to requirements, creating the ghettos and marginalized communities of often unemployed Muslim immigrants on the fringes of European society whose youths sporadically riot in protest at their degraded circumstances. Even where these Muslim youths are well educated and employed (as in the case of the leaders of both the London and Madrid bombers) they are still likely to experience social exclusion through racism, Islamophobia or – increasingly – through their own personal choice based on conflicting cultural and moral values. These young people are ripe for recruitment by the older generation of Islamic militants who are mostly veterans of the Afghan and Bosnian conflicts.

Abu Musʿab al-Suri (who is described in more biographical detail

further on in this chapter) wrote an account of life as an Afghan veteran living in Europe in the 1990s. It is very revealing both in terms
of how the *mujahedin* spent their time in Europe and how things
changed dramatically for them when Tony Blair came to power in
Britain in 1997:

> London was the centre for communications between Islamist
> groups and groups opposed to the governments of their own
> countries. We maintained communications with *jihadi* leaders
> outside Britain, in particular Dr Ayman al-Zawahiri who used
> to call me regularly and I would take his calls in a telephone
> box in the London suburbs – John Major's government was
> very clever and served the security of Britain and the interests
> of its people by accepting our truce by which we meant that
> we would never target Britain . . . as long as the security forces
> left us alone . . . When Tony Blair came to power in 1997 he
> tore up the unwritten understanding and stabbed the *muja-
> hedin* in the back by changing the laws and harassing us. I
> believe this showed early on that Tony Blair already had the
> intention of attacking the Muslim world under the American
> umbrella.

Germany, Italy, Spain, Holland, Belgium, Denmark and Britain all
hosted significant numbers of returning *mujahedin*. With their
Islamic dress and heroic tales from the battlefield these *jihadis* were
the exact antithesis of their European immigrant peers, flagging up
to angry Muslim youth the perceived passivity and weakness of their
parents' generation.

Islam also offered an answer to the identity crises experienced by
many disaffected Muslim youths in Europe. The concept of the
umma supersedes any question of nationality and provides the alienated and dispossessed with a sense of belonging. Mindful of the
backgrounds of its new generation of potential recruits, recent
videos by al-Qa'ida leaders al-Zawahiri and the late al-Zarqawi (of

27 April and 24 April 2006 respectively) have been subtitled in English. Al-Zarqawi's decision to present himself Rambo-style, with machine gun at the ready, was designed to appeal to a youth brought up on diet of Hollywood imagery. Most of the perpetrators of post-Iraq attacks on European soil were long-standing immigrants or the children of immigrants.

First-Generation Jihadi Leaders in Europe

Many key al-Qa'ida-linked figures took up residence in Europe during or before the 1990s, while maintaining their contacts with the central leadership. This migration of first-generation global *jihadis* was the basis for what is now an extremely elaborate and complex network of *jihad* cells throughout Europe. Al-Zarqawi had long recognized the strategic importance of the developing European network and until his death in June 2006 maintained a steady two-way flow of *mujahedin* between the West and Iraq. The following will give the reader a snapshot of how the European network was established and continued to evolve and expand.

Abu Mus'ab al-Zarqawi

It is believed that al-Zarqawi collaborated closely with Abu Mus'ab al-Suri in developing the *jihadi* cell network throughout Europe – even though insiders tell me that on a personal level the two men do not get along. In general the original leaders of the early cells most closely linked to al-Qa'ida (and particularly those responsible for attacks on mainland Europe) were Jordanian (like al-Zarqawi) or Syrian (like al-Suri).

Nowadays cells might not label themselves al-Qa'ida and might belong to up to 30 other organizations that are affiliated with al-Qa'ida, sharing similar theological and political ideas and goals – for example the Algerian Salafist Group for Preaching and Combat (GSPC) and the Moroccan Islamic Combatant Group (GICM).

Members of al-Zarqawi's Al-Tawhid wal-Jihad network (the

group he headed before formally uniting his fighters with the al-Qa'ida organization) dispersed in the aftermath of the 11 September attacks and several headed for Europe. Eleven members were arrested in Germany in April 2002 and wire-tapped evidence details regular contact with al-Zarqawi as they amassed weapons and made plans for attacks on Jewish targets in Berlin.[6] Members who migrated to other European countries are likely to have remained as active as these eleven men were.

A close al-Zarqawi collaborator, the Moroccan Amer Azizi, had settled in Spain and recruited fellow North Africans for Abu Dahdah's Soldiers of Allah cell, an al-Qa'ida-affiliated group established in 1995 and which would later evolve into the group that carried out the train bombings in Madrid in March 2004.

Of great importance to the al-Qa'ida network now is the two-way flow of European nationals to and from Iraq. On their return to Europe, such fighters, equipped with frontline training and experience in explosives and urban warfare, form the basis of the ideal al-Qa'ida sleeper cell. Through contacts established over a decade, al-Zarqawi can encourage and facilitate new recruits' travel and training.

Italian intelligence reports in 2004 identified at least two cells, one in Milan and one in Florence, that were actively recruiting suicide bombers and fighters for Iraq and highlighted links between the Milan cell and others in Germany, Spain and the Netherlands.[7] In 2006 the Spanish interior ministry broke up three al-Qa'ida-linked cells and arrested 50 people – some of whom were Afghan Arab veterans – who had been actively recruiting fighters to send to al-Zarqawi.[8] The *International Herald Tribune* reported that 40 or more Britons had been tracked heading for Iraq's Sunni Triangle, again with the aid of al-Zarqawi.[9]

There are many more such reports involving most European countries. Perhaps al-Zarqawi's most dramatic recruit was Muriel Degauque. His third female suicide bomber – she blew herself up attacking Iraqi police near the town of Baqubah – was a Belgian national who had converted to Islam on marrying a Belgian of

Moroccan descent, and who had been recruited for Iraq by her husband.

Abu Mus'ab al-Suri

Although he was arrested in September 2005 and his current whereabouts are unknown, Abu Mus'ab al-Suri remains a leading al-Qa'ida ideologue and strategist whose work is widely circulated and referred to on *jihadi* websites. I believe he played a key role in developing the *jihadi* network in Europe and pushed this as a strategic imperative within the organization.

Abu Mus'ab al-Suri is the *nom de guerre* of Mustafa Setmaryam Nasar, aka Omar Abdel Hakim, the red-haired, rather gruff Syrian whom I was astonished to meet in Osama bin Laden's caves at Tora Bora in 1996. Born in 1958, he studied mechanical engineering and while still a young man joined a Syrian group associated with the Muslim Brotherhood. He fought in the Afghan *jihad* where he formed his alliance with bin Laden and the nascent al-Qa'ida. From 1988 on he trained 'elite' fighters for al-Qa'ida in military strategy and methodology, the use of explosives and urban guerrilla warfare.

Following a dispute with bin Laden he left al-Qa'ida in 1997 and worked as media advisor to Taliban leader Mullah Omar. He ran independent training camps in Afghanistan from 1998–2001, tutoring recruits in chemical attacks and the use of poisons.[10] He was reunited with the al-Qa'ida leadership after the fall of the Taliban; as he recalls in a memoir posted on the Internet in 2005, 'I offered Sheikh Osama bin Laden my *bayat* for *jihad* and to fight against our enemies in November 2001.'[11]

In the same memoir, al-Suri affirms that many of his trainees held Western passports and he had extensive European connections of his own, having been based in London, Paris and Spain over a period of fifteen years. He had married Elena Moreno, a Spanish woman who had converted to Islam, in 1992 and held a Spanish passport; this, together with his red hair, green eyes and pale skin, enabled him to travel freely throughout Europe.

In 1995 al-Suri moved to London with Elena and their two children. There, he became intensely involved with the Algerian Armed Islamic Group (GIA) and edited their extremely radical newsletter, *Al-Ansar*. In 1998, with Afghanistan firmly under Taliban control and London no longer the 'safe haven' it had been under John Major's government, al-Suri moved his family to Jalalabad.

Al-Suri is formidably intelligent and has become a respected strategist and analyst, publishing vast tracts on the Internet dealing with *jihadi* experience and history.[13] His writings emphasize the necessity for *jihadis* globally to establish small anonymous and autonomous cells in every country, skilled in urban warfare and targeting tourist venues and oil and power installations. This seems to me to be very much in keeping with current observable *jihadi* activity outside Iraq.

While al-Suri steadfastly denies actual physical involvement in a series of attacks – the Paris Métro bombings in 1995, 11 September, Madrid and London – he affirms his role in instigating them. He admits that he 'advised the commander of the GIA Abu Abdullah Ahmad and his superiors [sic] . . . to strike deep inside the French mainland'.[14] He also admits that he had suggested the London Underground as a 'suitable target' to a group of trainees, adding, 'I am extremely happy that the seeds I planted have started to bear fruits.' Regarding his activities in Spain, he was certainly a member of the Soldiers of Allah. In 2001 he was charged *in absentia* with membership of the organization, having moved to Afghanistan fulltime in the late 1990s.

Although he is under arrest, al-Suri continues to exert a strong influence on the *jihadi* world. His inflammatory statements are widely available on the Internet, instigating the '*Mujahedin* who are spreading throughout Europe and other enemy countries to move as soon as possible to attack Britain, Italy, Holland, Denmark, Germany, Japan, Australia, Russia and France, to attack their interests in our countries and all over the world and also to attack countries which send troops to Iraq, Afghanistan and the Arabian Peninsula . . . the sleeper cells in Europe should wake up, the war is at its peak and the enemy is about to collapse.'

Abu Dahdah

Abu Dahdah is a Syrian, born in 1963, whose real name is Imad Eddin Barakat Yarkas. A member of the Syrian Muslim Brotherhood, he fled Syria in 1982,[15] eventually moving to Spain in 1986 where he married a Spanish woman, obtained Spanish citizenship and established several businesses.

In the mid-1990s Abu Dahdah and other ex-MB members established the Soldiers of Allah in Madrid. In keeping with the emerging pattern of al-Qa'ida activity in Europe, this apparently independent cell was affiliated to al-Qa'ida through shared members and ideology.

Spanish intelligence started wire-tapping Abu Dahdah in 1997 and collected extensive evidence of his connections with al-Qa'ida cells around the world from Indonesia to Hamburg. In 2001 Abu Dahdah facilitated a final planning meeting between Mohammed Atta and other plotters in Spain prior to the 11 September attacks. He was arrested in November that year and sentenced to twenty-seven years in jail: fifteen years for his role in the 9/11 plot and twelve years for 'leading a terrorist organization'. He was also charged with fundraising for al-Qa'ida and recruiting youths to attend training camps run by Abu Mus'ab al-Suri in Afghanistan from the late 1990s to 2001.

With Abu Dahdah in jail, the leadership of his group was eventually taken over in 2003 by the Tunisian Serhane bin Abdelmajid Fakhet. The initially Syrian Soldiers of Allah had by now been taken over by North Africans (largely due to the highly successful recruiting methods of al-Zarqawi collaborator Amer Azizi) and the group would later carry out the Madrid bombings under the banner of al-Qa'ida.

Abu Qatada

I had always been put off meeting Abu Qatada, who was usually described in the media as 'al-Qaʿidaʾs spiritual leader in Europe', horrified by his 1995 *fatwa* legitimizing the killing of the children of Algerian government officials. However, when he turned up at my office in the summer of 2005 (even though he was under house arrest and 'tagged' at the time) I found him to be warm and quick-witted although undeniably radical in his political and religious views.

A colourful character, the bearded cleric kept me entertained during the whole of his visit, talking eloquently about poetry, literature and other cultural matters as well as theology. However I remained mindful of just how dangerous this man is, if the accusations against him are true.

Abu Qatada, whose real name is Omar Uthman Abu Omar, is a Palestinian born in Bethlehem in 1960. He held Jordanian nationality and was closely associated with Abu Muhammad al-Maqdisi, the famous ideologue. The two travelled to Afghanistan in the late 1980s, as did Abu Musʾab al-Zarqawi. Indeed it was Abu Qatada who introduced the two men and he told me that it was he who accepted al-Zarqawiʾs *bayat* to Osama bin Laden

Abu Qatada came to the UK on a forged UAE passport and successfully applied for asylum in 1993. According to people who knew him during his time in London, the mid-1990s were when he was at his most extremist, agitating for, and (indirectly or directly) recruiting for the GIA. He subsequently discovered he had been duped by the Algerian secret services into adopting the most extreme positions – for example the *fatwa* I mentioned above – and a source close to him told me he was thrown into 'psychological shock . . . he felt compelled to ask forgiveness of the many Muslims he was associated with'.

He seems to have moved back into the al-Qaʿida fold thereafter and was identified by Jamal al-Fadhl (in his testimony in the Southern District Court of New York on 6 February 2001 regarding the August 1998 bombings of the US embassies in Nairobi, Kenya, and Dar-es-Salaam, Tanzania) as having been a member of the al-Qa'ida *Fatwa* Committee in 1998. In the same year he was sentenced *in absentia* to life imprisonment in Jordan for inciting a series of bomb attacks. In 1999 he was accused of funding a group mostly composed of Jordanians to attack a Christian settlement near Petra.

Abu Qatada was arrested and questioned in Britain in February 2001 accused of involvement in a planned attack on a Strasbourg Christmas market. He was in possession of £170,000 in cash but no charges were brought. After the 11 September attacks, videos of his speeches were found in the Hamburg flat of Mohammed Atta. He is also said to have been a mentor of Richard Reid, the British so-called 'shoe-bomber'.

He went on the run in December 2001 but was tracked down and arrested ten months later and put in Belmarsh prison. He was released in March 2005 and made subject to a control order. He was re-arrested in August 2005 and is currently in prison. Jordan and several European countries are seeking his extradition.

Target Europe

Osama bin Laden has often spoken of a long-standing Muslim anger towards France and, particularly, Britain. This stems from two historical events that were to have monumental implications for the *umma*. The Sykes-Picot agreement of 16 May 1916, which effectively divided up the Middle East into British and French areas of control was followed on 2 November 1917 by the infamous Balfour declaration, which outlined British support for Zionist plans for a Jewish 'homeland' in Palestine, apparently overlooking the fact that Palestine was already a homeland – to the Palestinians. For bin Laden these betrayals remain painfully relevant: 'the Bush-Blair agreement [has been] conducted under the same crusader banner of the cross and for the same purpose – the destruction and plunder of the Muslims'.[18]

The first attack by an al-Qa'ida operative on European soil actually took place as early as November 1991 when a Portuguese Muslim convert, Paulo Jose de Almeida, attempted to assassinate the former king of Afghanistan, Mohammad Zahir Shah, in Rome. De Almeida had trained in al-Qa'ida's camps in Afghanistan and had had three meetings with Osama bin Laden to plan the attack. He posed as a journalist to gain access to the King, who was planning to return to Afghanistan and who might have undermined the position of the Taliban and *mujahedin*. In a twist of fate worthy of a Hollywood melodrama the King was saved by a tin of cheroots he had in his breast pocket, which prevented the assassin's knife from penetrating his heart.[19]

As I have already determined, al-Qa'ida's presence in Europe is largely ideological rather than organizational: a network of loosely affiliated groups (some put the number of these at around thirty) sharing similar theological and political aspirations and often having personnel in common. This is not to suggest that ideology is compromised for the sake of pragmatism. I believe this situation has arisen organically following the dispersal of *jihadis* throughout Europe in the aftermath of the wars in Afghanistan and Bosnia and their subsequent association with local Islamist struggles, for example in Algeria.

Algeria's Armed Islamic Group (GIA), founded in 1992, had several hundred members who had fought against the Soviets and had ties with Osama bin Laden. The group was supported financially and practically by al-Qa'ida until the indiscriminate nature of its violence caused a rift and produced the breakaway Salafist Group for Preaching and Combat (GSPC) in 1998. The GSPC subsequently agreed to collaborate with al-Qa'ida and in September 2006 the relationship between the two groups was cemented in a formalized 'merger', widely publicized on *jihadi* websites. Other key figures linking the GIA and al-Qa'ida from 1992–1998 are Abu Mus'ab al-Suri and Abu Qatada. The GIA was the first al-Qa'ida-linked group to attack targets within Europe.

On Christmas Eve 1994, four GIA members hijacked an Air France aircraft carrying 170 passengers in Algiers. They killed three hostages, rigged the plane with dynamite and flew to France where they planned to crash into the Eiffel Tower in Paris. French commandos stormed the plane as it stopped to refuel in Marseilles and killed the four hijackers.

On July 25 1995, a gas canister loaded with nails exploded inside a train in St Michel station in Paris, killing seven and wounding more than 150. It was the bloodiest in a series of GIA bomb attacks targeting the French railways and Paris Métro that killed ten people and injured 180 others that year.

There were few actual attacks by al-Qa'ida or al-Qa'ida-affiliated cells in Europe until 2003, but several cells were broken up by intelligence services and police including one in Frankfurt, mostly composed of Algerians, which was planning an attack on the Christmas market in Strasbourg in 2000. Germany was also home to the infamous Hamburg Cell that spawned the 11 September attacks. Egyptian Mohammed Atta, the group's leader, and the majority of his six fellow cell-members came to Germany between 1992 and 1997 to study. Mounir Motassadeq, a Moroccan, (who was convicted of being an accessory to the murders of 3,000 people in the German Federal High Court in November 2006) met Atta in 1995 and introduced him to Said Bahaji, a German Moroccan who is still at large, and Zakariya Essabar, another Moroccan, who moved to Afghanistan just before the attacks. Essabar brought Ziad Samir Jarrah into the group and Atta met Marwan al-Shehhi from the UAE at a German language school in 1997. Ramzi Binalshibh, a Yemeni asylum seeker, met the group at the al-Quds mosque where the radical Moroccan imam al-Fizazi sometimes preached. Al-Fizazi is a recurrent figure in these narratives (he also preached at the mosque frequented by the Madrid bombers) and is currently in jail in Morocco for his part in the Casablanca bombings of May 2003.

According to interrogations of Ramzi Binalshibh, who was captured in Pakistan in 2002, some members of the Hamburg cell had decided to go to Chechnya and join the *jihad* there when a chance meeting on a German train with a Mauritanian businessman, Mohamedou Ould Slahi, changed their lives and the history of the world forever. Slahi has long since been suspected of having al-Qaʻida connections and is currently imprisoned in Guantanamo Bay, but neither German nor US intelligence services knew that he was living in Germany at that time. Slahi told Atta and the others that it was very difficult to get into Chechnya and suggested instead that they went to Afghanistan. In 1999 he arranged their trip and a meeting in Afghanistan with Osama bin Laden. The Hamburg contingent immediately swore *bayat* to bin Laden and came away with a mission – to prepare and train for the attacks on New York and Washington. A key planning meeting, facilitated by Abu Dahdah's Madrid cell, would take place in Spain in 2001.

Catalyst Iraq

Following the US-led invasion of Iraq on 19 March 2003 there was a dramatic escalation of al-Qaʻida-linked attacks against European and Jewish targets. On 16 May 2003 suicide bombers killed forty-five and wounded up to 100 in coordinated attacks on a Jewish cultural centre and other targets in Casablanca. One of the targets in the attack was a Spanish cultural centre, where four Spaniards were among the dead. Moroccan authorities linked the attackers to the Moroccan Islamic Combatant Group (GICM).

On 15 November 2003 an al-Qaʻida cell in Istanbul attacked the Neve Shalom and Beth Israel synagogues, killing twenty-five people and injuring at least 350 with two suicide truck bombs. My newspaper, *al-Quds al-Arabi*, received an email communication from a group called the Abu Hafs al-Misri Brigade, the military wing of what would later emerge as al-Qaʻida in Europe, claiming responsibility. Just five days later, British interests were targeted when two more trucks driven by suicide bombers detonated outside the British consulate and outside a branch office of HSBC bank. British

Consul-General Roger Short was among thirty-two people killed in the attacks, which also wounded 400.

Madrid, 11 March 2004

When ten bombs stuffed in bins or placed on luggage racks exploded on four trains in three of Madrid's busiest stations during the morning rush hour, more than 200 people were killed and up to 1,500 injured. Though the Spanish, British and American governments all rushed to blame ETA, *al-Quds al-Arabi* again received an email from the Abu Hafs al-Misri Brigade claiming responsibility. I was immediately struck by the reference to the Islamic territorial claim to Spain:

> The death squad (of the Abu Hafs al-Misri Brigades) succeeded in penetrating the crusader European depths to strike one of the pillars of the crusader alliance – Spain – with a painful blow. These bomb attacks were part of settling old scores with the crusader Spain for its war against Islam.

It seems likely that the plan to bomb Madrid was generated, or at least approved, by al-Qaʻida's central leadership. In October 2003 bin Laden had explicitly threatened Spain in his message to President Bush concerning the invasion of Iraq: 'We reserve the right to retaliate at the appropriate time and place against all countries involved, especially the UK, Spain, Australia, Poland, Japan and Italy'.[20] Also in October 2003, the Global Islamic Media website (the main al-Qaʻida Internet presence) called for an attack on Spain.

The reason behind the Western governments' reluctance to acknowledge the hand of al-Qaʻida in the most serious attack on European soil to date was clearly to avoid charges that it had been provoked by their invasion of Iraq. Clearly, the attack was timed to coincide with the Spanish general elections just three days later. An incredible 11,400,000 – more than one in four of the entire population – took to the streets across Spain, demanding to know who was behind the attacks.

On 13 March a videotape was placed in a bin near a Madrid mosque containing a message claiming responsibility for the train bombs from al-Qa'ida in Europe. This was the first time this 'umbrella' name had been used. The group responsible had evolved out of Abu Dahdah's Soldiers of Allah and consisted of Syrian founding members and a large number of North Africans – mainly Moroccans with links to the GICM and to Abu Mus'ab al-Zarqawi through Amer Azizi, who was alleged by the authorities to be a recruiter for the GICM.

The videotape showed a man with a Moroccan accent (probably not the author of the statement) claiming that the bombings were, 'A response to your collaboration with the criminals Bush and his allies . . . and the crimes you have caused in the world, and specifically in Iraq and Afghanistan.' The Spanish people spectacularly ejected Prime Minister Aznar's Partido Popular [People's Party] from power, replacing him with José Luis Rodríguez Zapatero, who had pledged to withdraw Spain's 1,300 troops from Iraq.

The Moroccan government sent its own team of investigators to examine the connections between the Madrid attacks and the multiple bombings in Casablanca the previous year. One link was Mustapha al-Mayouni, the brother-in-law of the Madrid cell's leader Serhane bin Abdelmajid Fakhet, who was a member of both the Soldiers of Allah group and the GICM cell that carried out the Casablanca bombings.

The Madrid attacks were unusual in the al-Qa'ida litany of horror in that they were not suicide attacks. It is probable that the group intended to strike again and that on a second occasion they would 'martyr' themselves. This is born out by the fact that when police raided their flat in Leganes, a satellite town of Madrid, the seven bombers present blew themselves up with suicide belts rather than face arrest.

Bosnian police have claimed that eleven of the Madrid cell

trained at a camp in Bosnia Herzegovina,[21] however this is not
borne out by other sources. It is not unlikely that the cell had no
need to travel for training – Abu Mus'ab al-Suri, who was a
member of the original Madrid network, Soldiers of Allah, was
one of al-Qa'ida's leading trainers in explosives and may well have
left trained personnel behind when he left Europe for Afghanistan.
The group certainly demonstrated the logistical know-how to prepare their bombs as well as a psychological acceptance of death as a
weapon.

Nearly all the members of the Madrid cell were North African
immigrants with low socio-economic status. The exception was
Serhane bin Abdelmajid Fakhet, who had a doctorate in economics
from a leading Spanish university, although despite this high level of
academic achievement he worked in the relatively lowly position
of salesman in a real estate company.[22] The backgrounds of the
Madrid bombers show that, apart from the socio-cultural factor
which must have motivated them to some extent, recruitment also
depends on existing social networks, for example family ties and religious institutions (three members met whilst working for Jamaat
al-Tabligh wal-Dawa, a Deobandi missionary group in Madrid).

Apparently revoking his 1998 *fatwa* against 'Jews and Christians',
Osama bin Laden offered the people of Europe a truce in the wake
of the Madrid bombings. In his 15 April 2004 communiqué he
proposed 'a commitment to cease operations against any state that
pledges not to attack Muslims or intervene in their affairs'. This
truce was 'available for a period of three months', and was roundly
ignored.

The Murder of Theo Van Gogh

In 2004 we saw the outbreak of what bin Laden has called 'cultural
and moral *jihad*' in Europe. The first incidence of this new phenomenon occurred in August that year when the French parliament
legislated against the wearing of conspicuous religious symbols,

including the Islamic headscarf, in state schools, which resulted in universal Muslim outrage and had serious repercussions including the kidnapping of two French journalists in Iraq.

In November 2004, Dutch filmmaker and writer Theo Van Gogh found himself the target of death threats from Islamists following the release of his film, *Submission*, which included shots of naked women draped in transparent cloth bearing verses from the Qu'ran. In his regular newspaper columns, Van Gogh had long been a vehement critic of Islam and often made insulting comments about Holland's Muslim population. He was also a vociferous champion of the US-led invasion of Iraq. None of this endeared him to the nation's 920,000 Muslims – 5.8 per cent of the population – many of whom who were outraged by *Submission*, perceiving it as insulting and blasphemous in the extreme.

In the early hours of 2 November, Van Gogh was shot eight times and had his throat slit by a second-generation Dutch-Moroccan, Mohammed Bouyeri. A five-page document pinned with the knife to Van Gogh's body threatened the writer of the film script, Somali refugee Ayaan Hirsi Ali, and was framed in terms of *takfir wal-hijra* [excommunication and flight] ideology – an exclusivist Salafist school of thought evolved in part by Abu Muhammad al-Maqdisi, al-Zarqawi's one-time mentor and a close associate of Abu Qatada.

Mohammed Bouyeri was arrested after a shoot-out with Dutch police and it was discovered that he was not acting alone. He was part of a Salafist-*jihadi* cell known as the Hofstad network, which had Europe-wide connections and links to the Casablanca and Madrid bombings. Dutch police subsequently arrested another thirteen suspected members of the group, mostly North African Muslims, including Rachid Belkacem, who was arrested in East London on 22 June 2005, just two weeks before the London tube bombs. Belkacem is accused of possessing weapons and recruiting for armed *jihad*.[23]

A group recruited in Spain called Martyrs for Morocco and led by Algerian Muhammad Achraf was discovered to have close links with Bouyeri and the Hofstad network when Spanish police thwarted an October 2004 plot to attack the National Court where investigations into the Madrid bombings are headquartered. Spanish police found that Achraf had provided funds to the Dutch group and had spoken on the phone to Bouyeri.

When arrested, a farewell poem heralding his own martyrdom called '*In bloed gedoopt*' ['Immersed in Blood'] was found in Bouyeri's possession. Bouyeri did not, however, end up a martyr and is currently serving a life sentence for murder.

The London Bombings

On 7 July 2005 three young British Muslim men of Pakistani origin and living in Leeds and one other Jamaican-born man from Buckinghamshire blew themselves up on the London transport system, killing fifty-six and injuring more than 700 people. Within hours of the attack 'the Secret Organization of al-Qa'ida in Europe' had claimed responsibility on the *jihadi* website 'al-Qal'ah'.

In a ghoulishly melodramatic gesture, the bombers intended to create a burning cross with the explosions, which were to have been located to the north, southeast and west of the Underground system. This religious symbolism was thwarted when one of the bombers, Hasib Mir Hussain, aged eighteen, left the Underground and instead boarded a bus, which he then blew up.

The other bombers were twenty-two-year-old Shehzad Tanweer, Germaine Lindsay, aged nineteen, and Mohammad Sidique Khan, aged thirty, who was the ringleader of the group. Relatives and friends of the bombers all expressed total shock and disbelief at what they had done. Shehzad Tanweer came from a hard-working, well-established and close-knit family of Pakistani origin. Shehzad has been described as the 'epitome of assimilation into British society' by a neighbour, Muhammad Ali.[24] An ambitious college student with many white British friends, he loved playing cricket and was described as calm and peaceful by most who knew him.

Hasib Hussain is unusual among the bombers in that some acquaintances recall incidents of aggression and violence in fights that were 'always whites against Asians'.[25] Two years before the bombings, when he was sixteen years old, he became involved in radical Islam, which had dramatically changed him, apparently for the better. He was due to begin university in September 2005 and had agreed to an arranged marriage.

Germaine Lindsay spent his teenage years in Huddersfield, twenty miles from Leeds. Although his Jamaican mother was an evangelical Christian, he converted to Islam in 2001 at the age of fifteen and changed his name to Abdullah Shaheed Jamal. He met the other bombers, in particular Khan, at the Grand Mosque in Leeds and subsequently joined them on paintballing excursions. He married another convert, Samantha Lewthwaite, when he was just sixteen and went to live in Luton with his nineteen-year-old bride. Samantha Lewthwaite initially refused to believe Jamal had been involved in the bombings. Only the infamous CCTV footage of the four at Kings Cross station at 8.20 AM on the fateful morning of 7 July 2005 finally convinced her.

All the bombers had been living double lives, even travelling abroad without the knowledge of those close to them, but no one was more of a chameleon than Mohammad Sidique Khan, the oldest of the group (born 20 October 1974) and undoubtedly the person most responsible for their radicalization.

Before he started work for the Department of Trade and Industry in 1995 – a job he described as 'dull' – the twenty-year-old Khan went on a trip to America. Friends recall that he came back wearing cowboy boots and completely rejected his Pakistani-Muslim identity, wearing Western clothes and calling himself 'Sid'. He even talked of emigrating to the US.

In September 1996 Khan left the DTI to study business management at Leeds Metropolitan University, where he met his wife, Hasina. Khan worked as a learning mentor at Hillside Primary School in the Beeston area of Leeds from 2001 until the end of

2004. His employment records from Leeds Education Department reveal excessively long periods of absence, the last of more than three months. His attendance was certainly not exemplary.

His employers' tolerance may have contributed to the apparent ease with which Khan led another, secret life. Intelligence reports suggest he had been in touch with senior al-Qa'ida figures for five years prior to the London bombs. In a 27 October 2005 article in the Australian paper the *Age*, terrorism researcher Rohan Gunaratna claims that Khan trained at a Jamaah Islamiah camp in the Southern Philippines in 2000 and was hosted on this visit by the organization's leader, Hambali, who was arrested in 2004 accused of having close ties to al-Qa'ida and of involvement in the atrocious October 2002 nightclub attacks on Bali.

Khan was exposed to radical Islam in 1999, when Jamaican-born *jihadi* cleric Abdullah el-Faisal (now in jail for incitement to murder) first preached at the Beeston mosque. That this was significant turning point in Khan's life is evidenced by remarks made to an undercover reporter in February 2006 by Hamid Ali, the Imam at the mosque; he praised Khan and the other bombers, saying they had forced people to take notice where peaceful demonstrations had not and called them 'children of Abdullah el-Faisal'.[26] El-Faisal preached at the Beeston mosque at least three times thereafter.

In 2001 serious rioting occurred in Burnley, Oldham and Bradford, mostly involving young Muslim men. Like the riots in France, Belgium and Denmark in November 2005, the perpetrators felt deprived and discriminated against and had, quite simply, had enough. The three Beeston youths became increasingly radical over a period of a few years, galvanized by key incidents like 11 September and the US invasion of Iraq.

With the local Islamic bookshop and the gym under the mosque as their headquarters they were at the centre of a fifteen-strong vigilante group known as the 'Mullah Crew', which waged war against Western decadence and excess. Its activities included forcibly detoxing Muslim-born heroin addicts, confining them in a room for days to go cold turkey. The Mullah Crew was known to the police who thought it was carrying out a useful social service. However, users of the gym were more aware of their radical agenda – before long it was nicknamed the 'al-Qa'ida gym'.

All three British Muslim bombers travelled to Pakistan in 2004; their journeys were picked up on the Pisces system, which photographs everybody legally entering and leaving Pakistan. Khan and Tanweer flew into Karachi together on Turkish Airlines flight 1056 on 19 November 2004 and left on Turkish Airlines flight 1057 on 8 February 2005. Records show Hasib Hussain arriving in Karachi in July 2004, on Saudi Arabian Airlines flight SV-714. His port of exit has not been established.

What the men did during their visits is not clear but it seems likely they were preparing for the 7 July attack. The Internet can provide detailed bomb-making information but it is highly unlikely that the mental and spiritual preparation required for a suicide mission could be gleaned solely online. Pakistan is a common entry point for people wishing to make their way to the mountainous border area with Afghanistan where many al-Qa'ida fighters, and probably bin Laden and al-Zawahiri, are in hiding. Although it is not known whether the London bombers met the al-Qa'ida leadership personally, they clearly had the means to communicate with them closely during this trip. Khan in particular seems to have had detailed dialogue at least with al-Zawahiri as the communiqués issued after the bombings imply. The statement claiming responsibility released after the bombings by 'the Secret Organization of al-Qa'ida in Europe' is framed in the radical ideological terms of the most militant Egyptian *jihadi* groups and I am almost certain that it was written by al-Zawahiri himself.

Khan's last will and testament – produced by al-Qa'ida's al-Sahab production company – was most likely made during this trip, as was Tanweer's, which was released some months after Khan's. If that was not the case, Khan clearly had the means to get it to al-Sahab, suggesting high-level al-Qa'ida contacts. Speaking in English (with a strong Yorkshire accent), Khan's words at times echo those used by bin Laden. For example, in his 'message to the Peoples of Europe', broadcast on 15 April 2004 in the wake of the Madrid bombings, bin Laden says, 'Security is a vital necessity for every human being. We will not let you monopolize it for yourselves.' Khan, in turn, warns, 'Until we feel security, you will be our targets.'

Khan's video is interesting in another way which also suggests it was made under supervision of top al-Qa'ida figures – he refers to 'today's heroes like our beloved Sheikh Osama bin Laden, Dr Ayman al-Zawahiri and Abu Mus'ab al-Zarqawi'. Given that the formal alignment of al-Zarqawi's group with al-Qa'ida was consolidated at exactly the time (December 2004) that the video was being made, this is unlikely to be mere coincidence. Linking the triumvirate in such a high profile way would have made an enormous impression on the *jihadi* audience.

The video is spliced together with a statement by al-Zawahiri who baldly states that the bombs were a direct response to UK foreign policy, 'Just as 9/11 was a response to America's.' Al-Zawahiri threatened more attacks in Europe in the near future because bin Laden's April 2004 offer of a truce had been ignored.

This is not to disregard the deeper underlying social causes for the London bombings. In common with many young Muslims who feel alienated, excluded and despised in Europe, Khan and his cohorts felt a strong sense of identification with the *umma*. Bin Laden homes in on this when he says in his 23 April 2006 audiotape, 'the West still believes in ethnic supremacy and looks down on other nations. They categorize human beings into white masters and coloured slaves.' Iconic Islamist leaders, such as bin Laden and the late al-Zarqawi, are perceived as redressing this long-standing injustice and inequality, and anecdotal evidence suggests that it is common for British Muslim youths to boost their 'tough' image by claiming to belong to radical *jihadi* groups.

On 21 July 2005 another bomb attack on the London Underground was prevented when all four bombs failed to detonate.

This time the accused were all from East Africa: Ibrahim Muktar Said, twenty-seven, a naturalized UK resident originally from Eritrea; Osman Hussain, a naturalized British citizen, originally from Ethiopia; and Yassin Hassan Omar, twenty-four, and Ramzi Mohamed, both from Somalia. The Abu-Hafs al-Masri Brigade again claimed responsibility and said attacks would continue in Europe until Iraq was left in peace.

The Danish Cartoons Crisis

The most extraordinary incidence of cultural *jihad* erupted at the end of 2005 when thousands of Muslims worldwide took to the streets in protest against a series of blasphemous cartoons of the Prophet Muhammad first published in *Jyllands-Posten*, the best-selling Danish newspaper, on 30 September. The protests continued for months, escalating into scenes of rage and passion that resulted in scores of deaths. In February 2006, for example, Pakistani police shot dead at least five protestors, and fifteen Christians were killed in Nigeria when Muslims attacked and burned churches.

The protests were historically remarkable for here we witnessed the global mobilization of the *umma* in response to a shared grievance, a perceived attack on Muslims' religion and dignity. Osama bin Laden frequently emerged as the figurehead of this uprising, with protestors in Ramallah for example, chanting: 'Bin Laden our beloved, Denmark must be blown up.'

By 23 April 2006, bin Laden had formulated his response to the cartoons crisis in the form of a *fatwa* reminiscent of that issued by Ayatollah Khomeini against British writer Salman Rushdie in 1990. Bin Laden urged fellow Muslims 'to punish the crusader-journalists who have committed horrible crimes against our prophet Muhammad . . . the *umma* has reached a consensus that he who offends or degrades the messenger must be killed'.

It was undoubtedly ill-considered and disrespectful of Western media outlets to first publish and then continue to reproduce the cartoons. Many Western commentators seemed genuinely baffled by the Danish cartoons crisis and responded with arguments upholding the right to free speech. However, as al-Zawahiri observed in a videotape of 4 March 2006, 'no one dares insult Jews . . . or homosexuals'. The lack of respect for Muslim values is particularly dangerous at a time when anger and resentment are so widespread among the Muslim population and makes it easy for al-Qa'ida to package the cartoons crisis as 'a continuation of the crusaders' war against Islam', thus furthering its own political agenda.

Conclusions

The *jihadi* element in Europe is well established and numerous with small networked cells operational or dormant in most countries. These cells are composed of members from various different militant Islamist groups which may have their own local agenda but which share the al-Qa'ida ideology and long-term political/theological ambitions and acknowledge its leadership.

These groups will often have members in common providing a channel to key al-Qa'ida figures, however indirect or tenuous such a channel might be. The Internet plays a crucial role in maintaining this network and providing a well-sourced, continuous stream of news, incitement and practical military information.

The *jihadi* presence in Europe is currently composed of three main groups. The Afghan Arab and Bosnia veterans who found asylum in the West in the 1990s are the first generation of Europe-based al-Qa'ida operatives. It is largely due to their connectivity that the European network exists at all. In the past such men would typically have been the recruiters and leaders of *jihadi* cells (and many that were are now in jail) but in the wake of 11 September and the atrocities on European soil they are under constant and intense surveillance. That is not to say that they no longer pose a danger – their knowledge and experience, whether processed in the form of actual military know-how, strategic analysis or ideology, remain immensely influential and no doubt they are capable of inciting the younger generation to radical action.

The most active group is composed of disaffected Muslim immigrant youths – often second- or third-generation – with serious cultural identity issues for which they seek resolution through identification with the *umma*. Most recent atrocities on European soil have been committed by such youths, radicalized in mosques, prisons, through personal contacts or *jihadi* websites, who have simply set up their own cells. There is also an increasing incidence of native European converts to Islam engaging in violence either in Iraq or at home. These 'home-grown' *jihadis* are almost impossible to police since there is often nothing to set them apart from thousands of other apparently similar youths. In many cases these cells plan and organize attacks autonomously, although in the case of suicide bombings I am certain some level of training is involved. Despite their apparent independence these youths are able to participate in the network of secretive links that inevitably lead to al-Qa'ida as we have seen in the case of the London bombers.

This group of, as it were, 'embedded' home-grown *jihadis* and the enormous potential to add to their ranks from among the alienated, increasingly ghetto-ized immigrant communities of Europe is of great interest to the al-Qa'ida leadership. This is evidenced by references to European issues in the most recent (April 2006) statements by both bin Laden (whose communiqué contained a *fatwa* against the Danish cartoonists) and al-Zawahiri (who, like bin Laden, addressed the persecution in France of Muslim women who wish to wear the veil).

Even more compellingly, both al-Zawahiri's 27 April 2006 broadcast and that of al-Zarqawi on 24 April carried English subtitles as if mindful of the fact that many second- and third-generation European Muslim immigrants would have no knowledge of Arabic. Furthermore, an increasing number of *jihadi* websites with military instructions, ideology and bulletin boards are being posted in English and other European languages.

In the past decade a new group has appeared in Europe. Almost entirely composed of North Africans, these are what could be called '*jihadi* tourists' who arrive in European cities with false documents and only one purpose – to recruit for and establish military cells. The majority are associated with the Algerian GSPC network which is very closely affiliated with al-Qa'ida and, while their primary focus is providing muscle for the ongoing insurgency in Algeria, the presence of these cells must be a matter for concern, offering an ideal vehicle for al-Qa'ida to 'sub-contract' attacks within Europe. Primarily based in Italy (and in particular Milan, which has become the hub of Islamist activity) this network has branches in most countries in Europe as well as extensive links with Takfir wal-Hijra, the organization which, the reader will recall, was implicated in the murder of Theo Van Gogh.

I believe that the al-Qa'ida leadership has its sights trained on Europe and that another attack is imminent. As long as Europe remains engaged in Iraq and continues to support the US agenda in the Middle East it will be considered a legitimate target by *jihadis*.

In his 24 April 2006 communiqué, al-Zarqawi referred to the rejected truce offered by bin Laden to the Europeans and added, 'It would have been better for you if you had accepted, but your arrogance pushed you to refuse.' Before his death, al-Zarqawi had diligently ensured a steady influx of European recruits for his forces in Iraq. We have yet to witness the impact of large numbers of returning European *mujahedin* from Iraq but they are likely to constitute an extremely militant and battle-hardened group, well versed in the military tactics of its Western enemies.

We already know that al-Qa'ida is committed to dismantling the US superpower and its allies in the West; what better way to undermine these regimes than from within? Al-Qa'ida strategist Makkawi's long term plan, referred to elsewhere in this book, delineates a 'fourth stage' where the organization will become a global network loosely linked by ideology and a set of guiding principles. We are already witnessing this stage in Europe.

*

Europe is fast emerging as the new battlefront both for military *jihad* and that new phenomenon, cultural and moral *jihad*. The latter is particularly dangerous since it can engage and harness the frustration and anger of all Muslims regardless of background, age or status, not just 'hot-headed' youths. The ridiculous tests for would-be Muslim immigrants implemented by German legislators, which include questions such as, 'How would you feel if your son announced he was a homosexual?'[27] are just one example of the hysterical Islamophobia that threatens to pervert European justice and values. Equally damaging are the ill-considered, possibly deliberately provocative, comments made by Pope Benedict XVI, who dug up an obscure quote from the fourteenth-century Byzantine Emperor Manuel II Paleologus in order to claim that in Islam, 'you will find only things evil and inhuman', and broadcast this analysis around the world. This kind of overt and unthinking prejudice can only exacerbate what is already an incendiary situation. Europe ignores this at its peril.

8

The Future of al-Qaʿida

Recent events, most notably the devastating attacks in Europe and in Sharm El-Sheikh in Egypt, have shown that al-Qaʿida is not only still in existence, but has a long-term strategy and a solid ideological base. At the same time it is capable of constantly transforming and adapting to changes in circumstances, history and strategy.

These attacks were carried out by local, secret cells and many of the perpetrators were home-grown suicide bombers. With no previous links to radical Islamic groups or the Afghan training camps, such operatives represent Western intelligence services' worst nightmare. They are impossible to trace or identify. As a result the intelligence agencies have proved utterly incapable of predicting these attacks, let alone preventing them. Even when they succeed in detaining key personnel, this does not seem to impact on the incidence of attacks.

All indications confirm that al-Qaʿida is, in fact, growing more powerful. Having transformed itself into an ideology, physical and geographical restrictions no longer apply. It has become a global umbrella for groups and individuals who share its agenda.

Al-Qaʿida's training manuals, ideology and long-term strategies are no longer an exclusive domain under the control of a centralized leadership. They are out there in cyberspace and easily accessible. Anyone so determined can participate in the al-Qaʿida project.

Bin Laden has filled the contemporary gap created by history for a strong Muslim leader to unify the *umma* in battle against the US and its allies, and to restore the Muslim world to its former glory. This is the way he is perceived by millions. Alive or dead, whether we like it or not, bin Laden is and will remain one of the key historical figures of our times.

Al-Qa'ida is unique in the history of radical organizations. It is the first to have such a significant global constituency, due to two factors – the diaspora of Muslims throughout the world and, even more critically, the Internet. Any Muslim anywhere in the world can immediately be part of the electronic *umma* whose *jihadi* wing is fronted by al-Qa'ida first and foremost.

Al-Qa'ida is unique in organizational terms: with a central leadership functioning as figurehead and inspiration, the day-to-day logistics have become the domain of field commanders in more than forty countries around the world. Again, this is possible because of the Internet, which provides, maintains and updates the ideological and strategic framework within which these commanders – and indeed, any group or individual – can operate.

Finally, al-Qa'ida is uniquely dangerous because it has the potential to mobilize thousands, perhaps millions, of the world's 1.3 billion Muslims by applying an interpretation of Islam which, alone among world religions, encompasses the obligation to fight among its tenets. However, it is important to note here that only a tiny minority of Islamists would endorse violence, let alone turn to it themselves.

A Long-term Strategy

What really sets al-Qa'ida apart and, I believe, makes it so 'successful' in its own terms, is that it has painstakingly developed a long-term strategy on the basis of experience, research and observation, which is strictly adhered to. This strategy will be the guiding principle for the future of al-Qa'ida.

The West should never underestimate the intellectual prowess or scope of the al-Qa'ida leadership, which is extremely learned, well-read and well-informed.

It seems to me that al-Qa'ida's strategy for defeating its enemy has four aspects: military, ideological/political within the Islamic world, ideological/political within the populations of the US and its allies, and, finally, economic.

Military strategy

On 11 March 2005 *al-Quds al-Arabi* published extracts from a document titled 'al-Qa'ida's Strategy to the Year 2020', which had been posted on the Internet by Muhammad Ibrahim Makkawi, al-Qa'ida's main military strategist. Makkawi is a shadowy figure, and little is known about him except that he used to be a war strategies expert in the Egyptian army.

The document shows that al-Qa'ida has already started on its master plan, to pursue a long-term campaign of *jihad* to rid the *umma* of all forms of oppression, and that this has five distinct stages.

In the first stage, al-Qa'ida aimed to provoke what Makkawi describes as 'the ponderous American elephant' into invading Muslim lands. The 11 September attacks, which had been planned since at least 1998, resulted in the US's full-scale attack on Afghanistan and the subsequent invasion of Iraq.

The second stage in the military plan was to reawaken another 'giant elephant' – the *umma* itself. According to Makkawi, the most effective way to do this was to bring large numbers of American soldiers onto Muslim soil, enraging the *umma* and provoking a full-scale confrontation. The religious aspect of this situation, so reminiscent of the medieval Crusades, would surely rouse the nation and generate the widespread hatred of America that al-Qa'ida was banking on. For there to be a *jihad*, al-Qa'ida had first to mobilize *mujahedin*. The escalating bloody insurgency, with its seemingly endless reservoir of foreign and native fighters, in Iraq testifies to al-Qa'ida's success in this arena. It might seem remarkably prescient of al-Qa'ida's leadership to have seen all this coming, but I can attest that bin Laden's stated objective back in

1996 when I met him was to 'bring the US to fight on Muslim soil'.

The third stage, according to Makkawi, is to expand the conflict throughout the region and engage the US in a long war of attrition. British and US forces have found themselves utterly unprepared for their battle with a ferociously resurgent Taliban, operating in alliance with al-Qa'ida, in Afghanistan. This additional military engagement is already diluting the coalition's strength and numbers, not to mention resolve, in Iraq. The aim is to create a '*jihad* Triangle of Horror' which would start in Afghanistan, run through currently neutral Iran and Southern Iraq, then via southern Turkey and south Lebanon to Syria.

The fourth stage is to become a global network through effecting organizational changes that will further take al-Qa'ida outside the scope and experience of international security forces. By converting al-Qa'ida into a set of guiding principles, an ideology, it transcends all national boundaries and makes affiliation or enfranchisement exceptionally easy. The perpetrators of recent attacks (for example, in Casablanca and London) had little overt connection with known radical Islamic groups or individuals. Identifying them prior to the atrocities would have been almost impossible. Field and local commanders have full autonomy in planning, choice of targets and tactics, giving the organization an immense flexibility while ensuring an ideological and strategic cohesion. The al-Qa'ida path is clearly delineated and easily accessible on the Internet.

The fifth and final stage sees the US stretched beyond even its megalithic capabilities, fighting wars on many fronts as it attempts to secure all the oilfields in the Gulf area and maintain the security of Israel. At this point, Makkawi says, the American military budget will be crashed into bankruptcy, the cost in personnel will become catastrophic and the mighty superpower will implode. If this all sounds far-fetched, it is sobering to consider that this virtually describes the downfall of the Soviet Union.

Following the demise of the US, according to sources, al-Qa'ida envisages the easy overthrow of hated Arab regimes and the re-establishment of the caliphate. An ultimate, definitive military clash between a mighty Islamic army and the 'nonbelievers', often mentioned by bin Laden, will result in the victory and global dominance of the caliphate. This, at any rate, is al-Qa'ida's dream.

Ideological and political strategy within the Islamic world

Al-Qa'ida has made many mistakes since its inception. Their 1998 *fatwa* stating that it was permissible to kill 'Crusaders and Jews' met with widespread opposition among its sympathizers, even from within its own membership. One of the high-profile opponents of that *fatwa* was bin Laden's 'ambassador in London' Khaled al-Fawwaz, who is currently being held in a British prison pending his extradition to the US. He published a statement in *al-Quds al-Arabi* expressing his conviction, which happens to be the conviction of many others like him, that it was not permissible to kill American citizens just because their government happens to be hostile. He said that there were Muslim Americans as well as many non-Muslim Americans who opposed the policies of their government. (It is worth noting that bin Laden has implicitly retracted this *fatwa* by offering a truce to the Spanish people following their troop withdrawal from Iraq; his address to the American public before that country's election, telling them they alone were responsible for their security, also seems to imply that a truce would be possible.)

Muslim opinion regarding the attacks of 11 September remains divided. Some see it as a catastrophic act of terrorism that resulted in the deaths of 3,000 Americans and the demise of the Taliban's Islamic government; that it distorted the image of Islam and Muslims, brought about the American invasion of both Afghanistan and Iraq and caused a clash between the strong West and the weak Islamic world. On the other hand, there are those who believe that the attacks exacted revenge against the American enemy, demonstrating that the free hand it has given itself in the Middle East, plus its support of Israel and of corrupt and dictatorial Arab regimes, will not go unchecked.

Bin Laden and al-Zawahiri have always been highly conscious of the 'PR' aspect of their mission. In the previously cited quote from *Knights Under the Prophet's Banner*, al-Zawahiri emphasizes: 'We must win the people's respect, confidence and affection. The people will not love us unless they feel that we love them, care about them and are ready to defend them.' He also acknowledges that al-Qaʿida 'wins over the *umma* when we choose a target that it favours, one that means it can sympathize with those who hit it' (also cited earlier).

In 2003 George W. Bush delivered what al-Zawahiri would call a 'target' that many Muslims favoured 'hitting': an occupation force of 150,000 US troops on Iraqi soil. Al-Qaʿida's PR worries were over. Whereas targeting Shiʿis had previously been unacceptable, this is now part of its agenda in Iraq. Civilian 'collateral' casualties had always been avoided wherever possible. Now hundreds have lost their lives in insurgency attacks, a situation justified thus by al-Zarqawi in an audio recording on 18 May 2005: 'The shedding of Muslim blood . . . is allowed in order to avoid the greater evil of disrupting *jihad*.'

While al-Qaʿida is once again thriving in Afghanistan in alliance with the Taliban, Iraq is in many ways a better base for al-Qaʿida than Afghanistan. It provides an Arabic-speaking environment and culture. Geographically, Iraq is the heart of the region. In Islamic terms, Iraq is as important as Saudi Arabia and Palestine, the ancient seat of the caliphate. Al-Qaʿida's supporters in Iraq are Sunni Arabs who have been marginalized by the aftermath of the occupation, isolated from the state institutions in a rather humiliating manner and who are eager for revenge and the resumption of power. If there were a sectarian civil war in Iraq, neighbouring Sunni-majority countries could well ally themselves with the Iraqi minority, leading to the establishment of a new Islamic state in the region. Al-Qaʿida has identified this step as key to its long-term project of re-establishing the caliphate.

Al-Qa'ida remains implacably opposed to many regimes in the Muslim world, and much of its effort is directed at fomenting insurrection, mobilizing people against their own governments as well as the US. Al-Zawahiri has often stated that he would much prefer to live in a state of utter lawlessness than be subjected to the rule of tyrants. Both he and bin Laden have broadcast scathing criticisms of these corrupt Arab regimes, accusing them of collaborating with Zionists and the US. These tapes meet with broad approval throughout the Muslim world, and facilitate al-Qa'ida's recruitment of *jihadis.*

For a significant group within the Muslim world, al-Qa'ida continues to provide a unique and compelling vision where faith, Islamic identity and the desire for political justice converge, creating a heady sense of the possibility of change that the region has lacked for many decades.

Whether or not a majority of Muslim people would welcome the sort of Taliban-style, *shari'ah*-based rule al-Qa'ida champions is questionable. But this problem will not exercise them while US troops remain on their lands and al-Qa'ida continues to deliver on its promises to rid the *umma* of the occupiers.

Ideological and political strategy regarding the US and its allies
More than 80 per cent of Muslims believe that America's war is against Islam, and not against terrorism. Al-Qa'ida wishes to foment a 'clash of civilizations', with Christian fundamentalism opposed to Islamic fundamentalism, resulting in an eventual all-out war between the 'believers' and the *kafir*. However, al-Qa'ida would like to see the US fighting this battle alone.

Al-Qa'ida aims to effect a division between the US and Europe. The organization has already had a massive impact in this regard with the Madrid and the London bombings. Al-Zawahiri told the British people in an audiotaped message on 4 August 2005 that 'Blair has brought destruction to the heart of London', and many British people do indeed consider him to be personally responsible because of his decision to participate in the invasion of Iraq.

Al-Qaʻida sets great store by reasoning with people rather than governments, according to sources close to the leadership. The thinking is that if the people turn against their rulers, perceiving them as responsible for their misfortunes, even states like the US can implode. Aiming to sow popular dissatisfaction, bin Laden has made much of the Bush administration's interests in Iraq, reminding the American people in a speech on 29 October 2004 of 'the scope of the contracts won by large dubious corporations like Halliburton and others that have ties to Bush and to his administration', adding: 'The losing side is in fact you, the American people, and your economy.'

A general public that faces being bombed on the way to work is unlikely to approve of a government that not only fails to protect them but has brought terrorism to their doorstep. The lingering sense of unease, mistrust and insecurity such attacks leave in their wake can further alienate the people from their leaders. Governments who seek to capitalize on fear, as the US and Britain have done with a rush to implement more restrictive legislation, do so at their peril. The US Patriot Act of 2001 has been compared to Hitler's Reichstag Fire Decree of 1933 in that it limited civil liberties with the declared purpose of protecting the people. The Patriot Act has been criticized widely for eroding the principles of habeas corpus, freedom of press and speech, freedom to organize and assemble and the right to privacy of communication. Tony Blair's 2005 Prevention of Terrorism Act has been sharply objected to on the grounds that it compromises the right to a fair trial enshrined in British judicial history for 800 years, ushering in measures that, as the Tory Member of Parliament Boris Johnson commented, 'would be instantly recognizable to the old BOSS security service in South Africa and every secret police force including the CHEKA'.[1]

Recent UK measures (published in August 2005) to facilitate the deportation of alleged 'terrorist sympathizers' might actually have the effect of radicalizing British Muslims. Nor is this problem confined to Britain, as the same response has been observed across Europe and the US. A 'witch hunt' against Islamists, based on the assumption that all are in favour of violence – which is certainly not the case – could create a network of sympathy and outrage. The more such actions are seen to constitute extreme oppression, blind prejudice and injustice, the more legitimate and justified an extreme response will seem, especially to Muslims who may already feel marginalized and alienated.

Al-Qaʻidaʼs economic strategy

Waging war on the economic front is a concept that appeals to al-Qaʻida and its multimillionaire leader, Osama bin Laden. In a speech addressed to the American people on 29 October 2004, he rather gleefully noted that 'al-Qaʻida spent $500,000 on the event [11 September 2001] while America lost, in the event and its subsequent effects, more than $500 billion dollars; that is to say that each of al-Qaʻidaʼs dollars defeated 1 million American dollars, thanks to Allahʼs grace'.

The attacks had other economic repercussions: Arab investors, worried that their assets might be frozen, withdrew billions of dollars from Western financial institutions and invested them instead in the Muslim world. Huge oil revenues resulting from the vastly inflated current price of oil are also now being invested in the Gulf states themselves, resulting in an economic boom.

Regular insurgency attacks on oil pipelines and installations in Iraq have also already impacted on oil prices with the so-called 'terror premium' leading to the highest prices on record. Al-Qaʻida has frequently urged OPEC ministers to reduce oil production, resulting in higher prices which squeeze Western economies. However, oil prices are not the only drain on the US.

Sources close to the al-Qaʻida leadership say that al-Zawahiri is a great admirer of Yale historian Paul Kennedy's book *The Rise and Fall of the Great Powers* and that he uses it as a reference in the context of strategic planning. Kennedy's theory, in summary, observes that great empires fall for three main reasons: spiralling costs for maintaining internal security; an expanding military presence in the world with an attendant increase in personnel and financial commitments; powerful foreign competition in trade and commerce.

Al-Zawahiri believes that the US is just such an empire in decline and that it has already met Kennedy's first and second conditions. Internal security has already become very costly largely due to al-Qaʿida's actual or threatened operations. George W. Bush has frequently reiterated his claim that he invaded Iraq to tackle terrorism 'over there' so that it would not come to America's doorstep. But many commentators believe another military attack on the US, similar in scale and impact to 11 September, is imminent.

The US has significant military commitments in parts of Europe, Northeast Asia, East Asia, the Middle East and Southwest Asia, and is engaged in actual conflicts in Afghanistan and, most notably, Iraq. It is also adopting an increasingly bellicose stance towards Iran, which took the opportunity to resurrect its nuclear programme while the US was busy in Iraq.

The war in Iraq is rapidly becoming a war of attrition and represents a great drain on the US economy. By October 2006 the cost of the war had reached about $337 billion at a monthly rate of $7.8 billion according to most estimates, with some commentators suggesting it might ultimately exceed $700 billion. As bin Laden put it in a speech to the American people: 'The *jihad* fighters have recently forced Bush to resort to an emergency budget in order to continue the fighting in Afghanistan and in Iraq, which proves the success of the plan of bleeding [America] to the point of bankruptcy, Allah willing.'

The third condition posited by Kennedy brings global commercial competition from an emerging rival superpower into the picture. According to al-Zawahiri (and most economists) both China and India already pose such a challenge and will constitute a real threat to the US and its economy in the next decade.

What if bin Laden is Captured or Killed?

Bin Laden has repeatedly affirmed that he will not be taken alive. The US has spent billions of dollars and lost thousands of soldiers in its bid to capture bin Laden and destroy al-Qa'ida. It has achieved very little, and every day that bin Laden and al-Zawahiri remain at large will be seen as a political and propaganda victory for al-Qa'ida.

No one really knows where these men are hiding, but theories abound. There are those who believe that they move from one location to another in the tribal regions along the Afghan-Pakistani borders which extend for about 1,500 miles. This area is almost entirely outside the jurisdiction of the Pakistani government and its troops. It is a rough, mountainous region inhabited by tribes loyal to bin Laden, whom they view as a heroic *mujahed* who struggled for the liberation of Afghanistan and gave up wealth and comfort in order to support his brothers.

General Asad Durrani, former head of Pakistan's intelligence service, believes that big cities are the best places for bin Laden to remain hidden. It is true that most of the arrests of key al-Qa'ida figures in Pakistan have been made in cities like Karachi, Faisalabad, Peshawar, Quetta and Rawalpindi.

I was told by one of bin Laden's close associates that he had been staying in the same house as Abu Zubaydah, the al-Qa'ida member in charge of mobilization and recruitment who was arrested in Faisalabad in March 2002. This source said bin Laden had left the house three days before the raid, which was conducted by a joint US-Pakistani force. This seems quite feasible, and I would not rule out the possibility that bin Laden has now left Pakistan completely.

When I met bin Laden he intimated that he might move to the Yemeni mountains. I have since learned that he despatched envoys to Yemen in order to establish links with the tribes there and investigate the possibility of a move. One of the tribal chiefs he apparently contacted was Sheikh bin Shaj from the Sadr region. (His fourth wife, the Yemeni Amal al-Sadah, returned there in 2002.)

Other possible havens for the fugitives include Kashmir or the Islamic republics of the former Soviet Union such as Uzbekistan, Azerbaijan or even Chechnya.

The quality of the audio- and videotapes bin Laden has released in recent months do not give the impression that he is living in a backward tribal region. His statements indicate that he and al-Zawahiri are staying in a comfortable and secure location, and that they are able to follow political developments in the Arab region and the entire world as events unfold.

Bin Laden told me that since he returned to Afghanistan following his deportation from Sudan he had not used any modern communication equipment such as mobile or satellite phones, the Internet or email. He now prefers to communicate information and instructions in handwritten letters delivered by messengers. He is kept up to date by followers who download the latest news and information in Internet cafés, putting it onto disks or printing it out for him.

Bin Laden and al-Zawahiri are proving very difficult to track, not least because of their intelligence and alertness. They have made their personal security their own business. Bin Laden moves with one bodyguard and a small group of trusted companions in a region very well known to him. It is not at all true that it is easy to recognize him because of his height (6 feet, 3 inches) – if he is indeed in the mountains between Pakistan and Afghanistan, most men in this tribal region are tall, bearded and dress just the way he does.

It is indicative of the extraordinary success of bin Laden's security measures that he currently has two wives and around twenty sons and daughters in hiding in Afghanistan. Until now the whereabouts of his wives and children and those of al-Zawahiri remain unknown.

The US had more luck tracking down Saddam Hussein because he was arrogant, careless and moved within the same area. Even though he was on the run, he continued to behave like a head of state; he visited tribal chiefs, communicated with his followers and had untrustworthy bodyguards. Furthermore, there were 140,000 US soldiers in Iraq, and more than three-quarters of the Iraqi people were against him.

When Saddam was ousted from power many of his followers deserted him and popular support dwindled. The exact opposite has been happening in the case of bin Laden – he only moves in areas where people are known to support al-Qa'ida, and his followers are fiercely loyal and prepared to die to protect him. The US presence in the tribal regions including Afghanistan does not exceed 20,000 soldiers. There are few US personnel dedicated to the task of tracking bin Laden in the other countries where he might be hiding.

As long as they remain alive, bin Laden and al-Zawahiri will continue to influence events from behind the scenes. They will produce more recordings and post statements inciting *jihad* and violence on the Internet. In the past these statements have often been followed by an attack. On 6 October 2002, bin Laden urged his followers to strike at Western economic interests; on the same day the French supertanker Limburg was punctured by a suicide bomber in a small boat. Six days later, a nightclub on the Indonesian island of Bali was bombed, killing 200 young people. (The club was frequented by foreign tourists, especially from Australia, a US ally in the wars on Afghanistan and Iraq.) In December 2003, al-Zawahiri condemned Pakistani President Parvez Musharraf; shortly afterwards, the president miraculously escaped an assassination attempt. Prior to the Madrid bombings in 2004, both bin Laden and al-Zawahiri released tapes in which they threatened to avenge the innocent victims of the war on Iraq.

It seems to me that the only way bin Laden will be detained or killed is by pure chance or a lucky strike. But alive or dead, bin Laden would pose a whole new set of problems for the US. If he is captured alive, the question will be how to prosecute him, according to which law and in which country. Killing him, on the other hand, will turn him into a martyr or a saint, and could result in bloody revenge operations.

The detention of Saddam has not produced any sense of hope-lessness or desperation among his followers, and it certainly did not halt the insurgency – in fact quite the opposite is true. When Sayyid Qutb was executed by Nasser in 1966, he was transformed into a hero. Previously almost unknown as a writer, demand for his books spiralled after his death.

If bin Laden is removed, one way or another, this will not result in the demise of al-Qaʻida, just as al-Zarqawi's death did nothing to diminish the strength of al-Qaʻida in Iraq. The pattern of recent al-Qaʻida operations shows that the organization has a life of its own, independent of any one person or group, it is a collective ideologi-cal entity which has become more solid, more integrated and is demonstrably capable of enduring long after the death of its leader. Alive or dead, bin Laden will remain the figurehead, the inspiration of the organization.

What is to Be Done?

As we have seen, the US has provided al-Qaʻida with the geograph-ical base it urgently needed in Iraq as well as the opportunity to train *jihadis* and allow them to gain combat experience. Meanwhile, the organization itself has become truly global.

In order to carry out the attacks of 11 September, al-Qaʻida oper-atives had to travel to the US and penetrate that country's security barriers. This is no longer necessary. Al-Qaʻida now has branches that are absolutely autonomous and independent in Iraq, Afghanistan, Pakistan and Europe. There are reports of further branches in many countries including Algeria, Uzbekistan and even Palestine, each enjoying full independence and possessing consider-able powers.

The *emir* of a local branch does not need to obtain direct instruc-tions from the supreme leader of the entire organization, bin Laden, or from al-Zawahiri, in order to carry out small operations aimed at causing a security breach or attracting media attention. However, 'consultation' does take place regarding major operations which require 'permission'. The plan for the Madrid bombing was arrived at through consultation and coordination. In keeping with the new shape of al-Qa'ida, the actual attacks were carried out by the local cells independently.

Al-Qa'ida's first objective is to destroy the current US neo-conservative project because it considers it responsible for all the evils – political and moral – that plague the Islamic world. Al-Zawahiri, and latterly al-Zarqawi, have succeeded in persuading bin Laden that any actions that can weaken the US are legitimate.

Bin Laden remains unchallenged as al-Qa'ida's spiritual leader, and al-Zawahiri has emerged as its supreme military leader. But there is a new generation of al-Qa'ida leaders in waiting and the influence of the late al-Zarqawi is clear in his legacy of an even more hardline agenda. There is a new ruthlessness about relentless violence directed at a wide range of targets in Iraq, which is clearly designed to shock and terrorize their enemies.

What makes al-Qa'ida different to other Islamist organizations such as the Muslim Brotherhood is the flexibility of its ideology and its wide range of aims. While the leadership's own theological plat-form is essentially Salafi, the organization's umbrella is sufficiently wide to encompass various schools of thought and political leanings. Al-Qa'ida counts among its members and supporters people associated with Wahhabism, Shafi'ism, Malikism and Hanafism. There are even some whose beliefs and practices are directly at odds with Salafism, such as Yunis Khalis, one of the leaders of the Afghan *mujahedin*. He is a mystic who visits tombs of saints and seeks their blessings – practices inimical to bin Laden's Wahhabi-Salafi school of thought. The only exception to this pan-Islamic approach is Shi'ism. Al-Zarqawi fomented the bloody sectarian conflict between Sunni and Shi'i in Iraq which today places the nation on the brink of civil war. While Osama bin Laden explicitly opposed this policy, his reservations are only temporary since the Shi'i – whom he regards as heretics – would have no place in any future caliphate.

In his 2004 book *Against All Enemies: Inside America's War on Terror*, Richard A. Clarke, the former White House counter-terrorism coordinator, says that senior administration figures failed to understand the nature and level of the threat al-Qa'ida poses to the US. Thinking within a Cold War analytical framework, top officials were searching for the power behind al-Qa'ida instead of directly addressing it as the source of menace. This, Clarke explains, is why the US has failed so singularly in its battle against terrorism.

The dominant conviction within White House circles even prior to the events of 11 September, according to Clarke, was that behind every terrorist network there is a state that protects it and sponsors it – once such a state is destroyed, the terrorist network and the threat it posed will come to an end. This is one reason why the US has been so keen to prove a link between Saddam Hussein and al-Qa'ida and why, having announced – with no evidence – that there was such a link, the American neo-conservatives were able to acquire the support they needed for their plan to attack Iraq.

It is impossible to defeat an enemy you cannot see or understand. Al-Qa'ida is something entirely new in the history of terrorism. It has the strategic audacity of a nation-state and yet it has no geographical location; its membership is distributed across the globe and cyberspace and has no obvious identifying features.

The war on al-Qa'ida has, right from the start, been premised on the wrong assumptions. The enemy is invisible, and therefore the use of force on its own is utterly futile. The oft-repeated Bush mantra that he is 'destroying the infrastructure of terrorism' is simply untrue when it comes to al-Qa'ida. It is not at all possible to carpet-bomb al-Qa'ida's positions, or attack its soldiers, who develop their military skills and receive their instructions by sitting in front of a PC and connecting to the Internet.

Security solutions alone will not eliminate al-Qa'ida because the success and survival of the network does not depend on individuals or even groups; bin Laden himself is no longer indispensable. Giving security agencies additional money, manpower and jurisdiction might slightly reduce the level of attacks, but will not bring them to an end.

The prospect of opening negotiations with al-Qaʿida seems remote indeed, and one cannot negotiate with ghosts. However, this notion should not be completely ruled out. Who could have envisaged that Britain would one day negotiate with the Irish Republican Army, or Israel with Yasser Arafat, once labelled a brutal terrorist? The problem, of course, is that al-Qaʿidaʾs demands are global, and not confined to a particular state or territory.

The only way forward that I can see is for the US to acknowledge that armed action does not emanate from a void. Al-Qaʿidaʾs is not mindless violence. It is military aggression with a set of objectives, and survives on a diet of popular sympathy, cover and human ammunition.

Support for groups like al-Qaʿida is born of political, social and economic circumstances that people find unacceptable. Al-Qaʿida offers them the chance to fight back – something that, for the Muslim world as a whole, has not been possible for a very long time. Muslims might not like what al-Qaʿida has to offer in the long term – how many of them really want to live under a Taliban-style regime? – but that is not the issue at present.

To lessen the power and range of al-Qaʿida it would first be necessary to dry the wellsprings of recruitment by tackling the root causes for disaffection, dissatisfaction and the massive amount of hatred the US has managed to generate – by its military interventions above all, but also because of what Muslims often perceive as its inherently corrupt, greedy and amoral way of life.

Democratic reform throughout the Arab region would go some way to addressing some of the region's underlying problems, and bin Laden would have played a major role in bringing it about. The attacks of 11 September, for which he claimed responsibility, brought about an increased awareness in the West regarding the level of corruption and dictatorship in the Arab world. It is very likely that overt and covert US support for dictatorial and oppressive regimes in the region are another major reason why it is hated throughout the Islamic world.

Not only that, the US also has to face up to heavy political, security and economic demands that support for these regimes places on it, particularly when its own economy faces enormous problems and deficits. Condoleezza Rice, the US Secretary of State, recently acknowledged that successive American administrations have erroneously based their policies on the rationale that stability in the Arab region is maintained at the expense of democracy. Now it is clear that neither have been achieved. There is direct correlation between the level of corruption and repression among a regime's rulers and the prevalence of Islamic extremism which targets the US and the West. Saudi Arabia is a case in point – it is the most corrupt and repressive regime in the region, and it has produced 70 per cent of al-Qa'ida's fighters as well as the leader himself.

In dealing with al-Qa'ida for the time being, the focus must be on Iraq. The situation in Iraq, more than anything else, has provided al-Qa'ida with a safe haven and with endless hordes of fighters eager to die opposing the US occupation of the country. The US presence there has also brought al-Qa'ida greater support, or at least non-opposition, among people in much of the Islamic world. Of course, without a resolution to the enduring Palestinian-Israeli conflict, no lasting or credible peace in the region is likely. However, this is a subject for another book.

As long as connections continue to be made between US policy, actual or perceived, and the continuing instability in much of the Middle East, we can expect that al-Qa'ida will grow stronger and expand the sphere of its activities.

Notes

Chapter One

1. Salafism, derived from the Arabic word *salaf* ('predecessors' or 'early generations'), is a religious school of thought which holds that only the first three generations of Muslims adhered to the true path. Hence, the argument goes, the decline and fall of the *umma* as theological deviation set in. Salafis are also known as al-Salaf al-Saalih ('The Righteous Predecessors').
2. BBC, 3 January 2002.
3. Interview with Saad al-Faqih, 28 April 2005, London.
4. The interview was conducted by al-Hammadi and published in *al-Quds al-Arabi* on 3 August 2004.

Chapter Two

1. A *fatwa* is a legal opinion or ruling issued by an Islamic religious scholar.
2. The General March is the principle, according to Ibn Taymiyyah, whereby the entire *umma* is commanded to mobilize as one, marching to the site of an infringement on Muslim land and embarking on *jihad*.

Chapter Three

1. Dale, S., 'Religious Suicide in Islamic Asia: Anticolonial Terrorism in India, Indonesia and the Philippines', *Journal of Conflict Resolution*, 23: 37–59, 1988.
2. Interview with Dr Zaki Badawi, London, 11 April 2005.
3. Ashley Tellis, quoted in *The San Francisco Chronicle*, 20 March 2005 ('Iraq Desert Becomes Chief Training Ground for Killing Americans').
4. See Merari, A., 'The readiness to kill and die: Suicidal terrorism in the Middle East', in W. Reich (ed.), *Origins of Terrorism: Psychologies, Ideologies, Theologies, States of Mind* (Washington, DC:

Woodrow Wilson Center Press, 1990, pp. 192–210) and Robert S. Robins and Jerrold Post, *Political Paranoia: The Psychopolitics of Hatred* (New Haven: Yale University Press, 1997).

5. Nasra Hassan, www.electronicintifada.net/v2/article2637.shtml, 7 May 2004.
6. Interview conducted by the author, December 2001.
7. AFP news agency, 7 April 2002.
8. Al-Jazeera,12 September 2002.
9. Interview with al-Jazeera, 15 September 2002.
10. Robert A. Pape, *Dying to Win*, p. 233.
11. Press Trust of India,18 May 2004.
12. Strategic Studies Institute, US Army, June 2004.
13. Hala Jaber, 'The Avengers', *The Sunday Times*, 7 December 2003.

Chapter Four

1. ETA is an acronym for Euskadi Ta Askatasuna ('Basque Country and Liberty').
2. Bruce Scheier, expert on Internet espionage, www.theregister.co.uk, 3 October 2001.
3. Will Knight, *The New Scientist* , 18 November 2001.
4. www.pcworld.com, 20 November 2002.
5. John Lasker, 'US Military's Elite Hacker Crew', *Wired*, 18 April 2005.
6. Ibid.

Chapter Five

1. The survey, conducted in October 2001, was referred to in a classified US intelligence document as reported in *The New York Times*, 29 January 2003. *The New York Times* also reported that Prince Nawwaf bin Abdul Aziz, Director of Saudi intelligence services, confirmed the existence of the document, but would not specify the exact level of support for bin Laden – which he attributed to anti-American sentiment.
2. Reported on CNN by Nic Robertson, 9 December 2004.
3. Raid Qusti, 'How Long Before the First Step?', *Daily Arab News*, 5 May 2004.
4. www.eia.doe.gov/emeu/cabs/saudi.html.
5. *Jihad* in this context means a 'war for the cause of Islam', although it can also mean striving in a moral sense – against temptation, for example.

6. The *ulama* are Islamic religious leaders who as a group provide edicts to guide Saudi governance.

7. Osama bin Laden interviewed by Robert Fisk, *The Independent*, 6 December, 1996.

8. Lend-lease assistance from the US to its allies during World War Two started in 1941. Under the programme, the US 'loaned' materials with the understanding that it would be paid back. Fifty billion dollars was made available for this programme, which also allowed for 'reverse lend-lease' whereby the Allies would repay the US with certain materials and services in lieu of money.

9. Saudi citizens are still entitled to free education and health care, but lack of continuous investment has led to a catastrophic decline in standards.

10. Saad al-Faqih, based on official Saudi government records.

11. Jonathan Randal, *Osama*, p. 100.

12. Richard Beeston et al, *The Times*, 9 November 2002 and 5 July 2004.

13. Dr Muhammad al-Masari, interviewed in London, March 2005.

14. Michael Scott Doran, 'The Saudi Paradox', *Foreign Affairs,* pp. 35–51, January/February 2004.

15. 'What If?', special report, 27 May 2004.

16. Jane Padgham, *Evening Standard* (London), 3 June 2004; quoted in Mark Hollingsworth, *Saudi Babylon*.

17. *Al-Quds al-Arabi*, 2 May 2005.

18. *The Economist*, 'Pumped Up: Saudi Arabia's Stock Market Soars', 20 August 2005.

Chapter Six

1. Abu Mus'ab al-Suri ('The Syrian') is a *nom de guerre* of the Syrian ideologue and al-Qa'ida trainer Mustafa Abdul-Qadir, also known as Mustafa Setmaryam Nasar and Omar Abdul Hakim.

2. Abu Qatada was formerly based in London, but at the time of writing (August 2005) was under a deportation order. Interview with Abdel Bari Atwan, London, June 2005.

3. The caliphate was established following the death of Muhammea in 632 CE. The first *kalifa* or 'successor' to the Prophet was his father-in-law, Abu Bakr. Under the first *caliphs* the Islamic world expanded way beyond the Arabian Peninsula. Baghdad was the seat of the caliphate from 750–1258.

4. www.globalpolicy.org/security/oil/2002/12heart.htm.

5. Jeremy Rifkin, in *Hydrogen Economy*, quoted by Robert Fisk, *The Independent*, 18 January 2003.

6. *60 Minutes*, CBS-TV, 5 December 1996.

7. *The New York Times*, 1 July 2003.

8. Interview with Yassir al-Sirri, London, 27 April 2005.

9. Yusef Rababa'a quoted in Paul Harris, 'Profile: Abu Mus'ab al-Zarqawi', *The Observer*, 29 May 2005.

10. Jordanian journalist. Interview with Abdel Bari Atwan, April 2005.

11. *The Observer*, 29 May 2005.

12. Paul McGeough, *Good Weekend*, p. 23, 16 October 2004.

13. BBC News, 23 April 2002.

14. Dilip Hiro, *Secrets and Lies*, p. 541.

15. BBC interview, *Breakfast with Frost*, 29 June 2003.

16. Discussion between Hassan Juma'a Awad al-Asade, President of General Union of Oil Workers in Iraq and David Bacon, veteran *Washington Post* labour journalist, broadcast on *Democracy Now*, independent American television programme, 13 June 2005. See www.democracynow.org.

17. Sarah Left and agencies, 'US Troops Kill Iraqi Protesters', *The Guardian*, 29 April 2003.

18. Dilip Hiro, *Secrets and Lies*, p. 414.

19. An annual Shi'ite ritual commemorating the death of Imam Hussein.

20. Dilip Hiro, *Secrets and Lies*, p. 413.

21. Ibid., p. 515.

22. Ibid., p. 354.

23. Al-Jazeera profile, 6 May 2004.

24. Allawi served from 1 June 2004–7 April 2005.

25. *USA Today*, 30 April 2004.

26. *The Washington Post*, 20 June 2005.

27. www.rebuild-iraq-expo.com.

28. *The Age*, 'Corruption: The Growth Industry of New Iraq', 2 May 2005.

29. *The Independent*, 30 September 2003.

30. Dilip Hiro, *Secrets and Lies*, p. 442.

31. In an *Observer* report, senior medical staff in the US forces predicted that one in five returning soldiers would suffer from post-traumatic stress disorder. With 150,000 American troops currently deployed in Iraq, that means a staggering 30,000 will suffer psychological damage as a result of their combat experiences (up to 86 per

cent of US troops in Iraq have been involved in actual battle, compared with only 31 per cent in Afghanistan. See Peter Beaumont, 'Stress Epidemic Strikes American Forces in Iraq', *The Observer*, 25 January 2004.

32. James Sterngold, 'Casualty of War: the US Economy', *The San Francisco Chronicle*, 17 July 2005.

33. See www.globalsecurity.org.

34. http://www.whitehouse.gov/news/releases/2005/05/images/20050516_webp44882-165-515.html.

Chapter Seven

1. In September 2004, the French government introduced a ban on female students wearing headscarves in schools.

2. Author's interview with Hani al-Sabai, Director, al-Maqrizi Centre for Historical Studies, London, April 2006.

3. Evan F. Kohlman, *Al-Qa'ida's Jihad in Europe, the Afghan-Bosnian network,* (Oxford / New York: Berg, 2004, p. xii).

4. Several sources. In particular, journalist Eve-Ann Prentice testifying at the trial of Slobodan Milosevic in The Hague, who said she and Renate Flotel from *der Spiegel* saw Osama bin Laden going into the office of the late Bosnian President Alija Izetbegovic in November 1994. www.un.org/icty/transe54/060203IT.htm.

5. Several sources, including *Wall Street Journal*, 1 November 2001.

6. *The Times* online, 'Al-Zarqawi's Europe cell jailed', 27 October 2005.

7. Jamestown Foundation, Global Terrorism Analysis, *Terrorism Monitor*, Volume 3, Issue 4 24 February 2005.

8. *New York Times*, 'Spain arrests suspected leader of Islamic [sic] recruiting cells', Renwick McClean, 12 January 2006.

9. *International Herald Tribune*, 'Al-Qa'ida's second front: Europe', Robert S. Leiken and Steve Brooke, 15 July 2005.

10. Evan F. Kohlman, www.globalterroralert.com, 'Abu musab al-Suri: Dirty Bombs for a Dirty Nation'.

11. Statement by Omar Abdul Hakim (alias, al-Suri) published on *International Islamic resistance* website, August 2005.

12. *Chicago Tribune*, 'Reports Emerge of Suspect', John Crewsdon, 12 July 2005.

13. The most influential of these is an 18-chapter work, published in 1987, *Mulahazat hawl al-Tajriba al-Jihadiya fi Suria* [*Observations on the* jihadi *experience in Syria*]. In December 2004 he produced a

1,600 treatise called *Da'wat al-Muqawama al-Islamiyya al-Alamiyya* [*The Call of the International Islamic Resistance*] outlining future strategies for *jihad.*

14. August 2005 statement.

15. The Syrian army massacred up to 10,000 Muslim Brothers in 1982.

16. From the wire-tap transcript quoted in www.cbc.ca/fifth/warwith-outborders/suspect.

17. www.cbc.ca/fifth/warwithoutborders/suspect.

18. Statement issued by Osama bin Laden, 16 February 2003.

19. www.telegraph.co.uk/news/main.jhtml?xml=/news/2002/04/14/wafg14.xml.

20. english.aljazeera.net/NR/exeres/8E8EA580-943C-4FBF-9ABD-21B47627FECD.htm.

21. Sofia News Agency, Bulgaria, 11 May 2005.

22. *El Mundo,* 8 April 2004.

23. Channel 4 special report, Simon Israel, 23 June 2005.

24. *Rai,* Milan, '7/7 The London Bombings, Islam and the Iraq War', p. 31.

25. ibid., p.45.

26. *The Sunday Times,* 'British imam praises London Tube bombers', Ali Hussain, Jonathan Calvert and Gareth Walsh, February 12 2006.

27. http://news.bbc.co.uk/2/hi/europe/4655240.stm.

Chapter Eight

1. www.boris-johnson.com/archives/2005/02/prevention_of_t.html.

Select Bibliography

Bergen, Peter, *The Holy War, Inc.: Inside the Secret World of Osama Bin Laden*, London: Phoenix, 2002.

Burke, Jason, *Al-Qaeda: The True Story of Radical Islam*, London: Penguin Books, 2004.

Clarke, Richard A., *Against All Enemies: Inside America's War on Terror*, New York: Free Press, 2004.

Gambetta, Diego (ed.), *Making Sense of Suicide Missions*, Oxford: Oxford University Press, 2005.

Gunaratna, Rohan, *Inside al-Qa'ida*, London: C. Hurst & Co., 2002.

Hobsbawm, Eric, *Age of Extremes: The Short Twentieth Century 1914–1991*, London: Michael Joseph, 1994.

Hollingsworth, Mark, and Mitchell, Sandy, *Saudi Babylon*, Edinburgh: Mainstream Publishing Company, 2005.

Kepel, Gilles, *Jihad: Expansion et déclin de l'islamisme*, Paris: Gallimard, 2000.

Lewis, Bernard, *The Crisis of Islam: Holy War and Unholy Terror*, London: Phoenix, 2003.

Lewis, Bernard, *What Went Wrong? Western Impact and Middle Eastern Response*, London: Phoenix, 2002.

Pape, Robert A., *Dying to Win: The Strategic Logic of Suicide Terrorism*, New York: Random House, 2005.

Randal, Jonathan, *Osama: The Making of a Terrorist*, New York: Alfred A. Knopf, 2004.

Scheuer, Michael, *Imperial Hubris*, Dulles, Virginia [US]: Brassey's, 2004.

Sifaoui, Muhammed, *Sur les traces de Ben Laden*, Paris: Le Cherche-Midi, 2004.

Willliams, Paul, *Osama's Revenge: The Next 9/11*, New York: Prometheus Books, 2004.

Al-Zawahiri, Ayman, *Knights Under the Prophet's Banner*, Cairo: Al-Sharq al-Aswat, 2001.

Index